Understanding Children's Testing
Psychological Testing

Understanding Children's Testing
Psychological Testing

Elizabeth H. Aylward, Ph.D.
Johns Hopkins University School of Medicine
Baltimore, Maryland

pro·ed
8700 Shoal Creek Boulevard
Austin, Texas   78758

© 1991 by Elizabeth Aylward

All rights reserved. No part of this book may be reproduced in any form or by any means without the prior written permission of the publisher.

Printed in the United States of America

Library of Congress Cataloging-in-Publication Data

Aylward, Elizabeth H., 1954–
    Understanding children's testing / Elizabeth H. Aylward
      p.   cm.
    Includes bibliographical references.
    Contents: v. 1. Psychological testing.
    ISBN 0-89079-413-8
    1. Psychological tests for children. I. Title.
BF722.A94   1990
155.4'028'7 – dc20   89-13813
                                                  CIP

pro·ed
8700 Shoal Creek Boulevard
Austin, Texas   78758

1 2 3 4 5 6 7 8 9 10   95 94 93 92 91

Contents

Preface		vii
Chapter 1	**Basic Concepts Underlying Psychological Testing**	1
	Types of Tests	2
	Types of Scores	3
	Reliability	9
	Validity	14
	Other Considerations in Test Selection	18
	Summary	20
Chapter 2	**Test Administration and Scoring**	21
	Test Administration	22
	Scoring	28
	Summary	29
Chapter 3	**Multi-Scale Tests of Intelligence and Cognitive Development: "The Big Three"**	31
	Wechsler Intelligence Scale for Children–Revised (WISC-R)	32
	Kaufman Assessment Battery for Children (K-ABC): Mental Processing Scales	40
	Stanford-Binet Intelligence Scale (Fourth Edition)	47
	Considerations in Selecting the WISC-R, K-ABC, or Stanford-Binet	60
	Summary	64

v

Chapter 4	**Other Multi-Scale Tests of Intelligence and Cognitive Development**	**67**
	Wechsler Preschool and Primary Scale of Intelligence (WPPSI)	68
	Wechsler Preschool and Primary Scale of Intelligence– Revised (WPPSI-R)	74
	Woodcock-Johnson Psycho-Educational Battery– Revised (Test of Cognitive Ability) (WJ-R COG)	82
	Woodcock-Johnson Psycho-Educational Battery (Part I: Tests of Cognitive Ability)	94
	McCarthy Scales of Children's Abilities (MSCA)	104
	Hiskey-Nebraska Test of Learning Aptitude	111
Chapter 5	**Single Scale Tests of Intelligence and Cognitive Development**	**117**
	Slosson Intelligence Test (SIT)	118
	Columbia Mental Maturity Scale (CMMS)	123
	Peabody Picture Vocabulary Test–Revised (PPVT-R)	126
	Standard Progressive Matrices (SPM), Advanced Progressive Matrices (APM), and Coloured Progressive Matrices (CPM)	129
	Bayley Scales of Infant Development (Mental Scale)	137
	Leiter International Performance Scale (LIPS)	142
Chapter 6	**Tests of Visual-Spatial and Visual-Motor Skills**	**149**
	Developmental Test of Visual-Motor Integration (VMI)	150
	Motor-Free Visual Perception Test	155
	Bender Visual Motor Gestalt Test	158
Chapter 7	**Tests of Adaptive Behavior**	**165**
	AAMD Adaptive Behavior Scale	166
	Vineland Adaptive Behavior Scales	172
	Woodcock-Johnson Psycho-Educational Battery Scales of Independent Behavior	184
	References	193
	Index	199

Preface

Understanding Children's Testing: Psychological Testing is designed as a practical guide to children's testing, to be used both by psychologists and nonpsychologists. General information is presented here regarding testing, including explanations of various types of tests and scores, important considerations for determining whether a test score is reliable and meaningful, and discussion of the importance of standardized administration. The nonpsychologist will find this information useful in understanding the psychologist's role in the evaluation process, in developing a critical approach to using test data, and in appreciating what types of questions can and cannot be answered by test results.

The nonpsychologist will also be able to use this book to understand and clarify data from individual tests. For example, a pediatrician who is provided with conflicting scores from the Wechsler Intelligence Scale for Children–Revised (WISC-R) and the Peabody Picture Vocabulary Test–Revised (PPVT-R) can read the reviews on these two tests to learn what the child had to do to obtain the given scores on each test, evaluate how well the tests were developed and normed, and appreciate the strengths and weaknesses of each test. With this understanding, the pediatrician will be able to decide which of the two scores, if either, should be used in guiding the diagnosis and management of the child's difficulties. This book can be of particular assistance in educating nonpsychologist members of interdisciplinary teams whose responsibility it is to evaluate, diagnose, and plan treatment for children with various disabilities.

The experienced psychologist will find reviews of some of the newest tests and can use these reviews to determine which tests should be included in his or her repertoire. Additional information on some of the older tests may suggest new uses for test data, or additional limitations and considerations of which the psychologist needs to be aware. In addition, psychologists involved in research will be able to determine which tests might be most useful and appropriate for studying particular cognitive functions in specific populations.

Reviews have been organized according to test types, with three chapters devoted to tests of intelligence, one chapter to tests of visual-spatial and visual-motor skills, and one chapter to measures of adaptive behavior. I attempted to select those tests that are most commonly used in clinical work and in research. Inclusion of a test in this book certainly does not imply that the author recommends its use. In fact, many of the tests reviewed have been found to be lacking in major critical areas, including reliability, validity, and adequacy of the norming sample. When possible, I have attempted to describe some of the ways the tests can be used that will circumvent their weaknesses.

Each test review contains information regarding the purpose and possible uses of the test; a description of the test and its administration; scoring and interpretation procedures; technical qualities of the test (norms, reliability, and validity); and other considerations, including strengths and limitations of the test in comparison to other tests of similar purpose.

E. H. A.

CHAPTER 1

BASIC CONCEPTS UNDERLYING PSYCHOLOGICAL TESTING

Over the years, psychologists, educators, and others have developed tests to measure children's performance or potential for performance in many diverse areas. Some have attempted to quantify the child's "innate" abilities or his or her developmental level on a particular skill, whereas others have attempted to determine how much of a particular body of knowledge the child has mastered. Regardless of the stated purpose of a given test, practitioners must be extremely cautious in its use and interpretation. They must not assume that a test claiming to measure a particular skill does so accurately, and must not use test data for making decisions about a child or group of children until they are confident that they know whether and how well the test does what it claims. The information in this chapter will help the practitioner understand what he or she should consider in choosing a test or in using available test data. Understanding the concepts presented in this chapter is essential for understanding the test reviews in following chapters.

TYPES OF TESTS

Cronbach (1970) defines a test as "a systematic procedure for observing a person's behavior and describing it with the aid of a numerical scale or a category-system" (p. 26). Most psychological tests fall into one of two basic categories: norm-referenced or criterion-referenced tests. Norm-referenced tests provide data that allow the child to be compared in one or more areas of functioning with his or her peers. Criterion-referenced tests, on the other hand, are designed to determine if a child does or does not exhibit certain characteristics, has or has not mastered specific material, meets or does not meet certain objective criteria. Intelligence tests, for example, are almost always norm-referenced. They attempt to answer the question "How does the tested individual compare with same-age peers on tasks designed to tap cognitive abilities?" On the other hand, a third-grade teacher who wants each student in class to be able to accurately solve 50 single-digit multiplication problems in 2 minutes will administer a criterion-referenced test. In this case, the purpose of the test is to determine whether or not a certain level of mastery of multiplication facts has been obtained, and the student's score does not imply anything about his or her standing within a group. Indeed, the teacher wants *all* of the students to achieve 100% accuracy.

Both norm-referenced and criterion-referenced tests can employ one or more approaches to obtain information about the individual being tested. Most tests that will be discussed in the following chapters require the child to respond to questions or perform specific tasks. These can involve many different formats, including paper-and-pencil tasks (e.g., copying geometric figures), oral responses to orally presented questions (e.g., answering orally presented arithmetic problems), manipulation of materials (e.g., arranging blocks to match a model), or completing a checklist (e.g., choosing which of four statements best describes one's feelings toward school). Some of the tests described in the following chapters are based on an observer's report of the child rather than on the child's actual performance in the testing situation. For example, a child's behavior can be evaluated by having a teacher or parent complete a checklist describing which behavior problems are observed at home or in the classroom. Regardless of the format, the test can be criterion-referenced only if its purpose is to determine whether or not some set of criteria has been met. It can be norm-referenced only if the data are interpreted with reference to others who have taken the same test. Interpretation of norm-referenced tests usually involves an objective numerical score (e.g., indicating what percentage of children score more poorly than the child being tested). Results from some norm-referenced tests can, however, be interpreted subjectively, based on the examiner's awareness of what constitutes "normal" performance (e.g., as on a projective test that requires the child to tell a story about each of a standard set of pictures).

All of the tests that are described in this book are norm-referenced. However, some of the tests yield information that, in addition to norm-referenced interpretation, can be used in a criterion-referenced fashion. For example, a raw score from a test of adaptive functioning can be interpreted in reference to the child's standing among a group of peers being evaluated with the same test. The same test might also yield data that indicate the child is unable to brush his or her teeth without assistance, thus allowing a criterion-referenced interpretation as well.

TYPES OF SCORES

Results from criterion-referenced tests are generally presented as *raw* scores that indicate how many items were answered correctly (e.g., the child correctly spelled 30 out of 40 words chosen randomly from the first-grade reader) or as percentiles (e.g., the child correctly solved 88% of 50 single-digit addition facts). These data can be interpreted only in relationship to some artificially set criterion (e.g., all children must be able to solve 90% of 50 single-digit addition facts before being promoted to second grade).

Scores from norm-referenced tests can be a bit more complicated. Most norm-referenced tests will yield, at a minimum, percentile scores. Grade-equivalent and age-equivalent scores are sometimes provided. The best developed tests, however, allow the examiner to calculate one of several "standard scores," which are able to take into account the average performance of the norming group, as well as the amount of variance within the group. Psychologists usually find the standard score most useful because it allows comparison between two or more tests. Stanine scores, which are based on standard scores, are often used in reporting scores to parents. Each of these scores will be discussed in the following sections.

PERCENTILES

A percentile score indicates what percentage of peers taking the same test under approximately the same conditions performed at or below the level of the individual being tested. For example, the performance of a child at the 66th percentile on a given test is the same as or better than that of 66 out of 100 of his peers. Of course, the 50th percentile represents the average or mean score, as one-half of children taking the test will be expected to perform at or below this level. Most tests involve comparison of the child with same-age peers, providing separate norms for age ranges spanning anywhere from 1 month to several years. Other tests, especially tests of academic achievement, allow the child to be compared with peers at the same grade level. Separate sets of norms are usually provided for each grade level or for students in the first or second half of each grade level. When possible, it is often desirable to calculate percentile scores from both age- and grade-level norms, especially for children who are not in the same grade level as most children their age.

GRADE-EQUIVALENT AND AGE-EQUIVALENT SCORES

Properly used, a grade-equivalent score tells at what grade level the *average* child performs at the same level as the child being tested. That is, it tells at what grade level one-half of the children perform better than the child being tested and one-half do as well or poorer than the child being tested. For example, if the average child in the 2nd month of third grade obtains a raw score of 18 on a given spelling test, then a child at any level who gets a raw score of 18 on the same spelling test can be said to be performing at the 3.2 grade level.

Similarly, an age-equivalent score tells at what age level the *average* child obtains the same raw score as the child being tested. For example, if the average child of 3 years 6 months obtains a raw score of 14 on a vocabulary test, then a child at any age level who gets a raw score of 14 on the same vocabulary test can be said to be performing at an age level of 3–6. (Note that grade-equivalent scores are usually reported with a decimal separating the grade from the month, whereas age-equivalent scores are usually reported with a hyphen separating the year from the month. It is important to remember that grade-equivalent scores are usually based on a 9- or 10-month year, whereas age-equivalent scores are always based on a 12-month year. Thus, a child with average performance who is just starting second grade would be at the 2.0 grade level, whereas the same child in the last month of second grade would be at the 2.9 grade level.)

Age-equivalent and grade-equivalent scores are appropriately used only when norms are based on the actual performance of children at various age and grade levels on the *same* test that has been administered to the child being evaluated. For example, the same achievement tests from the Woodcock-Johnson Psycho-Educational Battery are administered to all individuals, regardless of age or grade level. That is, the 6-year-old child is presented with the same sheet of arithmetic problems as is the 16-year-old. (Children at different ages might be allowed different starting points, but they must reach basal levels that assure they would be able to solve all problems below the starting point.) Thus, the test developers can say with assurance what level of performance is average for a child of any given age level.

Norms for some standardized tests, especially group-administered achievement tests, are based on performance of children at only one age or grade level. For example, items for an achievement test designed for third graders may have been administered *only* to a sample of third graders, not a sample of children at all grade levels. Thus, it would be impossible for the test developers to determine with certainty the grade-equivalent score for any child whose performance is either above or below third-grade level. Grade-equivalent scores for these children would be based on extrapolations, not on real data. If a third grader received a grade-equivalent score of 2.5 on this test, practitioners must understand that the child's performance is not being compared directly with any child who is actually in the 5th month of second grade. Therefore, practitioners must be much more cautious in assuming that a grade-equivalent score from one of these tests is reflective of the average performance of a child at that grade level. However, standard scores and percentiles can still be accurately determined, since they are based on comparison of the child with other children of the same age or grade level.

Even when age-equivalent and grade-equivalent scores are properly obtained, most psychologists and educators caution against their use. Age-equivalent and grade-equivalent scores are susceptible to misuse, based on the inaccurate assumption that they represent an equal-interval scale. With the assumption of an equal-interval scale, it would be the case that first graders make the same amount of progress in reading each month as do fifth graders. There is substantial evidence indicating that the rate of learning is not constant and, thus, the assumption that grade-equivalent scores and age-equivalent scores represent an equal-interval scale is inaccurate. For this reason, it is invalid to use arithmetic operations such as addition or subtraction on these scores. For example, it would be invalid to claim on the basis of grade-equivalent scores that a child made half as much progress in reading in second grade as in first grade. For these and other reasons (see Berk, 1984), the use of grade-equivalent and age-equivalent scores cannot be recommended as the primary scores to be considered.

Age- and grade-equivalent scores are useful, however, in providing parents, as well as professionals, with a *rough* idea of the child's level of functioning in a way that may be easier to comprehend than a percentile or standard score. For example, a parent of a retarded child may better be able to understand how to work with the child if told that the child's understanding of language is about at a 2-year level, rather than being told that the child is functioning at less than the first percentile for age level.

STANDARD SCORES

A standard score is based on both the mean and standard deviation of scores obtained by the norming sample. The mean score, of course, is obtained by summing all of the raw scores of individuals within the norming sample and dividing by the number of individuals. This gives the average score—the level above which half of the children performed and at or below which half performed. The standard deviation is a measure of the spread of scores. It tells, for example, whether the scores of the group clustered closely around the mean, with little deviation between the highest and lowest, or whether the scores were widely spread with a great deal of difference between the highest and lowest scores. It is calculated by first measuring the amount of deviation of each score from the mean (i.e., each score is subtracted from the mean, resulting in a positive or negative number). Each of these deviations is squared, and the average of the squared deviations is calculated. The average of the squared deviations is called the variance of the distribution. The square root of the variance is the *standard deviation.*

As stated previously, standard scores provide a comparison of the child's performance with the average (mean) performance of the group, while taking into account the amount of deviation within the group's scores. Most sophisticated tests are developed so that the scores obtained from a random sample of children fall into a nearly normal distribution. That is, when scores from the random sample are plotted against the number of children obtaining each score, a normal curve is obtained. Because of the mathematical properties of a normal curve, almost all scores will fall between $+3$ and -3 standard deviations. Figure 1-1 shows the percentage of cases that fall within each standard deviation when test scores fit a normal curve.

The mean and standard deviations of the normal curve are arbitrarily set. Most currently published tests use a mean of 100 and a standard deviation of 15. These scores are sometimes referred to as "deviation IQs."* Other scores that are sometimes reported include z scores, which have a mean of 0 and a standard deviation of 1, and T scores, which have a mean of 50 and a standard deviation of 10. The Stanford-Binet

---

*When the term IQ ("intelligence quotient") was first used, it represented a true quotient, derived by dividing Mental Age by Chronological Age. None of the well-developed standardized tests uses this procedure now, although the term IQ has remained popular and is still used.

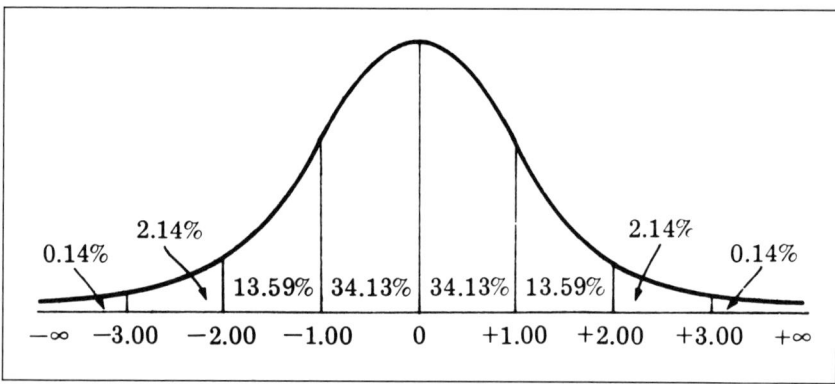

Source: From F. Kviz and K. Knafl, *Statistics for Nurses: An Introductory Text*, Little, Brown and Company, 1980, p. 118.

Figure 1-1. Percentage of cases that fall within each standard deviation of a normal curve.

Intelligence Scale, among others, uses a mean of 100 and a standard deviation of 16.

Most psychologists and educators prefer to work with standard scores when using test data to make decisions about individual students. Unlike grade-equivalent and age-equivalent scores, standard scores do reflect an equal-interval scale. It is, therefore, appropriate to use mathematical and statistical operations on standard scores. Most important, standard scores allow the valid comparison of scores from different tests. This characteristic is very important in the diagnosis of learning disabilities, which requires that the student's cognitive ability (usually represented by an IQ) be compared with his or her academic achievement (usually represented by standard scores on tests of reading, math, and written language). Standard scores are also useful in the comparison of results from tests of cognitive functioning with those of adaptive functioning for children suspected of mental retardation.

STANINES

Stanines are standard scores with a mean of 5 and a standard deviation of 2. Scores can range from 1 to 9, with each stanine encompassing a band of raw scores one-half standard deviation wide. Because they do not permit as great a level of discrimination as do deviation IQs, they are rarely used for decision-making purposes. Psychologists and educators often use stanines, however, in reporting scores to parents, as these scores can provide a general idea of the child's performance without the danger of parents misinterpreting them as exact measures of ability.

In selecting a test to administer or in interpreting an available test score, practitioners must consider the types of scores available. If the score from one test is to be compared with the score from another test, it is imperative that standard scores be provided. Of course, the scores being compared must have the same mean and standard deviation or must be converted to standard scores that do have common means and standard deviations. Tests that provide only grade-equivalent or age-equivalent scores should not be used in making diagnoses such as learning disabilities, and will not be particularly useful in other decision-making processes.

RELIABILITY

The reliability of a test refers to "the degree to which the results of testing are attributable to systematic sources of variance" (American Psychological Association, 1974, p. 48). It is often thought of as the test's ability to *consistently* measure what it measures. When evaluating a test for its usefulness or in reviewing a test score, it is essential that practitioners know the test's level of reliability in as many areas as possible (e.g., stability over time or consistency among examiners). Too often psychologists and educators blindly use test scores to make decisions without consideration of the accuracy of the scores. If a given test score is used, despite lack of proven reliability, the practitioner is seriously abusing the trust placed in him or her. It is the practitioner's responsibility to evaluate tests and select for use only those that will result in reliable information.

Berk (1984) lists five types of reliability, which are summarized in Table 1-1. Each type will be described briefly in the following sections. In addition, a statistic known as the standard error of measurement will be discussed as it relates to the test's ability to provide consistent information.

Table 1-1. Characteristics of five types of reliability

Type of reliability	Question posed	Method for answering
1. Stability	How stable are the test scores over time?	*Test-retest:* Administer one test twice to the same group with an intervening period of time between the two administrations
2. Equivalence (parallel forms)	To what extent are the two test forms equivalent?	*Equivalent forms:* Administer two forms of the same test to the same group at the same time
3. Stability and equivalence	To what extent are the test scores on two equivalent forms stable over time?	*Test-retest and equivalent forms:* Administer two forms of the same test to the same group with an intervening period of time between the administration of each form
4. Internal consistency	To what extent do all of the test items measure the same construct?	*Split-half:* Administer one test to one group; split the test into halves (e.g., even-numbered and odd-numbered items); correlate the scores from the halves; then substitute the correlation in Spearman-Brown formula to obtain estimate for full-length test *Kuder-Richardson:* Administer one test to one group; score the test and apply $K-R_{20}$ formula

Table 1-1. *(continued)*

Type of reliability	Question posed	Method for answering
5. Interscorer consistency or interobserver consistency	To what extent do different scorers produce the same results? To what extent do different observers record the same behaviors?	*Interclass correlation:* Obtain two sets of scores/observations from two independent scorers/observers at the same point in time; correlate the scores

Source: From R. Berk, *Screening and Diagnosis of Children with Learning Disabilities*, 1984, p. 49. Courtesy of Charles C Thomas, Publisher, Springfield, Illinois.

STABILITY OR TEST-RETEST RELIABILITY

The stability, or test-retest reliability, of an instrument refers to the extent to which the test consistently yields the same score for the same individual over time. A stability coefficient is obtained by administering the test to a group of students on two occasions and correlating the scores from the two administrations. The resulting coefficient should be at least .80, and preferably at least .90, for a test to be considered reliable over time. Of course, stability coefficients will be higher when the amount of time between the two test administrations is shorter. If the delay between the first and second administrations is too short, the students will remember their responses from the first administration. On the other hand, if the two administrations are spaced over too long a period of time, differences in test scores may reflect true growth or deterioration of ability. The practitioner must attempt to assess what would be a reasonable delay between the initial and retest administrations, based on the nature of the construct being measured. This assessment must be taken into consideration when determining the meaningfulness of the stability coefficient.

EQUIVALENCE OR ALTERNATE-FORM RELIABILITY

Some tests provide two or more alternate forms. Although the content of the two forms is similar, the exact items are not identical. Alternate forms are usually provided so that the evaluator can measure progress over time without being concerned that the student will remember items from one test administration to the next. Of course, the alternate forms are useful for measuring progress only if they can be proven to measure the same construct and have equivalent scores. As with the procedure for measuring a test's stability, a correlation is used to assess alternate-form reliability. One form of the test is given to half the students in a group, while the other form is given to the other half. Retesting occurs soon after, with students receiving the form they did not receive on the initial administration. Scores from the two administrations are correlated, resulting in a measure of consistency between the two forms. Berk (1984) recommends that a coefficient of .90 or above be considered adequate proof that the two forms of the test are measuring the same material. In addition, he suggests that the mean, standard deviations, and item analysis results (difficulty level and discrimination properties for individual items) for each test form be examined for consistency.

STABILITY AND EQUIVALENCE

This analysis is designed to determine how consistent the test scores on the alternate forms are over time. The procedure is identical to that used for obtaining the alternate-forms reliability coefficient, except that the two administrations are separated by a longer time period. As with the procedure for determining test-retest reliability, the evaluator must determine whether the amount of time between the two test administrations was appropriate.

INTERNAL CONSISTENCY

Internal consistency refers to the degree to which items within a test are all measuring the same construct. A "split-half" procedure is used, whereby students' scores on one-half of the test items are correlated with their scores on the other half of the items. Of course, the items must be divided in such a way that the two halves are of approximately equal difficulty. The resulting correlation coefficient is subjected to a statistical formula that provides an estimate of internal consistency for the entire test. Alternatively, procedures using statistical formulas, such as the Kuder-Richardson formulas, or "coefficient alpha," will yield a coefficient that is equal to the average of all the split-half coefficients. Whichever method is used, the coefficient derived reveals the extent of homogeneity among test items and indicates whether the test is measuring one or more than one construct. Berk (1984) recommends that in order to ensure adequate subtest homogeneity, the coefficient of internal consistency be at least .90 for standardized test batteries consisting of numerous subtests. Evaluation of internal consistency is not appropriate for speeded tests (i.e., those tests that measure performance according to how quickly a task is completed).

INTERSCORER CONSISTENCY

Interscorer, or inter-rater, reliability refers to the degree to which two independent scorers will arrive at the same result for a given individual. This type of reliability is determined by having two scorers administer the test to the same group of students. For other types of measurement, it is possible to have the two scorers simultaneously observe each student's behavior and rate the behavior independently. Scores obtained by the two test administrators or observers are correlated. When tests involve objective scoring, the scores obtained by two different administrators should be nearly identical. More variation between the two scorers will occur when evaluation of the students' responses requires more subjective judgment. Berk (1984) considers interscorer reliability coefficients in the .90s necessary if decisions about individual students will be based on the test results.

STANDARD ERROR OF MEASUREMENT

The standard error of measurement is one more statistic that should be considered in evaluating a test's ability to provide reliable data. It represents the degree to which a single score from an individual can be assumed to accurately reflect his or her "true" level of performance on that test. It is calculated from the standard deviation of the test scores and the test-retest reliability coefficient. Theoretically, the standard error of measurement represents the standard deviation of the scores that would be obtained for an individual if he or she took the test an infinite number of times with no test-retest effects. It allows the examiner to determine a range of scores within which the true score would fall a certain percentage of the time. For example, if a test has a standard error of measurement of 3 points, it means that a child's *true* score will be no more than 3 points higher or lower than the *measured* score approximately 68% of the time. (Sixty-eight is the percent of cases that fall within +1 and −1 standard deviations on a normal curve.) If you wanted to give a more conservative estimate, you could say that the child's true score would be no more than 6 points (or 2 standard errors of measurement) higher or lower than the measured IQ approximately 96% of the time, with 96 being the percent of cases falling between +2 and −2 standard deviations on the normal curve. Of course, test consumers will be interested in using tests that have the smallest standard error of measurement. If the examiner wishes to use subtests to develop a profile of the child's performance, it is also important that he or she examine the standard errors of measurement of each of the subtests.

It is important to note that one kind of reliability data cannot be substituted for another. A test cannot be said to be reliable, for example, based solely on measures of internal consistency. Test consumers must consider all of the reliability studies reported by the test developers, judge the adequacy of the samples used in these studies, and consider how test results will be used before deciding whether the test's ability to measure consistently is sufficient for their purposes. It is also important that test consumers compare the samples used in the reliability studies with those individuals to whom they plan to administer the test. For example, if a test is designed for children between the ages of 2 and 18 years, but reliability studies only involved adolescents, the test cannot be assumed to be reliable for preschoolers.

VALIDITY

As stated in the previous section, reliability refers to the test's consistency in measuring what it measures. Validity, on the other hand, refers to the test's ability to actually measure what it purports to measure.

Establishing the validity of a test is an ongoing process that is never considered complete. In determining whether or not a particular test has adequate evidence of validity, the practitioner must consider what question he or she is trying to answer with the test results. For example, is the examiner planning to use test data to predict whether the child is likely to succeed in first grade, to determine whether a group of students has mastered the fifth-grade spelling list, or to diagnose mental retardation? The determination of a test's ability to provide valid information on each of these questions will require different types of validity data. As noted in the *Standards for Educational and Psychological Tests* (American Psychological Association, 1974), "no test is valid for all purposes or in all situations or for all groups of individuals" (p. 31). Thus, it is inappropriate to consider test validity as a unitary concept. It is the test's validity for answering specific questions for specific populations that must be considered.

The three major types of validity that are usually reported by test developers are content validity, criterion-related validity, and construct validity. Information regarding each of these types should be provided by the test developer in order to help the practitioner determine whether or not the test is valid for his or her purposes. Each type of validity is described briefly in the following paragraphs.

CONTENT VALIDITY

The establishment of content validity involves the subjective assessment of test items to determine whether they adequately sample the universe of tasks or behaviors the examiner wishes to measure. For example, if a test is needed to measure mastery of fourth-grade math skills, the examiner would want to make certain that the items cover the content of the math curriculum for fourth grade, not for fifth or third grade. He or she would also want to know whether items covered all of the concepts presented in the fourth-grade math curriculum, and were not, for example, limited to or weighted heavily in favor of addition with fractions. There is no statistical formula or quantitative method for summarizing content validity. Test manuals should, however, describe how items were developed and selected in order to help the test consumer make a judgment regarding the validity of the test for his or her purpose.

CRITERION-RELATED VALIDITY

Criterion-related validity refers to the test's ability to estimate or predict the student's behavior or performance on some related measure. There are two major types of criterion-related validity: concurrent validity and predictive validity.

Concurrent validity indicates the extent to which a test is able to estimate an individual's present standing on the criterion being measured. It refers to the extent to which test results agree with results from another assessment of the same construct at the same time. Practitioners are usually interested in the concurrent validity of a test if they wish to use it to replace a more cumbersome or inefficient method of evaluation. For example, a psychiatrist may wish to know whether a particular personality inventory can be used instead of a lengthy interview procedure to distinguish among psychotic and nonpsychotic patients. Assuming that the psychiatrist's interview method is considered to provide accurate results regarding the presence of psychosis, he or she would want to know how well the results from the personality inventory agree with the established diagnosis for a group of patients. Concurrent validity for a newly developed test often involves administering the new test to a group of students at the same time as another well-established test that is designed to measure the same or a similar construct. Scores from the two tests are correlated, providing an estimate of the extent to which the new test measures the same construct as the old test. As Berk (1984) notes, the adequacy of the criterion measure (i.e., the well-established test) must be considered in evaluating whether a high correlation between it and the new test is meaningful. It is also important to evaluate whether the sample used in the study of concurrent validation is large enough and adequately representative of the population for which the examiner wishes to use the test.

Predictive validity refers to the test's ability to predict performance on some future outcome measure. It is assessed by administering the test in question to a group of individuals and, at some later time, measuring the outcome criterion that the new test claims to predict. For example, if a test is designed to predict which children will be successful readers in first grade, it would be administered to entering first graders. Scores would be correlated with measures of reading achievement at the end of the first grade. As with studies of concurrent validity, the test consumer must consider the adequacy of the outcome measure and the adequacy of the study sample.

CONSTRUCT VALIDITY

Construct validity is more difficult to assess than content validity or criterion-related validity. A psychological construct is "a theoretical idea developed to explain and to organize some aspects of existing knowledge" (American Psychological Association, 1974, p. 29). Examples of psychological constructs include "intelligence," "anxiety," and "reading readiness." Constructs are understood or inferred from their "network of interrelationships."

Construct validity involves an ongoing process, based on studies of the test's usefulness in explaining the construct and the degree to which the test scores are consistent with psychologically based implications regarding the construct being measured. For example, if a test purports to measure the construct of student morale, one would hypothesize that students receiving high scores would be more involved in extracurricular activities, be more likely to attend football games, have better grades, and be rated by peers as more popular. It might also be predicted that the average score for the student body would increase following the school's victory in the basketball championship series and would decrease following the institution of a stricter dress code. Studies would be conducted to determine whether or not these hypotheses are true. To the extent that the hypotheses directly follow from one's understanding of the construct and to the extent that the test results support the hypotheses, the test can be said to have construct validity. There is, of course, no specified number of studies or particular correlation coefficient that must be obtained to say that a test has construct validity. The evaluator's judgment of the adequacy of construct validity data is subjective and must be based on his or her understanding of the construct and his or her purpose for administering the test.

OTHER CONSIDERATIONS IN DETERMINING TEST VALIDITY

Berk (1984) and others have argued that determination of a test's validity should involve more than individual consideration of the three types of validity discussed in the previous sections. A more unified approach is proposed that places more emphasis on the adequacy of the data-gathering process and on the types of inferences to be made with the scores. Although this approach is desirable, most currently published test manuals continue to present validity data (if it is presented at all) according to the three categories discussed previously. Practitioners are urged, however, to seriously consider their purposes for administering a test, to consider the type of decisions that will be based on test results, and to consider all available validity data before selecting and using any given test.

OTHER CONSIDERATIONS IN TEST SELECTION
NORMING PROCEDURES

As discussed previously, norm-referenced tests are those tests that evaluate the individual's performance in relationship to how others have performed on the test in the past. Most often, the test developer provides the user with information regarding what level of performance is average (or "normal") and what percentage of individuals can be expected to perform at other various levels. This information is obtained by administering the test to a group of individuals, called the norming sample. The test norms are based on the scores obtained from this group.

The test consumer's responsibility is to evaluate the adequacy of the sample on which the test was normed. It is important that the sample be of adequate size, so that any deviations resulting from a few very aberrant cases can be counterbalanced by the more typical performance of the majority. The test consumer must also evaluate the types of individuals included in the sample and determine to what extent the sample is similar to the individual or group of individuals with whom the examiner wishes to use the test. Most well-developed tests that are designed for national use attempt to have their sample mirror the national population on several important variables, including sex, race, socioeconomic status, and geographic region (i.e., urban vs. rural setting). Norming samples for children's tests sometimes are also matched to the national population on the basis of parental level of education. Because most tests for children expect different performance at different ages, separate norms are provided for each age group or grade level. Sometimes separate norms will be provided for different socioeconomic groups.

When interpreting test scores for an individual student, it is important that the examiner consider the similarities and differences between the child being tested and the children in the norming sample. If the child is not typical for the norming sample, the examiner should attempt to find a test that has special norms that would be more appropriate or, at the very least, state in the test report that the scores may not be a totally accurate representation of the child's abilities. Test users are being urged more and more to develop their own local norms for tests in order to increase the appropriateness of the norms for the individual students being tested. Finally, the test consumer must consider whether or not the norms are up-to-date. Because children are developing some skills at different rates than did children 20 years ago, it would be inappropriate to compare a child's performance on a test to that of a sample that, in effect, no longer exists.

TEST BIAS

An issue related to the appropriateness of the norming sample is that of test bias. Test bias occurs when the probability of an individual's success or failure on a given task is affected simply by that individual's membership within a particular group. The greatest concern is generally in the areas of racial and ethnic or sexual bias. Test developers should report separate means and standard deviations for different sexes and racial and ethnic groups. The test consumer can refer to these statistics to help him or her decide if the test contains bias. (Significant differences between sexes or racial and ethnic groups do not *necessarily* indicate bias. However, when significant differences are observed between groups, the test consumer should examine the test carefully in order to determine why this might be the case.) In addition, the consumer should also examine the individual test items for obvious bias before selecting a test for a particular group. As mentioned previously, some tests provide separate norms for different sexes, socioeconomic groups, or racial and ethnic groups. Although special norms do not negate any bias within test items, the individual's performance can at least be compared with that of others who might be equally affected by the bias.

In general, test bias is more of a concern when a test purports to measure the child's "potential" for some ability or to predict future outcome. Tests that are designed to simply measure mastery of a particular skill area (e.g., knowledge of subtraction facts) will not generally be challenged as containing bias unless test scores are interpreted in a way to suggest the child's potential (e.g., potential for becoming a mathematician). Constructs that are more difficult to define are more likely to be charged as being biased, as ideas about what constitutes the construct may differ according to one's background. For example, there has been much controversy over the years regarding what constitutes "intelligence." Because intelligence is demonstrated differently among different racial and ethnic and socioeconomic groups, a test of intelligence that emphasizes one particular type of knowledge may not be valid for all groups. The test consumer must determine whether a given test defines and measures a particular construct in a way that is appropriate for the individual or group being tested.

SUMMARY

This chapter has presented some of the factors that must be considered by the test consumer who is selecting tests for decision-making purposes. The professional who has access to test results for individual children will also want to be familiar with these factors in order to determine the extent to which the scores obtained are meaningful. Two primary considerations in evaluating a test or a test score involve the test's ability to *consistently* measure what it measures (reliability) and to *accurately* measure what it claims to measure (validity). Most well-developed tests will provide information regarding several types of reliability and validity, each of which was discussed briefly. Tests should also be evaluated for appropriateness of the norming samples and the possibility of test bias. In general, the test consumer should evaluate a test based on its appropriateness for answering the questions being proposed, its proven reliability and validity for a particular purpose, and the appropriateness of the available norms for the individuals or groups who will take the test.

CHAPTER 2

TEST ADMINISTRATION AND SCORING

TEST ADMINISTRATION

Even the best developed tests cannot provide accurate and reliable information if they are not administered and scored properly. Professionals who must rely on test results obtained by others can have confidence in the scores only to the extent that they have confidence in the person who administered and scored the test. When the professional using the test results is unfamiliar with the test administrator, it is not at all inappropriate for him or her to ask questions regarding the qualifications and experience of the test administrator, the administration and scoring procedures employed, and the child's response to testing. When parents and professionals are using test scores to make important decisions about an individual child, they should not hesitate to question the circumstances under which the scores were obtained.

NEED FOR STANDARDIZED ADMINISTRATION

The results of any given test can be reliable and valid only to the extent that the test was administered according to standardized procedures. Because it is presumed that all of the subjects in the norming sample were administered the test under standardized conditions, the norms are appropriate for interpretation of test results only if the test was administered to the individual student under these same standardized conditions. Test manuals for well-developed tests will provide very specific and detailed instructions for test administration. It is imperative that these instructions be followed carefully, especially in regard to the amount of time allotted for certain tasks, amount of prompting permissible by the examiner, order in which subtests are to be administered, and specificity of instructions presented.

PROVIDING THE OPTIMAL TESTING CONDITIONS

The environment in which the test is administered is also important in assuring valid and reliable results. The testing room must be quiet, free from excessive visual distractions, properly ventilated, of comfortable temperature, and equipped with furniture that allows the child to be seated comfortably at a table or desk.

The child should be tested in the morning, if possible, when he or she is well rested and alert. Tests should be administered in sessions no longer than 2 hours (or shorter for younger children). If tests must be administered in one session, the student should be allowed a short break in the middle of the session.

As stated in most test manuals, the examiner should attempt to build a good rapport with the child in order to elicit his or her best performance. Especially for children with cognitive, academic, behavioral, or emotional problems, the examiner will have to put forth extra effort to overcome the effects of the child's poor self-concept, low tolerance for frustration, inability to maintain attention, lack of motivation, or excessive anxiety. A relaxed atmosphere, in which the child feels respected and unthreatened, will generally result in the best testing and the most meaningful results.

OBSERVING TEST BEHAVIOR

Critical observation of a student's behavior may provide as much important information as the test results themselves. For this reason, it is very important that the examiner carefully observes the student's behavior and provides a detailed account of any unusual behavior in the test report. Some of the behaviors that should receive special attention from the examiner are listed:

Distractibility

- Did the student have difficulty paying attention and staying on task? Did the student appear to be daydreaming, or off in his own world?
- Did he often ask to have items repeated?
- Did she often comment about or seem attuned to unavoidable visual or auditory distractions (e.g., the squeaking of a chair, the examiner's clothing)?
- Did he make irrelevant comments or attempt to relate personal experiences that were brought to mind by the various test stimuli?

- Did she often talk to herself, especially on tasks that required manipulation of materials rather than a verbal response?
- Did he seem to "lose track" of the task presented?

Restlessness, Fidgetiness

- Did the student have difficulty staying seated, especially on the subtests that did not require manipulation of materials?
- Did restlessness increase as testing proceeded or stay at a constant level?
- Did the child engage in excessive purposeless movement (e.g., squirming, tapping fingers, swinging feet, kicking the table leg?) Were the child's hands overly "busy" (e.g., twirling his pencil, picking at himself)?
- Did he chew on his pencil, shirt collar, cuffs, or other objects?

Rushed, Careless, Impulsive Approach

- Did the child appear to give the first answer that came to mind?
- Did the child attempt to begin tasks before instructions were complete?
- Did she grab for materials before the examiner was ready to present them?
- Did the child appear totally oblivious to obviously incorrect responses?
- Did he noticeably increase his speed of responding when he was aware that performance was being timed? Did this result in careless errors?

Slow, Obsessive Approach

- Did the child take excessive time before responding?
- Did she meticulously check and recheck work? Did this result in penalties for slow performance?
- Were his verbal responses more complete than necessary?

- Did she often come up with correct responses *after* time was up?
- Did he spend excessive time "planning" before responding?
- Were tasks done with excessive precision?

Anxiety

- Did the child have difficulty separating from his parent or teacher?
- Did she appear nervous? Did nervousness subside or increase as testing proceeded? Did it diminish with positive reinforcement and reassurance?
- Did anxiety appear to increase when tasks were timed?
- Was more anxiety observed on certain types of tasks (e.g., those requiring a verbal response, those that were timed) than on other types of tasks?

Confidence

- Did the child ask often if his responses were correct?
- Was the child reluctant to guess at an item when she was uncertain of the correct answer?
- Could the child be encouraged to take a guess, and, if so, were guesses often correct?
- Did she start to give answers and then change her mind and refuse to respond?
- Did the child qualify many responses (e.g., by saying, "I don't know, but . . ." or "This is just a guess.")?
- Did he often comment on the difficulty of items (e.g., "These are *so* easy" or "I'll never get this one.")? Were these opinions of difficulty congruent with the child's performance?
- Did the child often say "I can't" or "I don't know" without putting forth good effort?
- Did the child often ask for assistance on items or look to the examiner for reassurance that he was "on the right track"?

Frustration - Perseverance

- Did the child often stop working on a task before time was called, claiming an item was too difficult? Could she be encouraged to continue and, if so, was she able to successfully complete the item?
- If unable to succeed on an item within the time limit, did the child request "just a little longer" to complete the task?
- Did he ever scatter materials in frustration?
- Did she act disgusted with herself or make disparaging comments when she could not succeed on an item?
- Did he ever ask to complete remaining items after failing the prescribed number of items for discontinuing the testing?

Pencil Grasp

- Did the child exhibit an immature or awkward pencil grasp?

Avoidance Behavior

- Did the child ask for excessive breaks (e.g., for bathroom visits, drinks)?
- Did he complain of stomachaches or other ailments in an apparent attempt to discontinue the session?
- Did she complain of being tired?
- Did he often ask how much longer the testing would last?
- Did she complain about the testing?

Hearing and Vision

- Were there any indications that the child had difficulty seeing materials or hearing questions (e.g., squinting, holding materials close to his face, often saying "huh?" or asking to have questions repeated)?

Speech and Language

- Did the child often ask to have verbal items repeated?
- Was the child slow to begin giving verbal responses?
- Did the child often appear to not understand verbal directions, but "catch on" quickly after a few demonstration items?
- Did the child have "word-finding" problems? Did he often give a long verbal explanation or use gestures when more concise terminology would have been more appropriate?
- Were verbal responses extremely limited? Did the child resist encouragement to elaborate on verbal responses?
- Did the child give totally inappropriate responses to verbal questions and then, upon repetition of the question, provide an accurate response?
- Did the child give responses that were related only to a portion of the question?
- Did the child have any observable speech impediments (e.g., stuttering, lisping, poor articulation)? Did they interfere with testing?

Personality Characteristics

- Was the child friendly, pleasant, well mannered, cooperative?
- Did the child appear well motivated?
- Did he appear to enjoy the testing and the individual attention of the examiner?
- Did she offer spontaneous conversation?
- Did he make eye contact with the examiner?
- Did she appear to take pride in her successes? Did she respond to praise?
- Did he respond to the examiner's attempts to build rapport?
- Was the child overly affectionate with the examiner?

Health

- Was the child on any type of medication that might have affected performance (e.g., methylphenidate, antihistamines)?
- Were there any other health conditions that might have affected performance?

Although this list of behavioral observations may seem quite lengthy and detailed, it is important that each area be considered and, when appropriate, mentioned in the test report. Some major difficulties experienced by some children may be reflected more in these behavioral traits than in any test score. For many children, especially those with cognitive, academic, behavioral, or emotional difficulties, a test score can be interpreted properly only if it is considered in conjunction with detailed observation from the examiner.

SCORING

Of course, the examiner must be extremely careful in scoring the test, following all guidelines provided in the manual. In evaluating a given test, the examiner will want to consider the completeness and clarity of scoring instructions. Many tests require only a judgment of pass or fail for each item, and the scoring criteria are quite objective. In these cases, the examiner's major responsibility is to mark responses correctly and do the necessary calculations correctly to arrive at an accurate score. For other tests, however, the examiner is required to assign a score to each item based on his or her judgment of the quality of a response. For these types of tests, test consumers must be convinced that the criteria for scoring responses are complete and unambiguous. Reports of interscorer reliability for these tests should receive particular attention (see Chapter 1). If there is any question about the examiner's ability to accurately score responses, attempts should be made to have the individual item scores reviewed by another experienced examiner.

SUMMARY

This chapter has reviewed factors that must be considered in the administration and scoring of a test. Regardless of the technical merits of a test, the scores it yields will be reliable and valid only to the extent that administration and scoring were done in accordance with the standardized procedures outlined in the test manual. In addition to carefully following administration and scoring procedures, the test administrator is responsible for providing an optimal testing environment and for carefully observing the child's test behavior for any condition that might affect the test results. Professionals who are using test results to make decisions about individual students are responsible for obtaining information regarding the qualifications of the examiner and regarding the circumstances under which test scores were obtained.

CHAPTER 3

MULTI-SCALE TESTS OF INTELLIGENCE AND COGNITIVE DEVELOPMENT: "THE BIG THREE"

When psychologists and educators wish to obtain a measure of a child's intellectual functioning or cognitive abilities, three major instruments come to mind: The Wechsler Intelligence Scale for Children–Revised (WISC-R), the Kaufman Assessment Battery for Children (K-ABC), and the Stanford-Binet Intelligence Scale. Each of these tests is presented separately in this chapter, followed by a discussion of some of the factors that should be considered when choosing one of these tests over the others for a certain student or group of students. Chapter 4 reviews other tests that measure two or more facets of intelligence, and Chapter 5 covers tests that measure a single facet of intelligence, such as receptive vocabulary or visual-spatial reasoning. As mentioned in the Preface, inclusion of a test in this book does not at all imply that it is endorsed by the author. It is hoped that the reader will critically evaluate the information presented in each review to decide which tests meet the technical standards and cover appropriate content to be useful for his or her clients.

WECHSLER INTELLIGENCE SCALE FOR CHILDREN–REVISED (WISC-R)

David Wechsler

The Psychological Corporation
555 Academic Court
San Antonio, Texas   78204-2498

PURPOSE

The WISC-R is clearly one of the most widely used of all psychological instruments and is generally considered to be one of the best tests, if not the best, for obtaining a global score of intelligence in children. The WISC-R manual defines intelligence as "the overall capacity of an individual to understand and cope with the world around him" (Wechsler, 1974, p. 5). The test was published in 1974 as a revision of the Wechsler Intelligence Scale for Children (WISC), which was originally published in 1949.

DESCRIPTION OF TEST AND ADMINISTRATION

The WISC-R is designed for use with children aged 6 years 0 months through 16 years 11 months. (Other Wechsler tests are available for preschoolers and adults.) It is administered individually by a psychologist, and administration requires a fair amount of practice, as well as total familiarity with the manual. Testing generally requires 50 to 75 minutes. The manual provides very explicit instructions, including verbatim directions that are to be used by the examiner in presenting the items. Because of the variety of formats and materials used, students generally find the experience interesting.

The WISC-R is divided into two sections. The Verbal Tests measure overall language abilities, whereas the Performance Tests measure primarily visual-spatial perceptual skills.* Verbal and Performance tests are alternated during administration, which helps to maintain the student's interest.

Verbal Subtests

The six Verbal subtests are all presented orally and require oral responses. Only the Arithmetic subtest limits the time available for each response. Some of the subtests have different starting points, depending on the age of the subject. Each subtest is described briefly:

Information General information questions, such as "How many inches make a foot?" or "Who was Frank Lloyd Wright?" There are 18 items, and the test is discontinued after five consecutive failures.

Similarities Asks the student to tell how two concepts are alike. For example, "How are an hour and a day alike?" There are 17 items, and the test is discontinued after three consecutive failures.

Arithmetic The easiest items involve counting. The more difficult items are "word problems." For example, "Bill made a dozen cookies and ate three of them. How many were left?" There are 18 items, and the test is discontinued after three consecutive failures.

---

*Simulated items adapted from the Wechsler Intelligence Scale for Children—Revised. Copyright © 1974 by The Psychological Corporation. Reproduced by permission. All rights reserved.

Vocabulary Requires the student to define a word presented by the examiner. For example, "What is a rodeo?" or "What does *fundamental* mean?" There are 32 items, and the test is discontinued after five consecutive failures.

Comprehension Requires the student to demonstrate understanding of a social situation or everyday phenomenon. For example, "Why should people wear seat belts when riding in a car?" "Why do children go to school?" There are 17 items, and the test is discontinued after four consecutive failures.

Digit Span Requires the subject to repeat series of digits forward and backward. Forward series range from 3 to 9 digits; backward series range from 2 to 8 digits. There are 14 each of forward and backward items, with each set being discontinued after failures on two series of the same length.

It should be noted that several of the Verbal subtests, particularly Information and Comprehension, may be substantially influenced by the child's exposure to the predominant white American culture. Scores on these subtests should, therefore, be questioned as valid measures of intelligence for children whose exposure to this culture is limited. In addition, Arithmetic and Vocabulary must be considered to be influenced by academic exposure and experience, both in the home and at school. Similarities and Digit Span are probably the least culturally influenced of the Verbal subtests.

Performance Subtests

Each of the six Performance subtests employs visual stimuli or materials manipulated by the student. Only the Picture Completion subtest requires a verbal response (the subject can respond to some of the items, however, by pointing to missing parts of pictures). All subtests have time limits. Some of the subtests have different starting points, depending on the age of the subject. The six subtests are as follows:

Picture Completion Requires the student to identify (verbally or by pointing) the part of a picture that is missing. There are 26 items, and the test is discontinued after four consecutive failures.

Picture Arrangement Requires the student to arrange a series of 3, 4, or 5 pictures in order to "tell a story that makes sense." There are 12 items, and the test is discontinued after three failures.

Block Design Requires the student to arrange red and white cubes in a pattern to match the examiner's model or a picture of a model. There are 11 items, and the test is discontinued after two consecutive failures.

Object Assembly Requires the student to complete six- to eight-piece picture puzzles of common objects. There are four items, all of which are administered.

Coding A paper and pencil task in which the student is provided with a series of 93 boxes, each with a numeral, ranging from 1 to 9, in the top portion of the box. The student is provided with a code that shows what symbol is associated with each numeral. For each box, the student must write the symbol that corresponds to the number. The student completes as many boxes as possible in 2 minutes. A similar simplified version is administered to children younger than 8 years. In this version, marks are associated with five different shapes. There are 93 items for older children and 45 for younger children.

Mazes A paper and pencil task that requires the child to follow a path from inside to outside of increasingly difficult mazes. There are nine mazes, and the test is discontinued after two consecutive failures.

SCORING AND INTERPRETATION

On some subtests, the subject is given 1 point for each item completed correctly (Information, Arithmetic, Digit Span, Picture Completion, Coding). On others, the examiner must determine the quality of responses and assign 0, 1, or 2 points for each item, based on detailed scoring guidelines (Vocabulary, Similarities, and Comprehension). On the remaining subtests, points are assigned according to the speed with which items are successfully completed (Picture Arrangement, Block Design, Object Assembly), or according to the number of errors made (Mazes and Object Assembly items that are not totally correct). Scoring is generally fairly straightforward, except for the Vocabulary, Similarities, and Comprehension subtests that require the examiner to judge the quality of the response. Scoring guidelines for these items are fairly complete and clear, but there is definitely room for some variability among scorers. Scoring by an experienced examiner generally takes about 15 to 30 minutes.

For each subtest, the subject's raw score is compared with performance of other children his or her own age and assigned a "scaled score" between 1 and 19. For each subtest, the average scaled score is 10, with a standard deviation of 3. Five verbal subtest scaled scores (Information, Similarities, Arithmetic, Vocabulary, and Comprehension) are totalled and converted to a Verbal IQ* (VIQ), using a table provided in the manual. Similarly, five Performance subtest scaled scores (Picture Completion, Picture Arrangement, Block Design, Object Assembly, and Coding) are used to obtain a Performance IQ (PIQ). The five Verbal and five Performance scaled scores are totalled and converted to a Full Scale IQ. VIQs, PIQs, and Full Scale IQs are standard scores with a mean of 100 and a standard deviation of 15. VIQs and PIQs can range from 45 to 155. Full Scale IQs can range from 40 to 160. Functional levels are defined as follows:

130 and above:	Very Superior
120–129:	Superior
110–119:	High Average (Bright)
90–109:	Average
80–89:	Low Average (Dull)
70–79:	Borderline
69 and below:	Mentally Deficient

It is also possible to convert the IQs to percentiles. A table is provided that allows conversion of raw subtest scores to age-equivalents, called "Test Ages."

TECHNICAL QUALITY

Norms

The WISC-R norming sample consisted of 2,200 children. One hundred children of each sex were tested at each 1-year age level between the ages of 6 1/2 and 16 1/2 years. The sample was matched to the national population (based on the 1970 U.S. Census) on race, geographic region, urban or rural residence, and occupation level of head of household. Separate norms are provided for every 4-month age interval. Anastasi

---

*The term IQ or Intelligence Quotient is derived from older tests in which the subject's cognitive abilities were summarized in a score obtained by dividing Mental Age by Chronological Age, and multiplying by 100. The term "IQ" has been retained, despite the fact that no *quotient* is directly calculated.

(1982) wrote that "the WISC-R standardization sample is more nearly representative of the U.S. population within the designated age limits than is any other sample employed in standardizing individual tests" (p. 258). Of course, the WISC-R norms are becoming somewhat dated now.

Reliability

Reliabilities were established for the subtests and the VIQ, PIQ, and Full Scale IQ for each of 11 age groups, using data from the entire standardization sample. The average of these reliabilities, obtained through the split-half method (which provides a measure of internal consistency), is .94 for the VIQ, .90 for the PIQ, and .96 for the Full Scale IQ. Split-half reliability coefficients, averaged across age, range from .77 to .86 for the individual Verbal subtests, and from .70 to .85 for the individual Performance subtests.

Test-retest reliability for each of the 12 subtests and the three IQs was established, using a sample of 303 children from six selected age groups. Retesting occurred approximately one month after the original testing. Test-retest reliability coefficients, averaged across all age groups and corrected for the average variability of the relevant normative age groups, ranged from .65 to .88 for the individual subtests. The average test-retest reliabilities were .93 for the VIQ, .90 for the PIQ, and .95 for the Full Scale IQ. Additional studies by Vance, Blixt, Ellis, and Debell (1981), and Tuma and Applebaum (1980), among others, have reported high stability coefficients for the IQs after intervals exceeding six months, leading Vernon (1984b) to conclude that "the reliability and stability of the Full Scale scores are as high as or higher than those of other tests of intelligence" (p. 746). Thus, both internal consistency and stability across time are quite acceptable.

Standard errors of measurement were calculated, which provide an indication of the confidence one can have in making judgments about a child's true ability on a particular test. Standard errors of measurement, averaged across age groups, range from 1.15 to 1.70 for the individual subtest scores (which have a mean score of 10). Standard errors of measurement, averaged across age groups, are 3.60 for the VIQ, 4.66 for the PIQ, and 3.19 for the Full Scale IQ (each of which has a mean score of 100). Thus, the possible difference between the obtained scores and the "true" scores is relatively small, allowing the examiner to have a great deal of confidence in the accuracy of his or her measurements.

Validity

The WISC-R manual reports data from a limited number of studies of concurrent validity. Administering both the WISC-R and Wechsler Preschool and Primary Scale of Intelligence (WPPSI) to fifty 6-year-olds yielded coefficients of .80 for the VIQ-VIQ correlation, .80 for the PIQ-PIQ correlation, and .82 for the correlation between the two Full Scale IQs. WPPSI IQs were found to be about 2 points higher than the corresponding WISC-R IQs. A similar study comparing scores from the WISC-R and Wechsler Adult Intelligent Scale (WAIS), conducted with 40 children aged 16 years 11 months yielded a correlation of .95 for the Full Scale IQs, .96 for the VIQs, and .83 for the PIQs. Comparison of WISC-R IQs from 118 children with the IQs obtained on the Stanford-Binet (Form L-M, 1972 norms) revealed correlations of .71 for the VIQ, .60 for the PIQ, and .73 for the Full Scale IQ.

Although the WISC-R manual provides limited information regarding validity, thousands of studies have been conducted subsequent to the publication of the test that confirm its validity as a measure of intelligence for most populations. Review of these studies led Vernon (1984b) to conclude that there is strong support for the WISC-R's construct validity. As he notes, content validity is harder to assess, given the WISC-R's broad definition of intelligence. Users will have to examine the test items themselves to determine whether or not they tap constructs that are consistent with the user's concept of intelligence for the group being tested.

OTHER CONSIDERATIONS

In addition to strong evidence for reliability and validity, another strength of the WISC-R is the inclusion in the manual of information regarding interpretation of scaled score differences. A table is provided in the manual that gives the differences between scaled scores required for statistical significance at the 15% level of confidence. This table should definitely be used by examiners who are attempting to use subtest profiles to develop hypotheses regarding an individual student's strengths and weaknesses. Similarly, information is provided regarding the size of difference between the VIQ and PIQ that is required for statistical significance for each age group. On average, a difference of 9 points is required for significance at the 15% level and a difference of 12 points is needed at the 5% level. Wechsler (1974) states that a difference of 15 points or more is worthy of further investigation. An excellent source of further information regarding interpretation of the WISC-R is Kaufman (1979).

As stated previously, the WISC-R is generally considered one of the best measures, if not the best, of intelligence for school-age children. Its scores correlate highly with academic achievement. When used in conjunction with a test of academic achievement, it provides valuable information in the diagnosis of learning disabilities. (Learning disabilities *cannot*, however, be diagnosed using the WISC-R profile alone!) It is widely used in the identification of mental retardation, although Full Scale IQs do not go below 40, making it less useful in distinguishing among levels of retardation. For those professionals needing to make use of test data, there should be no hesitation about accepting a WISC-R score for most children, assuming that the test was administered by a competent examiner. Interpretation of the data also requires a competent professional who is familiar with the information regarding size of differences between scaled scores necessary for statistical significance. Familiarity with Kaufman's data regarding the percentages of normal children with various levels of VIQ-PIQ discrepancy and various amounts of subtest scatter (presented in Kaufman, 1979) is also important for the individual who wishes to use the WISC-R profile to identify a student's strengths and weaknesses.

SUMMARY

The WISC-R is considered to be one of the best of all psychological instruments in terms of technical qualities, including reliability, validity, and norms. Scores from the WISC-R can be assumed to be a very good indication of intelligence for most populations, assuming the test has been administered and scored properly. Full interpretation of the results, including identification of the student's strengths and weaknesses through the profile of subtest scores, requires a fair amount of experience and familiarity with information obtained from outside sources as well as the test manual.

KAUFMAN ASSESSMENT BATTERY FOR CHILDREN (K-ABC): MENTAL PROCESSING SCALES

Alan S. Kaufman and Nadeen L. Kaufman

American Guidance Service
Publisher's Building
Circle Pines, Minnesota   55014-1796

PURPOSE

The K-ABC, published in 1983, is a measure of intelligence, a construct defined by the authors as the "ability to process information effectively as a means of solving unfamiliar problems" (Kaufman, 1983, p. 206). The test was designed to "minimize the role of language and acquired facts and skills" (Kaufman, 1983, p. 206).

DESCRIPTION OF TEST AND ADMINISTRATION

The K-ABC is intended for use with children 2½ through 12½ years. It is composed of the Mental Processing Scales and the Achievement Scale. Because the Achievement Scale is more similar to an academic achievement test than an intelligence test, it will not be discussed in this volume.

The K-ABC is administered individually by a trained examiner who is very familiar with the manual and the test materials, generally a psychologist. Because of the wide variety of formats and materials, children generally enjoy taking the test and find it interesting. The manual provides very clear instructions regarding administration and scoring. Each subtest contains teaching items that allow the examiner to use whatever means are necessary to teach the child how to perform the task. This allows the examiner to be certain that items are not failed as a result of failure to understand instructions. Administration time varies from approximately 35 minutes for the youngest age groups to up to 75 to 85 minutes for older children.

The Mental Processing Scales include 10 subtests, which are divided into the Sequential Processing Scale and the Simultaneous Processing

Scale. The Sequential Processing Scale "measures a child's ability to solve problems by mentally manipulating the stimuli in serial order" (Kaufman, 1983, p. 206), whereas the Simultaneous Processing Scale "measures problem-solving skill whereby many stimuli have to be organized and integrated in parallel or simultaneous fashion" (Kaufman, 1983, p. 206).

Sequential Processing Scale

The three Sequential Processing subtests are described briefly, with the age ranges to which they are administered:

Hand Movements (For ages 2½ through 12½ years.) The child performs a series of hand movements in the same sequence as the examiner performed them.

Number Recall (For ages 2½ through 12½ years.) The child repeats a series of digits in the same sequence as the examiner said them.

Word Order (For ages 4 through 12½ years.) The child touches a series of silhouettes of common objects in the same sequence as the examiner said the names of the objects. (More difficult items include an interference task between the stimulus and response.)

Simultaneous Processing Scale

The seven Simultaneous Processing subtests are described briefly, with the age ranges to which they are administered. All of the subtests are presented on pages of the K-ABC "Easel-Kits" except for Magic Window, Triangles, and Photo Series. The Triangles subtest allows the child to manipulate plastic triangles, and the Photo Series subtest allows the child to arrange cards in order. The Triangles subtest is the only one that limits the amount of time the child is given to arrive at a correct response.

Magic Window (For ages 2½ through 5 years.) The child identifies a picture that the examiner exposed by slowly moving it behind a narrow window, making the picture only partially visible at any one time.

Face Recognition (For ages 2½ through 5 years.) The child selects from a group photograph the one or two faces that were exposed briefly on the preceding page.

Gestalt Closure (For ages 2½ through 12½ years.) The child names an object or scene pictured in a partially completed "inkblot" drawing.

Triangles (For ages 4 through 12½ years.) The child assembles several identical triangles into an abstract pattern to match a model.

Matrix Analogies (For ages 5 through 12½ years.) The child selects the meaningful picture or abstract design that best completes a visual analogy.

Spatial Memory (For ages 5 through 12½ years.) The child recalls the placement of pictures on a page that was exposed briefly.

Photo Series (For ages 6 through 12½ years.) The child places photographs of an event in chronological order.

As indicated by the age ranges, some tests are administered only to younger children, some only to older children, and some to all children. Most subtests have different starting points, depending on the age of the child. Stopping points for each age group are also indicated, although a child who performs especially well can be given items beyond the normal stopping point for his or her age.

SCORING AND INTERPRETATION

All items are scored as either correct (1 point) or incorrect (0 points). Scoring criteria are clearly presented, and there is little room for disagreement among examiners, based on subjective judgment. Experienced examiners find that scoring takes approximately 15 to 30 minutes. Computer scoring is available.

For each subtest, a raw score is calculated that is the total of correct responses. The child's raw score is compared with performance of other children of the same age and assigned a "scaled score" between 1 and 19. Like scaled scores on the WISC-R, the average score is 10, with a standard deviation of 3. Three to five Simultaneous subtest scaled scores (depending on the age of the child) are totalled and converted to a Global Scale score for Simultaneous Processing. Similarly, 2 or 3 Sequential subtest scaled scores (depending on the age of the child) are totalled and converted to a Global Scale score for Sequential Processing. All subtest scaled scores are totalled and converted to a Global Scale for Mental Processing Composite. Each of the Global Scale scores has a mean of 100, and a standard deviation of 15, just as the WISC-R VIQ, PIQ, and Full Scale IQ. Standard scores for the Global Scales can range from 40 to 160.

The K-ABC Manual also provides instructions for obtaining "confidence intervals" (a statistically derived range of scores within which the subject's "true score" can be expected to fall), and percentile scores based on both national norms and special norms for various sociocultural groups. Stanines and age-equivalent scores can also be obtained. Verbal descriptions for commonly used standard score ranges are as follows:

130 and above:	Upper Extreme
120–129:	Well Above Average
110–119:	Above Average
90–109:	Average
80–89:	Below Average
70–79:	Well Below Average
69 and below:	Lower Extreme

A Nonverbal Global score can be derived for children who are hearing-impaired, have serious speech or language disorders, or do not speak English.

TECHNICAL QUALITY

Norms

Norms for the K-ABC were developed in 1982, and are based on the performance of 1,981 children. The standardization sample was matched to the population, stratifying within each age group, on gender, geographic region, socioeconomic status, race or ethnic group membership, community size, and educational placement of the child in either regular or special education classes. The thoroughness of the sampling process is documented in the *K-ABC Interpretive Manual* (Kaufman & Kaufman, 1983). The standardization group was certainly of adequate size and representativeness to allow test users to feel confident in most cases that test scores truly reflect the child's standing within his or her peer group.

Norms are provided for separate age groups spanning 2-month intervals for ages 2½ through 5 years, and 3-month intervals for ages 6 through 12½ years. Special norms, based on performance of 807 black and 1,569 white children, were developed for six different socioeconomic groups, based on race and parental education, at each age level. Supplementary norms were also developed for out-of-level testing of children aged 4½ and 5 years of age, in order to permit children of these ages to be tested on some subtests that would normally be too easy or too difficult for the average child of this age.

Reliability

The K-ABC authors must be commended for their thorough job of substantiating the reliability of the instrument. Data relevant to several types of reliability are presented briefly here. A much more thorough discussion of the test's reliability is presented in the test manual.

Split-half Reliability. Data from the standardization sample were used to calculate split-half reliability coefficients for each subtest, using the Rasch-Wright model. Resulting reliability coefficients ranged from .72 to .88 for the preschool level, and from .71 to .85 for the school age level. Internal consistency for the Global Scales (Sequential Processing, Simultaneous Processing, Mental Processing Composite, and Nonverbal) was supported by mean split-half reliability coefficients ranging from .86 to .91 for the preschool sample and from .89 to .94 for the school-age children.

Test-Retest Reliability. A sample of 246 children, spanning the entire age range, was administered the K-ABC twice, with an intervening interval of 2 to 4 weeks. Reliability coefficients were calculated for each of the Mental Processing Global Scales. Coefficients ranged from .77 to .83 for preschoolers, from .82 to .88 for early elementary children, and from .87 to .93 for older children. Thus, the test's stability over at least a short interval is supported. Additional data indicate that stability coefficients are adequate for nearly all subtests.

Standard Error of Measurement. The mean standard errors of measurement at the preschool level are 4.8 for Sequential Processing, 5.7 for Simultaneous Processing, 4.6 for Mental Processing, and 5.4 for Nonverbal Scale scores. The average standard error of measurement at the school-age level was 5.0 for Sequential Processing, 4.0 for Simultaneous Processing, and 3.5 for the Mental Processing Composite. Subtest scores have standard errors of measurement that range from about 1 to 1½ points for both preschool and school-age children.

Validity

Extensive research is described in the manual that is relevant to the issue of the validity of the K-ABC. Using an innovative method of providing small "grants" for individuals doing research using the K-ABC, Kaufman and Kaufman (1983) funded about 20 studies relevant to validity. These, along with about 20 other validity studies are reported in the manual, which is far more than is reported in any other manual for a newly developed test. These studies are discussed under the headings of Construct Validity, Predictive Validity, and Concurrent Validity. In addition to these studies, the content validity of the test should be considered acceptable, based on the extensive test development procedures described in the manual.

Construct Validity. Kaufman and Kaufman (1983) report a study conducted by Reynolds, Chatman, and Willson (1983) that found significant correlations between age and performance on each of the K-ABC subtests, supporting the construct validity of the K-ABC as a developmental measure. Internal consistency within the battery was tested by correlating each subtest score with the Mental Processing Composite, for each of 11 separate age groups. The resulting coefficients ranged from .40 to .76, providing support for the construct validity of the Mental Processing Composite. Using statistical procedures called factor analysis, Kamphaus, Kaufman, and Kaufman (1982), and Willson, Reynolds, Chatman, and Kaufman (1983) obtained results supporting the Sequential-Simultaneous dichotomy for all age groups.

Kaufman and Kaufman (1983) present 10 pages of discussion regarding studies that correlate the K-ABC scores with those from other major tests of intelligence, including the WISC-R, WPPSI, and Stanford-Binet. Samples included normal children, learning disabled, physically impaired, high-risk preschoolers, gifted, culturally different Native Americans, mentally retarded, behaviorally disordered, and hearing-impaired children. In general, the correlations between the K-ABC and other tests of intelligence were moderate, supporting the construct validity of the K-ABC, while at the same time indicating that the K-ABC taps unique aspects of mental functioning not measured by the other tests.

Predictive Validity. Six studies are reported in the manual that correlated K-ABC scores with four separate achievement tests. Intervals between administration of the K-ABC and the academic achievement tests ranged from 6 months to 1 year. Correlations were moderate, generally ranging from .35 to .68.

Concurrent Validity. Kaufman and Kaufman (1983) include extensive discussion of studies correlating K-ABC scores with scores from a wide variety of academic achievement tests, both individually and group administered. The Sequential and Simultaneous Processing Scales generally correlated well with diverse areas of school achievement, as well as with correlates of group achievement scores. The Mental Processing Composite generally correlated more highly with achievement criteria than did either the Simultaneous or Sequential scores by themselves, again suggesting that both styles of information processing contribute uniquely to the concurrent "prediction" of school achievement. Other studies correlating K-ABC scores with tests of general cognitive ability (e.g., McCarthy Scales of Children's Abilities, the Woodcock-Johnson Psycho-Educational Battery cognitive portion, and the Cognitive Abilities Test) and The Luria-Nebraska Children's Battery also resulted in moderate correlation coefficients.

In general, the K-ABC must be commended for providing a wide spectrum of validity research, almost all of which supports the validity of the K-ABC as a measure of global intelligence for all populations studied thus far.

OTHER CONSIDERATIONS

In addition to the excellent norming sample and extensive reliability and validity data, the K-ABC has several other strengths of which the test consumer should be aware. The test developers provide substantial data on the K-ABC profiles of various groups of exceptional students, including learning disabled, dyslexic, mentally retarded, behaviorally disordered, physically impaired, high-risk preschoolers, hearing-impaired, and gifted students. Although these profiles need further validation, they do provide the examiner with some clues regarding what strengths and weaknesses may be demonstrated by children with various types of special needs. Kaufman and Kaufman (1983) also provide information regarding profile differences related to sex, socioeconomic status, and ethnic group membership (for blacks, Hispanics, and Native Americans).

The K-ABC manual describes a thorough and unambiguous process for empirically determining strengths and weaknesses within the profile. An informative discussion regarding the meaning of various patterns of strengths and weaknesses is provided, as are case studies that illustrate interpretation of several subtest profiles. The final section of the manual contains suggestions for educational programming that would be appropriate for children whose learning styles are dominated by strengths in either sequential or simultaneous processing. Although support for the contention that a remedial program derived from the K-ABC sequential-simultaneous processing model can lead to significant improvement in reading is provided by summaries of two studies, more research is necessary to substantiate this claim.

Strengths and weaknesses of the K-ABC, in comparison with the WISC-R and Stanford-Binet (Fourth Edition) are provided later in this chapter.

SUMMARY

Because the K-ABC is a relatively new test, it is less widely used than the WISC-R, and its advantages and disadvantages are less widely understood. Within the past 5 years, however, it has definitely earned its place as one of the most promising tests of intelligence for children. The presentation of reliability and validity data in the manual is by far the most comprehensive and informative of that for any of the well-known psychological instruments. Practitioners should have no concerns about accepting the accuracy of K-ABC scores as measures of intelligence for almost all children.

STANFORD-BINET INTELLIGENCE SCALE (FOURTH EDITION)

R.L. Thorndike, E.P. Hagen, and J.M. Sattler

The Riverside Publishing Company
8420 Bryn Mawr Avenue
Chicago, Illinois   60631

PURPOSE

The Stanford-Binet (Fourth Edition) was published in 1986 as a revision of the 1960 Stanford-Binet Intelligence Scale: Form L-M.* Users familiar with the older test will find, however, that the new version represents a complete overhaul, including an entirely different format and scoring system. In many ways, the developers of the Stanford-Binet have altered their test so that it is now more similar to the other two major tests of intelligence for children, the WISC-R and the K-ABC, than it is to the previous version of the Stanford-Binet.

The developers of the Stanford-Binet have attempted to serve the following purposes in their construction of the test:

1. To help differentiate between students who are mentally retarded and those who have specific learning disabilities.
2. To help educators and psychologists understand why a particular student is having difficulty learning in school.
3. To help identify gifted students.
4. To study the development of cognitive skills of individuals from ages 2 to adult (Thorndike, Hagen, & Sattler, 1986).

The test is designed to measure cognitive abilities of individuals from 2 to 23 years of age. Particular efforts have been made to avoid items that are racially, ethnically, or sexually biased.

DESCRIPTION OF TEST AND ADMINISTRATION

The test developers adopted a three-level hierarchical model of the structure of cognitive abilities. The first level is composed of a general reasoning factor ("g"), which, in turn, is made up of three broad factors at the second level: crystallized abilities, fluid-analytic abilities, and short-term memory. At the third level, verbal reasoning and quantitative reasoning are considered to comprise crystallized abilities, whereas

---

*Throughout the remainder of this book, the name "Stanford-Binet" will refer to The Stanford-Binet Intelligence Scale: Fourth Edition, unless otherwise stated.

3. Multi-Scale Tests of Intelligence and Cognitive Development: "The Big Three"   49

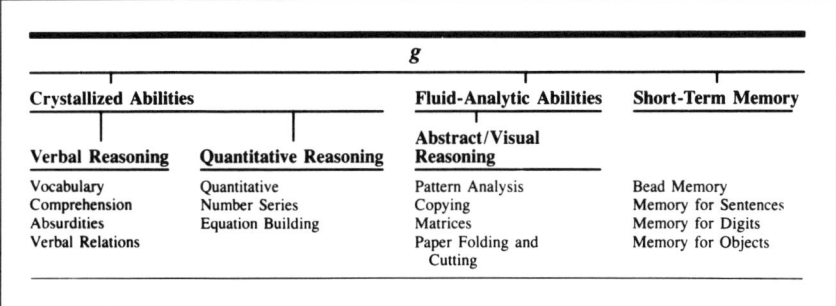

Source: Reprinted with permission of The Riverside Publishing Company from page 4 of *Stanford-Binet Intelligence Scale Guide for Administering and Scoring the Fourth Edition* by R. L. Thorndike, E. P. Hagen, and J. M. Sattler. The Riverside Publishing Company, 8832 Bryn Mawr Avenue, Chicago, IL 60631. Copyright 1986.

Figure 3-1. The Stanford-Binet's three-tier hierarchy and subtests that contribute to each area.

fluid-analytic abilities are represented by the abstract/visual reasoning factor. This three-tier hierarchy, as well as the 15 tests that measure the factors, are presented in Figure 3-1.

There are 15 subtests, but each child is administered only a portion of these (between 8 and 13), depending upon his or her age and "entry level." The entry level is established during administration of the first subtest, Vocabulary, which requires the child to name pictures of common objects or to orally define words. Performance on this test is used in conjunction with the child's age to determine an entry level, ranging from A to Q. Each of the remaining subtests is administered only to those children at the appropriate entry levels. The starting points for each subtest differ according to the child's entry level. Using this "adaptive-testing" format, children of the same age are not necessarily administered the same items or even the same tests.

For all subtests except Vocabulary, the examiner begins at the child's entry level. (The *Examiner's Handbook* [Delaney & Hopkins, 1987]* suggests some modification of this procedure, however.) Regardless of entry level, the examiner must establish a basal for each subtest, which is defined as the point at which all items at two consecutive levels are

---

*Both the *Examiner's Handbook* (Delaney & Hopkins, 1987) and the *Technical Manual* (Thorndike, Hagen, & Sattler, 1986) must be purchased separately from the test kit, but are essential for understanding and interpreting the Stanford-Binet.

passed. Ceiling levels for each subtest are established when the child passes at least three out of four items at two consecutive levels.

Delaney and Hopkins (1987) estimate that administration time averages approximately 30 to 40 minutes for students at Entry Levels A–C, 60 minutes for Entry Levels D–L, and 70 to 90 minutes for Entry Levels of M or higher. Several abbreviated batteries are suggested. In addition, Delaney and Hopkins (1987) suggest possible batteries that can be administered to individuals with limited English proficiency, for examinees who are deaf, motor impaired, visually impaired, or blind. Necessary test modifications are presented. However, separate norms for these special groups are not available.

Only one subtest, Pattern Analysis, is timed. Some time limits are suggested for other subtests.

The 15 tests are described as follows, and are organized according to the four areas presumed to be tapped by the various tests.* (Actual administration alternates tests from the four areas.) Within each test, items are arranged according to increasing difficulty, in levels A through Y.

Verbal Reasoning

Vocabulary This test contains two levels of items. The easier ones require the child to name pictures of common objects. The more difficult ones require the child to orally define words. There are 46 items, and the test is administered to all levels.

Comprehension This test contains two levels of items. The easier ones require the child to point to body parts on a picture of a child. The more difficult ones involve questions requiring understanding of social situations or everyday events (e.g., "Why do people go to the dentist?"). There are 42 items, and the test is administered to all levels.

Absurdities This test contains two levels of items. The easier ones require the child to point to which of three pictures shows something "wrong or silly." More difficult items require the child to explain what is wrong or silly about a depicted situation (e.g., a child painting with a spoon). There are 32 items, and the test is administered to all levels.

---

*The test examples provided here for illustrative purposes are similar to test items, but are not actual test items.

Verbal Relations The examiner reads a list of four words, and the student tells how three are alike and one is different. There are 18 items, and the test is administered only to those with an entry level of M or above.

Quantitative Reasoning

Quantitative There are two levels of items. The easier items require the child to use dice to match, count, add, subtract, or form logical series of numbers. The more difficult items are orally presented problems requiring application of math concepts. The child may use paper and pencil for these items. There are 40 items, and the test is administered to all levels.

Number Series The child is provided with a written set of numbers that are sequenced according to a certain rule. The child is asked to supply the next two numbers that would be consistent with the rule. There are 26 items, and the test is administered to those with an entry level of I or above.

Equation Building The student is provided with a written list containing several numbers and operational symbols and is required to arrange these numbers and symbols to make a mathematical statement that is true. There are 18 items, and the test is administered to those with an entry level of M or above.

Abstract/Visual Reasoning

Pattern Analysis There are two levels of items. The easier items require the child to complete a three-hole formboard with a circle, square, and triangle and then with combinations of pieces that together fit into the holes. More difficult items require the child to use black and white patterned cubes to match the examiner's model or a picture of a model. There are 42 items, and the test is administered to all levels.

Copying There are two levels of items. The easiest items require the child to arrange blocks to match the examiner's model. More difficult items require the child to draw copies of designs. There are 28 items, and the test is given only for entry levels A–J.

Matrices The child is presented with 2×2 or 3×3 matrices. In each of the cells except one are symbols or pictures that are related to one another according to some rule. The child must choose from four or five options the symbol or picture that completes the pattern. The four hardest items do not provide multiple-choice options, and the student must write the answer on the test form. There are 26 items, and the test is administered to those with an entry level of I or above.

Paper Folding and Cutting The child is shown a series of figures that demonstrate how a piece of paper is folded and cut. Using a multiple-choice format, the child must choose which of five drawings would look like the paper if it were unfolded. There are 18 items, and the test is administered to those with an entry level of M or above.

Short-Term Memory

Bead Memory For the easier items, the child is shown one or two beads and must identify them from memory by pointing to their pictures on a card showing the 12 different types of beads. On the more difficult items the child is shown a pattern of beads and is asked to reproduce it from memory, using beads of three colors and four shapes. There are 42 items, and the test is given to all ages.

Memory for Sentences The child is required to repeat a sentence exactly as spoken by the examiner. There are 42 items, and the test is administered to all levels.

Memory for Digits The child hears series of three to nine digits and is asked to repeat the series exactly as spoken by the examiner. Using series of two to seven digits, the child is asked to repeat the series in exact reverse order. There are 14 forward series and 12 reversed series. The test is administered to those with entry levels of I or above.

Memory for Objects The child is shown a picture of a common object or a series of pictures and then is asked to identify from a group of pictures the ones seen and the correct order of presentation. There are 14 items, and the test is administered to those with entry levels of I or above.

SCORING AND INTERPRETATION

For most of the tests, there is only one correct answer for each item. Five of the tests—Vocabulary, Comprehension, Absurdities, Copying, and Verbal Relations—require use of scoring guides presented in the manual. Guidelines indicate as clearly as possible the guiding principles involved in scoring and provide examples of correct, incorrect, and ambiguous answers that require follow-up. As with any tests that require a spontaneous verbal explanation, there is some room for disagreement in scoring, even among experienced scorers. All items are given 1 point if passed and 0 points if failed. Raw scores are calculated by totalling the number of correct items plus the number of items below basal level.

Raw scores on single tests are converted to Standard Age Scores using the norming tables. These Standard Age Scores have a mean of 50 and a standard deviation of 8. Standard Age Scores within each of the four areas (Verbal Reasoning, Abstract/Visual Reasoning, Quantitative Reasoning, and Short-Term Memory) are summed and converted to Area Standard Age Scores (Area SASs), based on a second set of tables. These four scores, each of which has a mean of 100 and a standard deviation of 16, are summed. The examiner then uses a third set of tables to convert the sum of the Area SASs to a Composite SAS, which also has a mean of 100 and a standard deviation of 16. To compare scores with other test scores that have means of 100 and standard deviations of 15, the *Technical Manual* provides a conversion table. Partial Composites, based on recommended abbreviated test batteries, can also be calculated. Composite Scores can be classified as follows (Delaney & Hopkins, 1987, p. 155):

132 and above:	Very Superior
121–131:	Superior
111–120:	High Average
89–110:	Average
79–88:	Low Average
68–78:	Slow Learner
67 and below:	Mentally Retarded

The lowest Area or Composite SAS that can be obtained is 36, preventing discrimination among levels of retardation below the moderate range. A table for computing age-equivalent scores for each subtest is provided in the *Technical Manual* and in the *Examiner's Handbook*.

The *Technical Manual* and the *Examiner's Handbook* provide statistics that allow the examiner to determine whether differences between SASs for the areas and composite are statistically significant. As Spruill (1987) notes, however, these values were computed without consideration of the fact that multiple comparisons are being made, which constitutes a "major error" (p. 552). To the test developers' credit, information is provided in the *Examiner's Handbook* regarding the mean and median discrepancies between the Composite SAS and each Area SAS, and among the Area SASs, based on the standardization sample. Tables in the *Examiner's Handbook* also indicate the percentage of the standardization sample that showed SAS discrepancies of various amounts (comparing the Composite with each of the Area SASs, as well as comparing each Area SAS with each of the other Area SASs). This allows the examiner to determine how unusual a given discrepancy between SASs is.

A "Profile Analysis" chart is provided in the test booklet for plotting subtest scores. Delaney and Hopkins (1987) suggest a difference of 7 points between individual subtests as an "arbitrary cut-off point" for determining strengths and weaknesses within the profile (p. 83). They include in their *Examiner's Handbook* a useful chart for interpreting strengths and weaknesses within the profile (p. 87). The "inferred abilities and influences" identified within a profile are, however, based on "the judgment of the authors of this *Handbook* and their interpretation of research literature" (Delaney & Hopkins, 1987, p. 85), and the validity of these interpretations remains questionable. Furthermore, as will be noted in the next section, some of the individual subtests are of questionable reliability. Thus, some discrepancies between individual subtests may not reflect true differences, but may be the result of measurement error. Wisely, Delaney and Hopkins recommend that inferences based on subtest strengths and weaknesses be confirmed or denied using qualitative data regarding the child.

TECHNICAL QUALITY

Norms

Standardization was carried out in 1985 on a sample of 5,013 individuals. The standardization sample was stratified according to the following variables: geographic region, community size, ethnic group, age, gender, parental occupation, and parental education. According to the test developers, the sample closely matched the U.S. population (based on the 1980 census) for all of the variables except parental occupation and parental education. The sample contained proportionately more in the college graduate or beyond and managerial and professional occupation groups than did the national population. The test developers claim that this bias was reduced by using a weighting procedure that counted each child from an "advantaged" background as only a "fraction of a case" (as little as 0.28), and counted each child from a "less advantaged" background as more than one case. This procedure suggests, however, that the sample of "less advantaged" children may not be truly representative of this group. As there is no shortage of children from less advantaged backgrounds, it is not clear why the developers used this weighting procedure instead of collecting additional data.

Norms are provided at 4-month intervals for children between 2–0 (2 years 0 months) through 5–11, at 6-month intervals for children between 5–11 and 10–11, and at 12-month intervals between 10–11 and 17–11. Only one set of norms is provided for the oldest group, spanning 17–11 through 23–11. It does not seem reasonable to expect so little change in performance between the ages of 18 and 24 that individuals within this age range can be compared to a single standardization group. Even the 1-year intervals for children between 11 and 18 years of age seem excessively large.

Reliability

Most of the reliability information available at this point regarding the Stanford-Binet is based on measures of internal consistency. As would be expected, the most reliable score is the Composite SAS. Across age groups, reliability coefficients ranged from .95 to .99, suggesting good consistency across subtests in the measurement of the general factor of intelligence. Standard errors of measurement for the Composite SAS ranged from 1.6 to 3.6 across age groups. Indices of internal consistency for the Area SASs were all at or above .80. Reliability is generally better when more subtests are involved in obtaining the Area SAS. Median reliability coefficients (across age groups) for individual subtests were all above .80, except for Memory for Objects, which was .73. Standard errors of measurement generally ranged from 1.6 to 4.1. Again, Memory for Objects yielded somewhat higher standard errors of measurement. For all scores, reliability coefficients are generally higher and standard errors of measurement are generally lower for older groups than for younger groups.

The *Technical Manual* reports test-retest reliability data from a total of 112 children, approximately half at 5 years of age and half at 8 years of age. The length of time between the two test administrations varied from 2 to 8 months. Reliability coefficients for the Composite SAS were .91 for the preschool sample and .90 for the elementary school sample. Reliability for the Area SASs ranged from .71 to .88 for the preschool sample. For the elementary school sample, Verbal Reasoning and Short-Term Memory Area SASs had test-retest reliability coefficients in the

.80s. Reliabilities for the other two areas, Abstract/Visual Reasoning and Quantitative, were somewhat low, at .67 and .51, respectively. Reliability coefficients for individual subtests ranged from .69 to .78 for the preschool sample, except for the Bead Memory Test, which had a coefficient of .56. For the elementary school sample, reliability coefficients for individual subtests were somewhat lower than desirable, ranging from .61 to .78, except for Comprehension (which had a coefficient of .86) and Quantitative and Copying (which had coefficients of .28 and .46, respectively). Thus, it appears reasonable to accept the Composite SAS scores and most of the Area SAS scores as reliable, at least for the age groups sampled. Reliability of some of the individual subtests is, however, more questionable.

Validity

Concurrent Validity. The *Technical Manual* presents comparison of scores from the Stanford-Binet with scores from Form L-M (the older version of the Stanford-Binet), WPPSI, WISC-R, WAIS-R, and K-ABC. With samples of "nonexceptional" students, ranging in size from 47 to 205, correlations between composite scores (Composite SASs, Full Scale IQs, or Mental Processing Composites) ranged from .80 to .91, suggesting that the Stanford-Binet Composite does measure general intelligence for normal individuals. The mean Stanford-Binet Composite SAS was 2 to 5 points lower than composite scores from the other tests, except for the WAIS-R, which yielded a mean Full Scale IQ that was 3.5 points lower, and the K-ABC, which yielded a Mental Processing Composite that was almost identical to the Stanford-Binet score.

Reviewing the data from studies presented in the manual and other studies that were conducted after the publication of the *Technical Manual*, Spruill (1987) concludes that the correlational data between the Stanford-Binet Composite SAS and other major tests of cognitive ability are acceptable, although "specific predicted patterns of results between the various scores of the Fourth Edition and other tests have not always been borne out" (p. 557).

Predictive Validity. The *Examiner's Handbook* presents data relevant to predictive validity that were not available at the time of publication of the *Technical Manual*. Scores from the Stanford-Binet were correlated with data from two achievement tests, the Wide Range Achievement Test–Revised (WRAT-R) and the Woodcock-Johnson Psycho-

Educational Battery (Part II: Tests of Achievement). With samples of "nonexceptional" students ranging in age from 5 to 13, and test intervals of 6 to 7 months, the correlations between Stanford-Binet Composite SASs and achievement test scores were generally between the .50s and .80s. This range of correlation coefficients is fairly standard for comparisons between tests of intelligence and tests of achievement.

Construct Validity. The *Technical Manual* presents data from two types of factor analytic studies. The first, using "a variant of confirmatory analysis" was carried out on the median correlations for the 17 age groups of the standardization sample. All tests demonstrated substantial loadings on the General Ability factor. Confirmation for the four areas—Verbal, Abstract/Visual, Quantitative, and Memory—was less convincing. In particular, Bead Memory had a low loading on the Memory factor, Paper Folding and Cutting had a low loading on the Abstract/Visual factor, and Copying and Matrices did not load appreciably on any of the group factors.

When separate factor analyses were conducted for three age ranges—2 through 6, 7 through 11, and 12 through 23, the results again confirmed the General Ability factor. However, the results were much less supportive for the existence of the four areas, especially for the younger groups. Spruill (1987) concludes that the claim of Thorndike et al. (1986) for conformation of the Stanford-Binet to the theoretical framework used to construct the test and good support for the theoretical rationale underlying the test is questionable.

OTHER CONSIDERATIONS

One strength of the Stanford-Binet is inclusion of a rating scale on the cover of the test booklet that may be used to summarize the examiner's clinical observations of the child. Although no further information is provided by the test developers regarding this scale (i.e., there are no norms or data on reliability and validity), it can be a handy device, especially for the less experienced tester. Another strength is the inclusion in the *Examiner's Manual* of many informative case studies.

Weaknesses of the test, however, overshadow its many strengths. These are discussed as follows: The older version of the Stanford-Binet was often used by psychologists for children who are too advanced for the Bayley Mental Scale (which provides norms through 30 months) and who are too young for the WPPSI (which provides norms starting at age 3 years 10 months). Unfortunately, the new Stanford-Binet is not a particularly valuable test for children in the 2½ through 4 year age range, especially if there are developmental delays (as there often are in children being tested this young). As the test developers note, many 2-year-olds obtain too many raw scores of 0 to allow calculation of IQs. At age 3, the developers claim, the test "adequately discriminates" among all except the lowest 2%. The author has many experiences with children at age 3 and older who were unable to achieve basal level on several subtests. Even if failure to reach basal level occurs in only 2% of 3-year-olds, one must keep in mind that it is often this 2% who are being seen for clinical evaluation. Because of this limitation with the new Stanford-Binet, some clinicians are actually continuing to use the older version with the population between 2½ and 4 years of age. This is difficult to justify, given that the norms are becoming quite dated and there are other excellent tests, such as the K-ABC, that cover this age range. In a related matter, Spruill (1987) reports that for older and very bright individuals, some of the subtests have a ceiling that is much too low.

Also of particular concern is the fact that several of the tests contain two types of items that seem quite dissimilar. For example, the easy items on the Comprehension test require children to point to body parts on a picture of a child. The more difficult items require the child to answer questions involving everyday events or social situations (e.g., "Why do people go to the dentist?"). It is not at all unusual for a child to be able to answer all of the easier questions and none of the more difficult questions. This is especially true for children with language delays, as they are often able to comprehend single words, but have great difficulty with comprehension of connected language. Similarly, children with expressive language difficulties might show the same pattern of performance, as the easier items require no verbal response, whereas the more difficult items require fairly sophisticated verbalization. It is doubtful, then, that the two types of items on this test are measuring the same construct for some children. In addition, the change in the nature of items can be quite confusing to the child if the examiner must go back to the easier type of item to establish a basal level and then return to the more difficult items to establish the ceiling. The same arguments can be made for the other tests that contain two types of items (Vocabulary, Absurdities, Copying, Bead Memory, Quantitative, and Pattern Analysis).

Because the Stanford-Binet is "essentially a power test" (Thorndike et al., 1986, p. 22), only one of the subtests, Pattern Analysis, has mandatory time limits for most of its items. For two of the more difficult tests, Number Series and Equation Building, Thorndike et al. suggest that most examinees who can correctly solve the items can do so in 2 minutes or less. "Suggested" time limits are provided, but the examiner apparently must rely on clinical judgment regarding enforcement of the limits. When using the test with adults, the author has found that it is affected dramatically by the perseverance of the examinee, especially if the suggested time limits are not enforced. Testing with a particularly persistent adolescent or adult could take in excess of 3 hours. It can also be questioned why the test developers do not consider a person's quickness in solving a problem as relevant to the measurement of intelligence.

To keep testing time to 60 to 90 minutes, the test developers suggest several abbreviated batteries. However, because the reliability is necessarily reduced by using an abbreviated battery, the examiner may prefer to administer the entire test over two sessions.

Although use of the "adaptive-testing" format (whereby tests are administered only to children at certain entry levels) prevents excessive frustration or boredom for the very dull or very bright child, it does make administration of the test more difficult to learn. The *Examiner's Handbook* suggests certain modifications for selecting an entry level (e.g., using Level A for all 2- and 3-year-olds). The effects of making these modifications, as opposed to applying the standardized procedure used with the norming sample, are unknown.

Another concern regarding the adaptive testing format involves adequacy of norms for very bright and very dull examinees. Because only a few bright children take some of the tests at the higher levels and only a few of the dull children take some of the tests at the lower levels, the norming samples for some tests at some age levels are inadequate. For example, an average 10-year-old would not take the Verbal Relations subtest, as his or her entry level would be below M, the minimum entry level required for administration of this test. As a result, few 10-year-olds in the standardization sample took this test, and the norms available on the Verbal Relations subtest for 10-year-olds cannot be considered representative. The examiner is, however, given the option to calculate scores only for those tests where adequate samples are available (i.e., where the standardization sample contained at least 100 subjects).

SUMMARY

The Stanford-Binet Intelligence Scale (Fourth Edition) represents a major overhaul in this veteran test. It appears, however, that the test developers attempted to create a test that was appropriate for too wide an age range. As a result, it is not particularly useful for the youngest age range (2½ through 4), especially for developmentally delayed children. This is a major loss, as the Stanford-Binet has, in the past, been particularly useful with this age group. Similarly, because norms for adults are represented by a single standardization sample of individuals 18 to 23 years of age, because of the excessive time sometimes necessary for administering the test to adults, and because of the low ceilings on some of the subtests, the adequacy of the test for this age group is also questionable. For the school-age group, there are many reasons, some of which have been presented here and some of which are mentioned by other reviewers (e.g., Spruill, 1987), that the Stanford-Binet cannot be considered the test of choice for measuring intellectual functioning. For the professional who has been given Stanford-Binet data as the primary measure of a child's intelligence, the Composite score can generally be considered to adequately represent cognitive skills. Interpretation of the Area scores and the subtest profiles should be done with caution and consideration of some of the test's weaknesses, as outlined in this section.

CONSIDERATIONS IN SELECTING THE WISC-R, K-ABC, OR STANFORD-BINET

Because the K-ABC and the Stanford-Binet (Fourth Edition) are relatively new tests (published in 1983 and 1986, respectively), both are still less widely used than the WISC-R, and their advantages and disadvantages are less widely understood. It is recommended that psychologists involved in evaluating children be familiar with all three of these major tests of intelligence and cognitive development. They will probably find it more appropriate to use one or another of the three tests in various situations. Although it is impossible to identify the K-ABC, Stanford-Binet, or the WISC-R as the "best" test for measuring intelligence, there are certain considerations that the psychologist should consider in each individual case:

• One of the major advantages of using the K-ABC instead of the WISC-R or Stanford-Binet is the availability of the K-ABC Achievement subtests, which were normed on the same sample as the K-ABC Mental Processing subtests. This allows the examiner to confidently compare results of the intelligence measure and the academic achievement measures, which is essential in making the diagnosis of learning disabilities. Unfortunately, however, the Achievement subtests do not adequately test several important academic skills (e.g., spelling, application of phonics skills, written calculations) that are commonly measured by achievement tests.

• The K-ABC, unlike the WISC-R, includes in its norming sample exceptional children (e.g., learning disabled, mentally retarded, gifted children) in the same proportion as occurs in the national population. The Stanford-Binet norming sample included some exceptional students, but it is not clear what types and what proportions of exceptional students were involved. Inclusion of exceptional students in the norming sample increases validity of the scores for the individual exceptional student.

• Because the K-ABC and Stanford-Binet are newer tests than the WISC-R, the children in their standardization samples are probably more similar to children currently being evaluated than the children in the WISC-R standardization sample, thus increasing the chance for validity. An important point to be noted in the use of tests for diagnosing learning disabilities is the necessity for a high degree of comparability of standardization samples for tests whose scores are being compared. That is, when the scores from two tests (e.g., an intelligence test and an achievement test) are to be compared, the samples on which those two tests were normed should be highly similar. The most widely used tests of academic achievement have been standardized within the past 10 years. Because the WISC-R was normed in the early 1970s, its standardization sample may be less similar to the standardization samples used in norming the widely used tests of academic achievement than are the K-ABC's and Stanford-Binet's standardization samples. Thus, comparisons between scores from a test of intelligence and scores from tests of academic achievement may be more valid if the K-ABC or Stanford-Binet is used.

- Racial and ethnic differences are less pronounced on the K-ABC, and perhaps the Stanford-Binet, than on the WISC-R. For example, Kaufman (1983) reports a 7-point average difference between the scores of black children and white children on the K-ABC, whereas an average difference of 16 points is reported for the WISC-R (Kaufman & Doppelt, 1976). A similar trend is reported for the differences between scores of Hispanic and white children. The developers of the Stanford-Binet had a large staff representing various minority groups review all of the test items for the possibility of racial, ethnic, or gender bias. This procedure resulted in some items being revised or dropped. However, the test developers do not provide information regarding differences in scores among various racial and ethnic groups or sexes.

- All K-ABC Mental Processing subtests include teaching or training items. These allow the examiner to use various means to make certain that the child understands the task. Although the WISC-R and Stanford-Binet provide sample items for most subtests (which allow the examiner to correct mistakes, using a clearly prescribed protocol), these sample items do not always ensure that the child understands what is expected. This, of course, is a more serious problem with younger or less intelligent children. The K-ABC teaching items allow the examiner to be more certain that a low score reflects a true weakness in a skill area rather than an inability to understand directions.

- The K-ABC provides a Nonverbal Scale, made up of subtests that can be administered in pantomime and responded to motorically. This is designed for children who are hearing impaired, who have serious speech or language disorders, or who use English as a second language. Although many of the WISC-R Performance subtests require no verbal response, it might be difficult to communicate the instructions for the task to a hearing-impaired child. Furthermore, this would definitely be considered "nonstandard" procedure for administration of the WISC-R subtests, thus invalidating norms. The Stanford-Binet suggests alternate batteries that can be given to students with limited English proficiency or hearing deficits, but special norms for these batteries are not provided.

- The K-ABC provides a variety of supplementary norms, including sociocultural norms (based on a cross-tabulation by race and by parental education). Thus, children can, when desired, be compared with peers from similar sociocultural backgrounds.

- The K-ABC provides specific strategies for teaching reading, math, and spelling, based on the child's profile of strengths and weaknesses on the Simultaneous versus Sequential Mental Processing tasks. (The effectiveness of these strategies, however, has not yet been proven.)

- Although the K-ABC intentionally omitted tasks that require extensive verbal expression, it cannot be denied that this is an ability that contributes greatly to school success. The examiner may want information comparing verbal and nonverbal skills, which can be obtained much more directly and thoroughly from the WISC-R, and to a lesser extent from the Stanford-Binet, than from the K-ABC.

- Just as the K-ABC may be useful for testing children who are hearing impaired or who have serious speech or language disorders, the WISC-R Verbal subtests may be useful for assessing cognitive abilities of children who are visually impaired. These children would be seriously disadvantaged on the K-ABC tests. The Stanford-Binet suggests alternative batteries for children who are blind or visually impaired. None of these tests provides special norms for visually impaired children.

- The WISC-R and Stanford-Binet allow the examiner to observe the child over a greater range of response modes than the K-ABC. Manipulation of objects, paper-and-pencil skills, single-word responses, elaborated oral responses, identification by pointing, and imitation of the examiner are all required by the various WISC-R and Stanford-Binet tasks. Although individual scores are not obtained for each of these response modes, the experienced examiner can use his or her observation to formulate some fairly sophisticated hypotheses regarding certain factors that will interfere with the child's learning. Most of the responses on the K-ABC require identification by pointing, although a few require single-word responses, manipulation of objects, or imitation of the examiner.

- The WISC-R and Stanford-Binet employ more manipulative materials than the K-ABC. Although this makes administration of the WISC-R and Stanford-Binet somewhat more cumbersome, it may be more effective in keeping the child's attention (especially at younger ages).

- Because of its "adaptive-testing" procedure, the Stanford-Binet is definitely the most difficult of the three tests to learn to administer. The WISC-R is generally considered to be a more difficult test to learn to administer than the K-ABC. Also, because scoring on several of the WISC-R and Stanford-Binet subtests is somewhat subjective, examiners with less testing experience may have more difficulty scoring these tests as accurately as the K-ABC.

• The three tests are designed to cover different age ranges, with the WISC-R covering ages 6 to 16, the K-ABC covering ages 2½ to 12½, and the Stanford-Binet covering ages 2 through adult. As mentioned previously, younger children or those with significant delays are often unable to reach basal level on several of the Stanford-Binet subtests. For very young children, the K-ABC would generally be the most appropriate test to use, although examiners might wish to supplement it with some measure of verbal ability. For older preschool children, the WPPSI-R should be considered. For individuals older than age 16, the WAIS-R should be considered, as the norms for older individuals on the Stanford-Binet only go up through age 23 years 11 months and are based on a large single sample for individuals between 18 and 24.

• Because the WISC-R has been available much longer, it is better known and better understood by most professionals than the two newer tests. The psychologist who chooses to use the K-ABC or Stanford-Binet will probably have to spend more time explaining the scales and their meaning. This consideration will, of course, become less valid if and when the K-ABC and Stanford-Binet become more widely used.

SUMMARY

This chapter has presented information regarding the purpose, administration, scoring, and technical qualities of three of the most popular tests for measurement of intellectual ability in children. The practitioner who is presented with scores from any of these three tests can, in general, be confident of the overall score of cognitive ability (the WISC-R Full Scale IQ, the K-ABC Mental Processing Composite, or the Stanford-Binet Composite SAS), assuming the test was properly administered and scored. Subtest scores available from these tests can generally be considered reliable and valid, although there are a few exceptions for particular age groups (especially for the Stanford-Binet). Interpretation of subtest profiles must be done cautiously, taking into consideration the discrepancies between subtest scores necessary for statistical significance, as well as data regarding the extent to which such discrepancies are commonly observed.

This chapter has also presented strengths and weaknesses of the WISC-R, K-ABC, and Stanford-Binet. It is impossible to identify one of these three tests as the "best." Each test's strengths and weaknesses must be considered in order to determine the most reliable and valid measure of intelligence for a particular child or group or children. As noted in previous chapters, practitioners must be cautious about using any single test score for decision-making purposes. The results from the tests of intelligence discussed in this chapter must be considered together with other data, including results from other tests, clinical observations during testing, teacher reports, and information on educational and cultural background.

CHAPTER 4

OTHER MULTI-SCALE TESTS OF INTELLIGENCE AND COGNITIVE DEVELOPMENT

Chapter 3 presented information regarding three of the most popular tests of cognitive ability for children. This chapter discusses other multi-scale tests of intelligence and cognitive ability. For the purpose of this book, a "multi-scale" test is one that provides scores in two or more areas of intellectual functioning (e.g., verbal and nonverbal). Chapter 5 presents information on single-scale tests that provide only one score reflecting overall intelligence. It is important to note, however, that some instruments designated as single-scale tests may include items assessing a variety of cognitive functions. They are termed single-scale tests based on the fact that they provide only a single *score* of intellectual functioning.

WECHSLER PRESCHOOL AND PRIMARY SCALE OF INTELLIGENCE (WPPSI)

David Wechsler

The Psychological Corporation
555 Academic Court
San Antonio, Texas 78204-2498

PURPOSE

The WPPSI, published in 1967, was designed with the same methodological and theoretical approaches to the measurement of mental ability as the WISC (see chapter 3). The test has been updated recently, and the new version, the WPPSI-R, is discussed in the next section. Information regarding the WPPSI has been included in this text because some practitioners may still be using it or may have access to scores from it.

DESCRIPTION OF TEST AND ADMINISTRATION

The WPPSI was developed for children from 4 to 6½ years of age. Like the WISC-R, it is administered individually by a trained examiner, usually a psychologist. Administration requires a fair amount of practice, as well as total familiarity with the manual. Testing generally requires 50 to 75 minutes and can be completed in one session. The manual provides very explicit instructions, including verbatim directions that are to be used by the examiner in presenting the items. Like the WISC-R, the WPPSI uses a variety of test formats and materials that help to maintain the child's interest.

The WPPSI contains six Verbal tests, designed to measure language skills, and five Performance tests, which primarily tap visual-spatial skills.* During the administration Verbal and Performance tests are given in an approximate alternate fashion.

Verbal Tests

The six Verbal tests are all presented orally and require an oral response from the child. Only the Arithmetic subtest involves time limits. The six tests are described as follows:

Information Requires the child to respond to orally presented questions involving general knowledge in a variety of areas. Typical questions would be "How many wheels does a car have?" or "What color is a lemon?" There are 23 questions, and the test is discontinued after five consecutive failures.

Vocabulary Requires the child to define individual words presented orally. For example, "What is a leg?" "What does *intelligent* mean?" There are 22 items, and the test is discontinued after five consecutive failures.

Arithmetic The easiest items involve demonstration of pre-arithmetic concepts such as "smallest" or "more." The next items involve counting objects, and the most difficult items require the child to answer "word problems," such as "Jack had three cookies and gave one to Mary. How many cookies did Jack have left?" There are 20 items, and the test is discontinued after four consecutive failures.

Similarities The easiest items require the child to complete sentences that involve two similar concepts. For example, "A mouse is little, an elephant is _____ ?" More difficult items require the child to describe how two concepts are alike. For example, "How are the sun and the moon alike?" There are 16 items, and the test is discontinued after four consecutive failures.

---

*Simulated items adapted from the Wechsler Preschool and Primary Scale of Intelligence. Copyright © 1967, 1963 by The Psychological Corporation. Reproduced by permission. All rights reserved.

Comprehension The child responds to orally presented questions involving understanding of social situations or everyday events. For example, "Why should children brush their teeth?" or "What is the thing to do if you get lost in a store?" There are 15 items, and the test is discontinued after four consecutive failures.

Sentences The child is required to repeat sentences exactly as spoken by the examiner. There are 13 items, and the test is discontinued after three consecutive failures.

Performance Tests

Each of the five Performance tests employs visual stimuli or materials manipulated by the child. Only the Picture Completion subtest requires a verbal response (the subject can respond to some of the items, however, by pointing to missing parts of pictures). All tests are timed except for Picture Completion and Geometric Design. The five subtests are as follows:

Animal House The child is presented with a board that has four different animals pictured at the top, each associated with a peg of a different color. Underneath are 20 pictures of the same four animals, each accompanied by an empty hole. The child is given a box of colored pegs and is required to place a peg in the hole under each animal, making certain that the color corresponds to the animal, as demonstrated in the model. There is a 5-minute time limit. Animal House can also be repeated as an optional subtest, and separate norms are provided for Animal House Retest.

Picture Completion The child is shown drawings of common objects, each of which is missing a part. The child must identify (verbally or by pointing) what part is missing. There are 23 items, and the test is discontinued after five consecutive failures.

Mazes A paper and pencil task, containing easy items that require the child to mark a path between a baby chick and its mother. More difficult items require the child to follow a path from inside to outside of increasingly difficult mazes. There are 10 items, and the test is discontinued after two consecutive failures.

Geometric Design A paper and pencil task that requires the child to copy increasingly difficult geometric designs. There are 10 items, and the test is discontinued after two consecutive failures.

4. Other Multi-Scale Tests of Intelligence and Cognitive Development 71

Block Design The child is required to arrange red and white blocks to match a model presented by the examiner or a picture of a model. There are 10 items, and the task is discontinued after two consecutive failures.

SCORING AND INTERPRETATION

For some of the tests (Information, Arithmetic, Picture Completion, and easy items on Similarities), 1 point is given for each correct response. For other tests (Vocabulary, harder Similarities items, and Comprehension), the examiner must determine the quality of responses and assign 0, 1, or 2 points for each item, based on detailed scoring guidelines. Mazes and Sentences are scored according to the number of errors made. Animal House is scored according to the speed with which the task is completed, along with number of errors. Block Design is scored according to whether the child was able to correctly arrange the blocks on the first or second trial, and Geometric Design is scored according to the quality of the drawings. Scoring is generally fairly straightforward, except for the Vocabulary, Similarities, Comprehension, and Geometric Design subtests that require the examiner to judge the quality of the response. Scoring guidelines for these items are fairly complete and clear, but there is definitely room for some variability among scorers. Scoring by an experienced examiner generally takes 15 to 30 minutes.

Converting raw scores to scaled scores and IQs is done exactly as with the WISC-R. Scores for all Verbal tests except Sentences are used in the calculation of the VIQ, and all Performance scores except Animal House Retest are used to calculate the PIQ. The Full Scale IQ is based on the five Verbal and five Performance scores used in calculating the VIQ and PIQ. As with the WISC-R, scaled scores have a mean of 10 and a standard deviation of 3. The VIQ, PIQ, and Full Scale IQ have means of 100 and standard deviations of 15, and can range from 45 to 155. Scaled scores and IQs can be converted to percentiles, and raw scores can be converted to Test Ages.

TECHNICAL QUALITY

Norms

The WPPSI standardization sample of 1,200 children was composed of 100 boys and 100 girls in each of six age groups, ranging by half-years from 4 to 6½ years. The sample was matched with the national population, according to the, 1960 U.S. Census, on the factors of geographic region, urban versus rural residence, race (white vs. nonwhite), and father's occupational group. The sample is judged to be adequate in size and representation, although the norms are now fairly dated and thus may result in inflated scores when compared with some of the more up-to-date tests.

Reliability

Reliability coefficients were calculated, using a split-half method, for each subtest and IQ score at each age level. When averaged across all ages, the reliability coefficients for the individual subtests range from .77 to .85, indicating fairly good internal consistency. The average reliability coefficient was .94 for the VIQ, .93 for the PIQ, and .96 for the Full Scale IQ. A test-retest study with an interval of approximately 11 weeks between the original testing and retesting was conducted on 50 kindergarten children. Stability coefficients, corrected for differences in variability, ranged from .60 to .93 for the subtests. The stability coefficients were .86 for the VIQ, .89 for the PIQ, and .92 for the Full Scale IQ, indicating good stability over time.

Standard errors of measurement, calculated for each subtest at each age level, ranged from .87 to 1.87. Because of the wide range of standard errors of measurement, examiners should take these into account when attempting to use individual subtest scores to identify a child's strengths and weaknesses. Errors of measurement ranged from 3.40 to 3.69 for the VIQ, from 3.44 to 4.35 for the PIQ, and from 2.66 to 3.12 for the Full Scale IQ. As would be suspected, errors of measurement were generally higher for younger children than for older children within the sample.

Validity

The WPPSI manual describes one study in which WPPSI scores were correlated with scores from three other individually administered intelligence tests: The Stanford Binet (Form L-M), the Peabody Picture Vocabulary Test (Form A), and the Pictorial Test of Intelligence. Mean scores yielded by the four measures were similar. Correlations between the WPPSI IQs and other test scores ranged from .53 to .76 for the VIQ, from .44 to .60 for the PIQ, and from .58 to .75 for the Full Scale IQ, with correlations generally higher between the WPPSI and the Stanford-Binet than between the WPPSI and either of the other two tests. Although validity data are sparse in the manual, many subsequent studies have been conducted that provide substantial support for the criterion-related validity of the WPPSI, when scores from either intelligence tests or academic achievement tests are used as outcome measures (Elbert & Holden, 1985). In addition, factor analytic studies provide support for separation of the WPPSI into Verbal and Performance scales (Elbert & Holden, 1985).

OTHER CONSIDERATIONS

As with the WISC-R, the test developer has included in the manual information regarding the amount of difference among subtest scores that is required for statistical significance. Similarly, the amount of difference between VIQs and PIQs that is necessary for significance is discussed. These statistics are important for proper interpretation of scores and subtest profiles. As with the WISC-R, examiners must be cautious not to "overinterpret" profiles when differences between subtests scores are not statistically significant.

One weakness of the WPPSI is the relatively small age range covered by the test. As a result, it is not particularly valuable for testing very bright children at the upper age range or very slow children at the lower age range. The manual states, for example, that it will be difficult to test children whose IQs are below 75 at age 4, below 69 at age 5, or below 50 at age 6. Because many preschool assessments are done for the purpose of diagnosing mental retardation, this test may not be appropriate for many clinic patients. Full Scale IQs below 45 cannot be calculated for any age group, which prevents discrimination among the lowest levels of retardation. Elbert and Holden (1985) note that the appropriateness of the WPPSI for identifying gifted children has been questioned because of limitations at the test ceiling. Elbert and Holden (1985) also note that some children fail on Performance subtests because their verbal skills are insufficient for understanding directions.

SUMMARY

In general, the excellent technical qualities of the WPPSI have made it one of the most widely used of all preschool measures. As with the

WISC-R, practitioners can have confidence in WPPSI IQs for most populations, assuming that administration and scoring of the test have been done properly. More in-depth analysis of WPPSI scores requires experience, as well as substantial information not presented in the manual, but available elsewhere. Practitioners should be wary of results for children who are significantly below or above average, especially at the extremes of the age range for which the test is intended. With the availability of the WPPSI-R, use of the WPPSI can no longer be recommended because of the obsolescence of the WPPSI norms. However, scores from previous evaluations employing the WPPSI can be used with confidence if practitioners remember that WPPSI scores may be somewhat higher than scores from more recently normed tests.

WECHSLER PRESCHOOL AND PRIMARY SCALE OF INTELLIGENCE–REVISED (WPPSI-R)

David Wechsler

Psychological Corporation
555 Academic Court
San Antonio, Texas   78204-2498

PURPOSE

The WPPSI-R, published in 1989, provides "standardized measures of a variety of abilities thought to reflect different aspects of intelligence" (Wechsler, 1989, p. 1). The WPPSI-R IQ serves "as an estimate of the individual's capacity to understand and cope with the surrounding world" (Wechsler, 1989, p. 1). The test is designed for children aged 3 years through 7 years 3 months, which is a somewhat broader age range than its predecessor, the WPPSI. The test developers suggest that the WISC-R continue to be used with normal children 6 years and older who are expected to have average or above-average cognitive and communicative abilities. The WPPSI-R can be used instead of the WISC-R for children in this age range who are expected to perform below average.

TEST DESCRIPTION AND ADMINISTRATION

Like the WPPSI and other Wechsler scales, the WPPSI-R is divided into Performance subtests, which primarily measure perceptual-motor skills, and Verbal subtests. The Verbal subtests of the WPPSI-R are the same as those for the WPPSI, although item format and content have been modified somewhat.*

Information This subtest requires the child to respond to orally presented questions regarding events or objects in the environment. The easiest items require a pointing response, whereas more difficult items require a verbal response.

Comprehension Items on this subtest require the child to "express in words his or her understanding of the reasons for actions and the consequences of events" (Wechsler, 1989, p. 7).

Arithmetic The easiest items on this subtest require the child to demonstrate understanding of basic quantitative concepts (e.g., "largest," "less than"). More difficult items require the child to count objects and solve word problems.

Vocabulary The easiest items require the child to name a pictured object. On more difficult items the child provides verbal definitions for orally presented words.

Similarities The easiest items on this subtest require the child to point to which of four pictured objects is most similar to a group of pictured objects that share a common feature. The next items require the child to complete a verbally presented sentence that reflects a similarity or analogy between two things. The most difficult items require the child to tell how two objects or events are alike.

Sentences This task requires the child to repeat a sentence exactly as spoken by the examiner. This test is optional.

No time limits are imposed for Verbal subtest items except for the word problems on the Arithmetic subtest.

---

*Simulated items adapted from the Wechsler Preschool and Primary Scale of Intelligence—Revised. Copyright © 1989 by The Psychological Corporation. Reproduced by permission. All rights reserved.

The Performance subtests of the WPPSI-R are the same as those for the WPPSI, with the addition of Object Assembly. Animal House has been retained in the WPPSI-R, but has been renamed Animal Pegs and is optional. The six Performance subtests are the following:

Object Assembly This subtest requires the child to fit puzzle pieces together to form a meaningful whole.

Geometric Design The easiest items on this subtest require the child to identify which of four geometric figures is identical to a model that is presented simultaneously. More difficult items require the child to copy a geometric figure from a printed model.

Block Design This test requires the child to "analyze and reproduce, within a specified time limit, patterns made from flat two-colored blocks" (Wechsler, 1989, p. 7).

Mazes This subtest requires the child to solve paper and pencil mazes of increasing levels of difficulty.

Picture Completion The child is required to "identify what part is missing from pictures of common objects or events" (Wechsler, 1989, p. 8).

Animal Pegs On this subtest the child matches pegs of four different colors with pictures of four different animals, according to a pattern presented in the model.

Items are individually timed for Object Assembly, Block Design, and Mazes, with bonus points given for fast performance on some Object Assembly and Block Design items. Animal Pegs has a time limit of 5 minutes. Other subtests are not timed.

As with the WPPSI, Verbal and Performance subtests are alternated during administration. Some tests have different starting points for children of different ages, although basal levels must be established when the subtest is not administered from the beginning. Each test is discontinued after a specified number of consecutive failures. All subtests except Arithmetic provide sample items or allow the examiner to provide the correct answer on the first item.

The WPPSI-R should be administered by an examiner experienced in the administration of standardized clinical instruments. Interpretation of results should be limited to those with appropriate training and experience in psychological assessment.

SCORING AND INTERPRETATION

Scoring for the WPPSI-R is basically the same as for the WPPSI. On some of the subtests (Information, figure-matching items on Geometric Design, Arithmetic, picture items on Vocabulary, Picture Completion, picture and sentence completion items on Similarities), items are scored as either correct (1 point) or incorrect (0 points). On other subtests (Comprehension, verbal items on Vocabulary, and verbal analogy items on Similarities), a response can receive a score of 0, 1, or 2, depending on its quality. Items on the Object Assembly subtest are scored according to the number of pieces correctly joined, with bonus points given for fast performance. On Geometric Design, several specific criteria are outlined for each of the figure-copying items. Each drawing is scored according to the number of criteria that are met by the drawing. Block Design items receive 2 points if performed correctly on the first trial and 1 point if passed on the second trial, with bonus points given for fast performance on the more difficult items. Mazes and Sentences are scored according to the number of errors made. For Animal Pegs, the score is based on the number of errors and omissions and the time taken to complete the task.

Scoring criteria are generally clear and sufficiently explicit. As with any test involving spontaneous verbal responses, some subjective judgment is involved in scoring. Scoring criteria for Geometric Design have been improved considerably over those provided by the WPPSI. The test kit even includes a template for assessing straightness of lines, angles, and gaps. Scoring for this subtest is, however, quite time consuming. In general, scoring is fairly easy and straightforward, although some practice is required to master criteria sufficiently for smooth administration.

Raw scores from each subtest are converted to scaled scores, according to tables of age-based norms. Scaled scores can range from 1 to 19, with a mean of 10 and a standard deviation of 3. Scaled scores from Information, Comprehension, Arithmetic, Vocabulary, and Similarities are totalled, and this sum is converted to the Verbal IQ. Scaled scores from Object Assembly, Geometric Design, Block Design, Mazes and Picture Completion are totalled and converted to the Performance IQ. Scaled scores from all 10 of these subtests are totalled and converted to the Full Scale IQ. The VIQ, PIQ, and Full Scale IQ each has a mean of 100 and a standard deviation of 15. Full Scale IQs range from 41 to 160. Subtest raw scores can also be converted to age-equivalent scores called Test Ages. Categorical descriptions for various IQ levels are as follows:

130 and above:	Very Superior
120 to 129:	Superior
110 to 119:	High Average
90 to 109:	Average
80 to 89:	Low Average
70 to 79:	Borderline
69 and below:	Intellectually Deficient

The WPPSI-R manual includes several tables that are useful in interpretation of test scores. These include a table regarding the difference between VIQ and PIQ required for significance at the 5% and 15% confidence levels, as well as a table presenting the frequency of given VIQ-PIQ discrepancies within the standardization samples. Other tables provide the minimum difference between subtest scaled scores that is necessary for statistical significance. Generally, a difference of 3 or more scaled score points is significant at the 15% level, whereas a difference of 4 or more points is necessary at the 5% level. Similarly, tables have been provided to determine whether a significant difference exists between an individual subtest score and the average scaled score on all subtests. Finally, another table presents the frequency of various discrepancies between scores on individual subtests and average subtest scores. All of these tables are helpful in preventing "overinterpretation" of WPPSI-R profiles. However, the examiner must have a fairly strong background in psychological testing in order to interpret the data in a way that is appropriate and meaningful.

TECHNICAL QUALITY

Norms

WPPSI-R norms are derived from a group of 1,700 children, with 100 boys and 100 girls in each of eight age groups, ranging by half years from 3 to 7 years, and one group of 50 boys and 50 girls ranging in age from 7 years 0 months through 7 years 3 months. The sample was selected to represent the United States population on geographic region, ethnicity, and parent education and occupation, as determined by census data from 1986. In general, the norming procedure appears to be quite appropriate.

Norms are provided at 3-month intervals for ages 2 years 11 months through 7 years 3 months.

Reliability

Split-half reliabilities were calculated for each of nine age groups of the norming sample for VIQ, PIQ, Full Scale IQ, and subtest raw scores. Correlations ranged across ages from .85 to .93 for PIQ, from .86 to .96 for VIQ, and from .90 to .97 for Full Scale IQ. Reliability coefficients for individual subtests, averaged across ages, ranged from .63 for Object Assembly to .86 for Similarities. Reliability coefficients were generally lower for the 7-year-olds than for the younger children because of ceiling effects.

Interscorer reliability was assessed for those subtests that involve some subjective judgment in scoring, namely Comprehension, Vocabulary, Similarities, Mazes, and Geometric Design. Two examiners independently scored protocols from 151 to 188 children who were randomly selected from the standardization sample. Interscorer reliability coefficients were .94 for Vocabulary, .96 for Similarities, .94 for Mazes, and .88 for Geometric Design. Thus, interscorer reliability is sufficient.

Test-retest reliability was assessed by retesting a sample of 175 children, divided into two age groups (3 and 4-year-olds, and 5 through 7-year-olds). Test-retest intervals ranged from 3 to 7 weeks. Stability coefficients, corrected to provide estimates of stability in the population, were .88 for the PIQ, .90 for the VIQ, and .91 for the Full Scale IQ. Corrected stability coefficients for the subtests ranged from .52 for Mazes to .82 for Picture Completion. Thus, although test-retest reliability is adequate for the VIQ, PIQ, and Full Scale IQ, it is somewhat low for some of the individual subtests.

Standard errors of measurement ranged across ages from 3.94 to 4.90 for the PIQ, from 3.09 to 4.98 for the VIQ, and from 2.81 to 3.91 for the Full Scale IQ. Standard errors of measurement for subtests were generally between 1.0 and 2.0, with higher standard errors obtained for the 7-year-olds than for the other age groups.

In general, reliability for the PIQ, VIQ, and Full Scale IQ is quite acceptable. Reliability data for individual subtests suggest that certain subtest scores should be interpreted cautiously. All measures of reliability compare favorably with those of the WISC-R and other intelligence tests for preschool children.

Validity

The manual provides some validity data from the WPPSI that is relevant to the validity of the WPPSI-R because of the similarity of the structure and content of the two tests. Factor analytic studies support the two-factor (i.e., Verbal and Performance) structure of the WPPSI. Concurrent validity studies generally show moderate to high correlations between scores from the WPPSI and other widely used measures of intelligence. Predictive validity studies have found the WPPSI to be a good predictor of both future intellectual ability and academic achievement.

Validity data for the WPPSI-R is more limited than for the WPPSI, but is substantial given the recency of the WPPSI-R's publication. A study of intercorrelations among the WPPSI-R subtests supports the two-factor structure of the test. As would be expected, Verbal subtests correlated more highly with other Verbal subtests (with an average correlation of .57) than with Performance subtests (with an average correlation of .33). Similarly, Performance subtests correlated more highly with one another (with an average correlation of .40) than with Verbal subtests. Factor analytic studies also resulted in a two-factor solution of the WPPSI-R for three age groups.

Concurrent validity was investigated by comparing WPPSI-R scores with scores from the WPPSI, WISC-R, Stanford-Binet Intelligence Scale (Fourth Edition), McCarthy Scales of Children's Abilities, and the K-ABC. High correlations were found between the WPPSI-R and WPPSI (with average correlations of .82 for PIQ, .85 for VIQ, and .87 for Full Scale IQ). WPPSI scores were approximately 8 points higher than the WPPSI-R score for Full Scale IQ, 9 points higher for PIQ, and 5 points higher for VIQ. These differences probably reflect the higher developmental level of today's preschool children compared with that of children 22 years ago when the WPPSI was normed.

The correlation between the WPPSI-R and WISC-R was conducted with a sample of 50 children ranging in age from 72 to 86 months (the age range for which the two tests overlap). WPPSI-R scores correlated with WISC-R scores .85 for Full Scale IQ, .75 for PIQ, and .76 for VIQ. The WISC-R Full Scale IQ is approximately 7 points higher than the WPPSI-R Full Scale IQ, with the VIQ being approximately 5 points higher and PIQ being approximately 9 points higher.

The Stanford-Binet Intelligence Scale (Fourth Edition) was administered to 115 children who had taken the WPPSI-R. The correlation between the WPPSI-R Full Scale IQ and the Stanford-Binet Composite was .74. The WPPSI-R VIQ correlated .73, and the PIQ correlated .56 with the Stanford-Binet Composite. Consistent with previous research with the WPPSI, the WPPSI-R PIQ correlated most highly with the Stanford-Binet Abstract/Visual Reasoning Area score (r = .54), and the WPPSI-R VIQ correlated most highly with the Stanford-Binet Verbal Reasoning Area Score (r = .63). The Stanford-Binet Composite was approximately 2 points higher than the WPPSI-R Full Scale IQ.

The WPPSI-R Full Scale IQ correlated .81 with the General Cognitive Index from the McCarthy Scales of Children's Abilities and yielded a Full Scale IQ that was approximately 2 points higher than the General Cognitive Index. The WPPSI-R Full Scale IQ correlated .49 with the Mental Processing composite of the K-ABC. The test developers hypothesize that this relatively low correlation may simply reflect sample bias within the small sample (N = 59) or may indicate that the two scales measure somewhat different constructs. The mean WPPSI-R Full Scale IQ was approximately 6 points lower than the mean Mental Processing Composite.

Further validity studies were conducted with various special populations. A sample of 16 children who were identified as gifted on the old Stanford-Binet (Form L-M) (IQs > 130) obtained lower WPPSI-R scores (mean Full Scale IQ = 122). This could be due to the obsolescence of the norms from the Stanford-Binet (Form L-M) or to the statistical phenomenon of regression toward the mean. The WPPSI-R was administered to a sample of 21 children classified as mentally retarded, based on scores from the Stanford-Binet (Form L-M), the PPVT-R, and the Beery Test of Visual-Motor Integration–Revised. The mean WPPSI-R Full Scale IQ was 65.2, suggesting that the WPPSI-R has an adequate floor for testing low-ability children.

In summary, results from intercorrelational and factor analytic studies indicate that the WPPSI-R is based on the same two-factor structure as the WPPSI and WISC-R. The IQs obtained from the WPPSI-R generally correlated highly with those from other measures of intelligence. The WPPSI-R can be expected, however, to yield somewhat lower scores than other IQ tests, especially those with older norms. In general, validity data are sufficient for a new test, and it is expected that future research will continue to support confident use of WPPSI-R scores.

SUMMARY

The WPPSI-R is a test of general cognitive function, designed for children between 3 years and 7 years 3 months of age. It appears to have all of the advantages of its predecessor, the WPPSI, including a well-founded and easily comprehensible structure that is based on verbal and visual-spatial factors. Other advantages shared with the WPPSI include comparability with other Wechsler scores, clear instructions for administration, and a variety of item types and response modes that help to maintain the child's interest. The major drawback of the WPPSI, its obsolete norms, has, of course, been remedied with a current standardization sample that is representative of the population. Other improvements include extension of the age range of the test both downward and upward, modification of the subtest structure to make the WPPSI-R more consistent with other Wechsler scales, clearer scoring criteria for some of the subtests (especially Geometric Design), inclusion of more sample items, and updating of visual stimuli. Reliability and validity data are sufficient to allow confident use of the WPPSI-R. It is expected that the WPPSI-R will become the test of choice for measuring intelligence of most preschool children.

WOODCOCK-JOHNSON PSYCHO-EDUCATIONAL BATTERY–REVISED (TESTS OF COGNITIVE ABILITY) (WJ-R COG)

Richard W. Woodcock
M. Bonner Johnson

DLM Teaching Resources
One DLM Park
Allen, Texas   75002

The Woodcock-Johnson Psycho-Educational Battery–Revised was published in 1989 as an update to the original version of this test, published in 1977. Like the older version, the Woodcock-Johnson Psycho-Educational Battery–Revised includes Tests of Cognitive Ability (WJ-R COG) and Tests of Achievement (WJ-R ACH). Only the Tests of Cognitive Ability are reviewed here. Because the revised version of this test has been published so recently, many readers may still be using the older version or may have access to scores from the older version. For this reason, the original Woodcock-Johnson Psycho-Educational Battery (Part I: Tests of Cognitive Ability) is also reviewed in the next section.

PURPOSE

The WJ-R COG is "an operational representation" of the Horn-Cattell theory of intellectual processing and contains tests that are designed to measure seven of the broad intellectual abilities defined by this theory. These abilities are fluid reasoning ("capability to reason in novel situations"), comprehension-knowledge ("breadth and depth of knowledge and its effective application"), visual processing ("capability in perceiving and thinking with visual patterns"), auditory processing ("comprehension and synthesis of auditory patterns"), processing speed ("performing relatively trivial cognitive tasks quickly"), long-term retrieval ("effectiveness in storing information and retrieving it over extended periods of time"), and short-term memory ("apprehending information and utilizing it within a short period of time") (Woodcock & Mather, 1989, pp. 19–20).

The WJ-R COG is designed for individuals from age 2 years through adulthood, with norms provided up through 90 years and older.

DESCRIPTION OF TEST AND ADMINISTRATION

The WJ-R COG is composed of a Standard Battery and a Supplemental Battery. Within the Standard Battery are seven tests, one for each of seven of the broad intellectual abilities theorized by the Horn-Cattell model. The tests are as follows:

1. *Memory for Names.* For this test, the individual is shown a picture of a "space creature" and is told its name. The individual must then identify from a group of nine pictures the creature just introduced. A new creature is introduced on each item, and the individual must identify the new creature, as well as those from all previous items.

2. *Memory for Sentences.* The individual must repeat phrases and sentences exactly as spoken by a model.

3. *Visual Matching.* This test requires the individual to locate and circle the two identical numbers in a row of six numbers.

4. *Incomplete Words.* The individual hears words with one or more phonemes missing and must identify the complete word.

5. *Visual Closure.* This test requires the individual to name a drawing or picture that has been distorted, has missing lines or areas, or is partially covered by a superimposed pattern.

6. *Picture Vocabulary.* The individual identifies pictures of objects, either by pointing to the object named or by naming the object presented.

7. *Analysis-Synthesis.* This test requires the individual to analyze the presented components of an incomplete logic puzzle and to determine the missing components.

The Supplemental Battery consists of an additional 14 tests:

8. *Visual-Auditory Learning.* This test measures the individual's ability to associate new visual symbols (rebuses) with familiar words and to translate a series of symbols into verbal sentences.

9. *Memory for Words.* The individual is required to repeat lists of unrelated words in correct sequence.

10. *Cross Out.* The individual is given a page containing rows of 3 drawings, with 20 drawings per row. He or she marks the five drawings in a row that are identical to the first drawing in the row.

11. *Sound Blending.* The individual must integrate and say whole words after hearing parts (syllables or phonemes) of the word.

12. *Picture Recognition.* This test requires the individual to recognize a subset of previously presented pictures within a field of distracting pictures.

13. *Oral Vocabulary.* This test has two parts, Synonyms and Antonyms. Synonyms requires the individual to state a word similar in meaning to the word presented. Antonyms requires the subject to state a word that is opposite in meaning to the word presented.

14. *Concept Formation.* The individual must identify the rules for concepts when shown illustrations of both instances of the concept and noninstances of the concept.

15. *Delayed Recall–Memory for Names.* This test requires the individual to identify (after 1 to 8 days) the space creatures presented in Test 1 (Memory for Names).

16. *Delayed Recall–Visual-Auditory Learning.* This test requires the individual to recall (after 1 to 8 days) the words associated with the symbols (rebuses) presented in Test 8 (Visual-Auditory Learning).
17. *Numbers Reversed.* The individual must repeat series of random numbers in exact reverse order.
18. *Sound Patterns.* This test requires the individual to state whether pairs of complex sound patterns, presented by tape, are the same or different.
19. *Spatial Relations.* The individual must select, from a series of shapes, the component parts needed to make a given whole shape.
20. *Listening Comprehension.* The individual listens to a short passage and must supply the last word in order to complete the passage sensibly.
21. *Verbal Analogies.* This test requires the individual to complete phrases with words that indicate appropriate verbal analogies.

As illustrated in Figure 4-1, a variety of measures can be obtained by administering various combinations of tests from the Standard and Supplemental Batteries. Broad Cognitive Ability, an overall measure of intelligence, can be obtained from the Standard Scale (Tests 1 through 7 of the Standard Battery), the Extended Scale (Tests 1 through 14), or the Early Development Scale (all of the Standard Battery except Visual Matching and Analysis-Synthesis), which is used for preschool children. Administration of the Extended Scale (Tests 1 through 14) also allows measurement of seven cognitive factors and four scholastic aptitude clusters. The scholastic aptitude clusters are designed to measure an individual's *expected* achievement level in four academic areas (reading, mathematics, written language, and knowledge of content areas). Tests 15 through 21 of the Supplemental Battery are generally selected individually to obtain additional information about a specific referral concern, to investigate a diagnostic hypothesis, or to further explore an observed pattern of strengths and weaknesses. Only two clusters, Oral Language and Oral Language Aptitude, require administration of any of the last eight tests of the Supplemental Battery.

The WJ-R COG is to be administered by examiners with training and experience in individual test administration and interpretation. The WJ-R COG manual provides complete guidelines for examiner training.

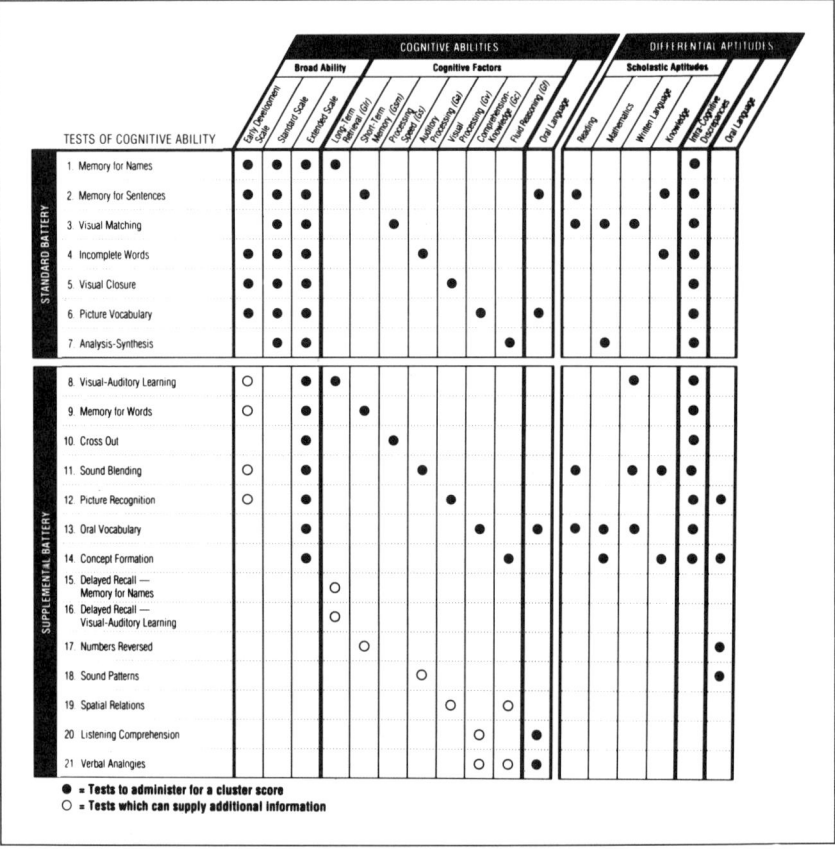

Source: From R. Woodcock and N. Mather, *WJ-R Tests of Cognitive Ability—Standard and Supplemental Batteries: Examiner's Manual*, DLM Teaching Resources, 1989, p. 12. Reprinted by permission.

Figure 4-1. Organization of the Woodcock-Johnson Psycho-Educational Battery—Revised tests of cognitive ability.

In general, the WJ-COG is easy to administer, with instructions for both the examiner and the subject presented conveniently and unambiguously.

The seven tests in the Standard Battery require 30 to 40 minutes to administer. Another 40 minutes is needed to administer Tests 8 through 14 of the Supplemental Battery. The Early Development Scale requires 20 to 30 minutes.

Seven of the tests, Memory for Sentences, Incomplete Words, Memory for Words, Sound Blending, Numbers Reversed, Sound Patterns, and Listening Comprehension, are presented by an audio tape that is provided to ensure standardized administration. Stimuli for two tests, Visual Matching and Cross Out, are presented in the Test Record. Stimuli for all other tests are presented in the easel test books. No manipulative stimuli are used, except for paper and pencil.

Starting points for various ages are suggested for Memory for Sentences, Incomplete Words, Picture Vocabulary, Memory for Words, Oral Vocabulary, Numbers Reversed, Listening Comprehension, and Verbal Analogies. Basal levels (based on a particular number of correct consecutive responses) must be established for these tests. For all other tests, the examiner begins with the first item for all subjects. Visual Matching and Cross Out have a time limit of 3 minutes, regardless of the subject's age. Cut-off points for the other tests are specified clearly in the Test Record. Because cut-off criteria are different for each test, the examiner must be particularly attentive to make certain the appropriate number of items is administered for each test. Time limits are set for individual test items on Visual Closure, Visual-Auditory Learning and some of the most difficult items on Analysis-Synthesis and Concept Formation. Otherwise, no time limits are prescribed.

Most tests have sample items, and some allow the examiner to give the subject limited feedback when errors are made.

SCORING AND INTERPRETATION

For all tests except Memory for Sentences, items are scored as either correct (1 point) or incorrect (0 points). Memory for Sentences allows scores of 2, 1, or 0, with partial credit being given for sentence repetitions that include only one error. In most cases, correct and incorrect responses are clearly defined. Some responses require additional questioning, as indicated by the scoring criteria. Only occasionally must the examiner use professional judgment to determine whether a response should be scored as correct or incorrect.

For most subjects, the raw score is based on the number of correct items plus credit for every item below basal level. The raw score for Visual-Auditory Learning, however, is the number of *errors* the subject makes, and the raw score for Sound Patterns is the number of "different" pairs identified correctly by the subject. Visual Matching and Cross

Out allow bonus points if all items are completed before the time limit. The raw score on the two Delayed Matching tests depends on the number of days elapsed between the original testing and the delayed memory tasks.

Raw scores can be directly converted to age-equivalent and grade-equivalent scores, using tables provided in the Test Record. In addition, the Test Record provides a "W score," which is an equal interval measure that is used to calculate cluster scores. The information available in the Test Record itself is sufficient for completing an "Age/Grade Profile," which allows a comparison of the subject's performance on the various tests.

The process for converting raw scores to standard scores or percentiles is quite complex and time consuming. Briefly, the W scores for the seven tests in the Standard Battery are averaged to obtain a W score for Broad Cognitive Ability. (W scores for other clusters are obtained by averaging the W scores from the appropriate tests for those clusters.) The examiner then refers to a table of age-based or grade-based norms to obtain a "reference W score" (REF W) and standard error of measurement for each test. This REF W score is the average W score for individuals at the same age or grade level as the individual being tested. The norms tables also provide two column numbers that will be used to locate the standard score and percentile ranks in another table. The W score for each test is subtracted from the REF W, resulting in a difference score (DIFF), which can be either positive (indicating above-average performance), zero (indicating average performance), or negative (indicating below-average performance). The examiner then uses the DIFF score and the column numbers obtained in the previous step to locate in another table the standard score and percentile for each test.

Standard scores have a mean of 100 and a standard deviation of 15. Standard errors of measurement can be added and subtracted from the standard score and percentile score to obtain confidence bands for these measures. Profiles are provided for plotting these confidence bands. In addition, a "Relative Mastery Index" (RMI) can be obtained. This measure allows the examiner to determine the subject's expected level of mastery on tasks similar to the ones tested. For example, an RMI of 90/90 indicates that the subject would be expected to demonstrate 90% mastery on similar tasks that average individuals in the comparison group would also perform with 90% mastery. Finally, standard scores can be converted to T scores (mean = 50, standard deviation = 10), stanines (mean = 5, standard deviation = 2), or normal curve equivalents (mean = 50, standard deviation = 21.06).

Standard scores from tests or clusters can be classified as follows:

131 and above:	Very Superior
121 to 130:	Superior
111 to 120:	High Average
90 to 110:	Average
80 to 89:	Low Average
70 to 79:	Low
69 and below:	Very Low

Because the scoring procedure involves so many steps, examiners must be extremely careful to avoid errors. The test developers suggest that available computer software be used for scoring, and this recommendation appears to be quite appropriate. The test developers also wisely advise examiners to calculate only those scores that will actually be used rather than calculating every available score.

A comment should be made regarding the age-equivalent and grade-equivalent scores provided by the WJ-R COG. These scores sometimes include a superscript, as in the age-equivalent score $4\text{-}0^{35}$ or in the grade-equivalent score $K.0^{10}$. These "extended" age- or grade-equivalent scores are used at both extremes of the age- and grade-level continuum to describe the abilities of individuals who perform below the average score for the youngest children in the norming sample or above the average score of mature adults. For example, if the subject's performance is below the average for 4-year-olds (the youngest children in the norming sample for some of the tests), the resulting score of $4\text{-}0^{35}$ would indicate that he or she performed at the 35th percentile for the comparison group of children aged 4 years 0 months. Similarly, a grade-equivalent score of $K.0^{10}$ is interpreted as performance at the 10th percentile for beginning kindergarten students.

A comment should also be made regarding "extended percentile ranks" and "extended standard scores" that are provided by the WJ-R COG. Most standardized tests provide percentiles between 1 and 99. Performance of individuals falling outside this range is usually assigned a score of <1% or >99%. The WJ-R COG provides percentile ranks of 0.1 up to 99.9. Similarly, most standardized tests allow calculation of standard scores of approximately 40 through approximately 160. Standard scores on the WJ-R COG can range from 0 to 200. These extended scores make the WJ-R COG particularly useful for assessing individuals with relatively severe retardation. (Individuals must, of course, have a mental age of approximately 2 years in order to reach basal level on the tests.) Professionals relying on extended scores must realize, however, that they are based on extremely small samples, and thus may be less reliable than scores closer to the mean. Furthermore, most professionals do not have experience interpreting standard scores at the extremes of the continuum and may not be able to use this additional information to much advantage.

If the Extended Battery has been administered, the examiner can calculate "intracognitive discrepancies" that allow for interpretation of possible strengths and weaknesses within the cognitive profile. If the Woodcock-Johnson Tests of Achievement have been administered, the examiner can also calculate discrepancies between aptitude and achievement in four academic areas. Computer scoring is also recommended for these calculations.

TECHNICAL QUALITY

Norms

The standardization sample included 6,359 individuals from more than 100 geographically diverse U.S. communities. All age ranges were adequately sampled. The subjects were selected in such a way as to reflect the population on the variables of geographic region, community size, sex, race, occupational status (employed vs. unemployed) and level (white collar, blue collar, or service) for adults, education level for adults, and types of college (4 year vs. 2 year) and funding of college (private vs. public) for college students in the sample. Norming data were gathered between 1986 and 1988.

Separate norms are provided at 1-month intervals for ages 2 years 0 months through 18 years 11 months and at yearly intervals for ages 19 through 90 years. A single norming table is provided for individuals older than 90 years. Grade-based norms are provided at monthly levels from K.0 (beginning kindergarten level) through 16.9 (graduating college senior).

In general, the norms for the WJ-R COG appear to be quite adequate and are, in fact, among the most complete of any individually administered standardized test. Because the norms extend from preschool through elderly adult age levels, this test would be ideal for longitudinal or cross-sectional studies of cognitive development.

Reliability

Split-half reliabilities (corrected by the Spearman-Brown formula) were calculated for each test and cluster at nine age levels. The median reliabilities (across ages) for the tests ranged from .692 (for Visual Closure) to .934 (for Concept Formation). Median reliabilities for the clusters ranged from .805 to .970, thus indicating adequate internal consistency. Standard errors of measurement for the tests, averaged across age levels, range from 3.0 to 8.6. Standard errors of measurement for the clusters range from 1.5 to 5.3. Thus, available information suggests that scores from the clusters and from most of the individual tests can be used confidently. Data regarding test-retest reliability will be necessary before the reliability of the WJ-R COG can be more fully assessed.

Validity

Little information is provided regarding content validity, except that the test items were selected using item validity studies as well as expert opinion. Concurrent validity was studied by correlating the WJ-R COG Broad Cognitive Ability scores (from the Standard Scale, the Extended Scale, and the Early Development Scale) of children and adolescents with the K-ABC Mental Processing Composite, the Stanford-Binet Composite, and the WISC-R or WAIS-R Full Scale IQ. Correlations were generally in the .60s and .70s for the Standard and Extended Scales and in the .50s for the Early Development Scale. The Broad Cognitive Ability score from the Early Development Scale was correlated with the K-ABC and Stanford-Binet, as well as with several other preschool measures (Boehm Tests of Basic Concepts, Bracken Basic Concepts Scale, McCarthy General Cognitive Index) for a group of 3-year-olds. Correlations were generally in the .50s to .60s.

Scores from the Oral Language Cluster and the cognitive factors of the WJ-R COG were correlated with special clusters of other cognitive batteries (WISC-R VIQ and PIQ, Stanford-Binet Verbal Reasoning, Quantitative Reasoning, and Short-Term Memory, and K-ABC Sequential Processing, Simultaneous Processing, and Achievement) for groups of 9-year-olds and 17-year-olds. In general, the WJ-R COG Oral Language, Short-Term Memory, Comprehension-Knowledge, and Fluid Reasoning clusters correlated fairly high with the other tests (r's generally in the .40s to .50s). The other WJ-R cognitive factors (Long-Term

Retrieval, Visual Processing, Auditory Processing, and Processing Speed), which the test developers say are not as well represented in other batteries, had lower correlations with the other measures (r's generally below .40). Considering that the WJ-R COG is based on a theory of intelligence that is somewhat different from those of the other intelligence tests, these results seem reasonable.

Construct validity was investigated by correlating the WJ-R COG tests among themselves and the WJ-R COG cluster scores among themselves. In general, the correlations were low among the tests, but tests within the same cluster intercorrelated more highly than tests representing different clusters. These findings are consistent with the test's model. The scores from cognitive factors were not highly intercorrelated, suggesting that the factors are measuring different aspects of cognitive functioning.

A study of children in two age groups (9 and 17 years) also provides support for construct validity. Normal children were compared with age-matched gifted, learning disabled, and mentally retarded subjects. As would be expected, the test scores increased with age and decreased with extent of mental impairment.

Additional support for construct validity is provided by a factor analysis conducted on a large number of subjects from the norming sample. When a seven-factor varimax rotation was specified, the resulting factors generally had loadings of .7 or .8 for the two WJ-R COG tests that were associated with the factor. No test had a loading greater than .4 on a factor that it was not designed to represent.

Although validity is still somewhat sparse, the available data are quite encouraging.

OTHER CONSIDERATIONS

The primary complaint regarding the 1977 version of the Woodcock-Johnson Tests of Cognitive Ability concerns the unusual assortment of cognitive tasks chosen to represent the construct of intelligence. In fact, as discussed in the next section, the developers of the original version did not even consider the test to be an intelligence test per se. Because the WJ-R COG is clearly based on a model of intelligence, the user can have more confidence that the constructs being measured by the tasks are related to intelligence. Nevertheless, the seven tests selected for the

Standard Battery are a somewhat unusual representation of overall cognitive functioning, appearing to be rather heavily weighted toward tasks that are at a fairly low level of cognitive complexity (e.g., rote memory, psychomotor speed). The argument might be made that the seven areas of intellectual functioning outlined in the Horn-Cattell theory should not all be given equal weight in the measurement of intelligence, as has been done in the WJ-R COG.

Considering the entire battery, fully 8 of the 21 tests can be considered to be measures of rote memory. Although this construct seems to be over-represented, the inclusion of the two Delayed Memory tests is a unique contribution of the WJ-R COG.

On behalf of the test developer's selection of tasks, most of the tests do not appear to be heavily influenced by environmental stimulation (with Picture Vocabulary being the major exception). Thus, like the K-ABC, this test will probably prove to be relatively culture-fair. Unlike the K-ABC, the WJ-R COG has the advantage of sampling a fair number of verbal skills, except for verbal expression using connected language (as is tested by the WISC-R or Stanford-Binet Comprehension tests).

One particular advantage of the WJ-R COG in comparison to the other major tests of intelligence is its wide age range. For most of the WJ-R COG tests, items have been devised that can be presented at a level easy enough for preschoolers and progress to a level that is challenging enough for mature adults. Unlike the Stanford-Binet (Fourth Edition), the WJ-R COG has managed to span a wide age range without significantly changing the nature of items or the combination of tests administered to different age groups. This quality makes the WJ-R COG especially appealing for research involving comparison of different age groups on cognitive abilities.

SUMMARY

The Woodcock-Johnson Psycho-Educational Battery–Revised Tests of Cognitive Ability has many of the strengths of the original version of this test, including easy administration, norms for a wide age range, large standardization sample, provision of scores that can be compared confidently with achievement measures, and a wide variety of cognitive measures that can be obtained from various combinations of test scores. The standardization of the test appears to be good. Reliability and validity data are somewhat sparse, but the available information is encouraging.

The major concern regarding the original Tests of Cognitive Ability involves the unusual combination of tasks chosen to reflect the construct of cognitive functioning. For this reason, it is felt, the original version has not been widely used as a measure of cognitive ability. The WJ-R COG appears to have improved on this situation, at least partially, by selecting its tasks based on a theoretically sound model of intelligence.

It remains to be seen whether test consumers will accept the WJ-R COG's interpretation of this model as a useful one for the measurement of intelligence. Even if the measure of Broad Cognitive Ability does not become widely used as a measure of overall intelligence, there appears to be a substantial number of well-normed tasks that will be useful in assessing individual cognitive strengths and weaknesses. The WJ-R COG thus appears to be quite well suited for neuropsychological evaluations and for research.

WOODCOCK-JOHNSON PSYCHO-EDUCATIONAL BATTERY (PART I: TESTS OF COGNITIVE ABILITY)

Richard W. Woodcock and M. Bonner Johnson

DLM Teaching Resources
One DLM Park
Allen, Texas   75002

PURPOSE

The Woodcock-Johnson Psycho-Educational Battery, published in 1977, consists of three sections: Tests of Cognitive Ability, Tests of Academic Achievement, and Tests of Interest Level. An additional section, the Scales of Independent Behavior (SIB), was published in 1984. Only the Tests of Cognitive Ability are addressed in this chapter. The SIB is discussed in Chapter 7. The rationale underlying the Tests of Cognitive Ability was "to develop measures of cognition (i.e., intellectual performance) that accurately predict academic achievement specifically.

Therefore, the Tests of Cognitive Ability were not designed as measures of general intellectual functioning, as is the case with, for example, the WISC-R" (Hessler, 1982, p. 384). Thus, the Woodcock-Johnson should be used only as a predictor of academic achievement, not as a measure of general intelligence or cognitive development. The test is designed to cover ages 3 years 0 months through 80 years and older.

DESCRIPTION OF TEST AND ADMINISTRATION

The organization of the Woodcock-Johnson Psycho-Educational Battery Tests of Cognitive Ability is presented in Figure 4-2. As indicated in this figure, the Tests of Cognitive Ability provide scores in three areas:

- Broad Cognitive Ability: Cluster scores in this area are intended as "general or broad measures of cognitive functioning" (Hessler, 1982, p. 5).
- Cognitive Factors: Cluster scores in this area are designed to "permit the user to determine the nature of a subject's performance in more narrow cognitive areas" (Hessler, 1982, p. 5).
- Scholastic Aptitude: Cluster scores in this area "provide an estimate of the subject's expected achievement in reading, math, written language, and knowledge" (Hessler, 1982, p. 5).

Within each area, several Cluster scores can be obtained (see Figure 4-2). Each Cluster score is based on a combination of some or all of the 12 subtests (Table 4-1). The subtests are described as follows:

1. *Picture Vocabulary* requires the child to name pictures.
2. *Spatial Relations* requires the child to select from a series of drawings of shapes the ones that would combine to produce a given shape.
3. *Memory for Sentences* requires the child to repeat sentences exactly as spoken by the examiner.
4. *Visual-Auditory Learning* assesses the child's ability to associate visual symbols (rebuses) with familiar words and to translate series of symbols into verbal sentences.

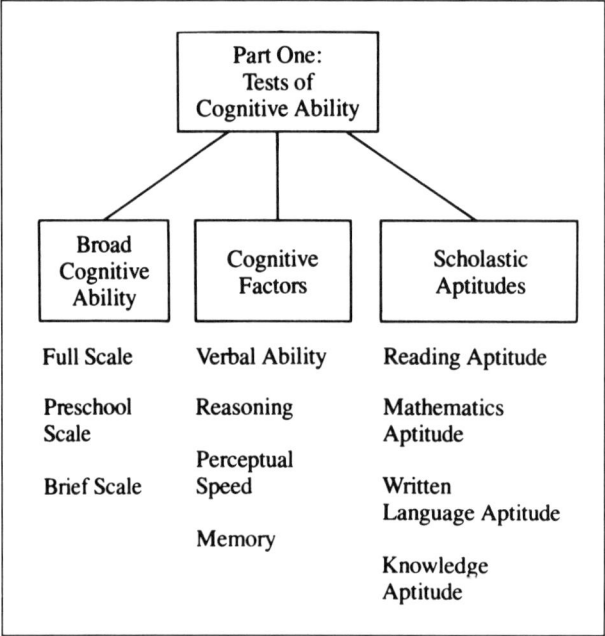

Source: From G. Hessler, *Use and Interpretation of the Woodcock-Johnson Psycho-Educational Battery*, DLM Teaching Resources, 1982, p. 7. Reprinted by permission.

Figure 4-2. Organization of the Woodcock-Johnson Psycho-Educational Battery: Tests of cognitive ability.

5. *Blending* requires the child to integrate and then verbalize whole words after hearing components (syllables or phonemes) of the words spoken in correct order by the examiner.

6. *Quantitative Concepts* requires the child to respond to questions about quantitative and mathematical concepts, symbols, and vocabulary, but does not require any calculation.

7. *Visual Matching* items require the child to find and circle the two identical numbers in a row of six numbers. The task is timed, and the child is told to work as quickly as possible.

8. *Antonyms-Synonyms* involves two parts, the first of which requires the child to give a word that is the opposite of the one spoken by the examiner. The second part requires the child to give a synonym for each of the orally presented words.

Table 4-1. Clusters of the Woodcock-Johnson Psycho-Educational Battery and the subtests that are used to obtain them

	Cognitive ability			Cognitive factors				Scholastic aptitude			
	Broad ability										
Required subtests	Full scale	Brief scale	Preschool scale	Verbal ability	Reasoning	Perceptual speed	Memory	Reading	Math	Written language	Knowledge
1. Picture vocabulary	•										
2. Spatial relations	•		•								
3. Memory for sentence			•				•				
4. Visual-auditory learning			•					•			
5. Blending								•			
6. Quantitative concepts	•								•		
7. Visual matching	•	•				•					
8. Antonyms-synonyms	•	•		•				•		•	•
9. Analysis-synthesis	•				•				•	•	
10. Numbers reversed	•									•	
11. Concept formation	•				•				•		
12. Analogies	•			•							•

Source: From G. Hessler, *Use and Interpretation of the Woocock-Johnson Psycho-Educational Battery*, DLM Teaching Resources, 1982, p. 12. Reprinted by permission.

9. *Analysis-Synthesis* items require the child to analyze the components of an equivalency statement and reintegrate them to determine the components of a novel equivalency statement.

10. *Numbers Reversed* requires the child to repeat a series of numbers spoken by the examiner in exact reverse order.

11. *Concept Formation* items require the child to identify rules for concepts when given both instances of the concept (drawings or series of drawings involving two shapes in two colors and in two sizes) and noninstances of the concept.

12. *Analogies* requires the child to give the word that completes an orally presented analogy.

Most of the subtests involve visual stimuli presented in the easel binders or verbal material presented by the examiner. The child is generally asked to give an oral response or to point to visual stimuli. The test has been criticized because of the lack of manipulative tasks, which might make it difficult for the examiner to keep the attention of younger children (Cummings, 1985).

Only two of the tests, Spatial Relations and Visual Matching, are timed, with the student being given a certain amount of time to complete as many problems as possible. The Visual-Auditory Learning test specifies the maximum amount of time that may be spent on any one item. For Picture Vocabulary, Memory for Sentences, Quantitative Concepts, Antonyms-Synonyms, Numbers Reversed, and Analogies, a starting point is suggested, based on the examinee's grade level. For each of these tests except Numbers Reversed, the examiner is then required to establish a basal level of five consecutive correct responses and a ceiling of five consecutive errors. For the Numbers Reversed, basal level is achieved when all three test items within a group are passed (all items within a group are series of the same length), and the ceiling is established when all three test items within a group are failed. For Visual-Auditory Learning, Blending, Analysis-Synthesis, and Concept Formation all examinees start at the beginning of the test, and the test is discontinued when a specified number of errors has been made. All tests except Picture Vocabulary, Quantitative Concepts, and Visual-Auditory Learning have sample items.

Administration of all 12 subtests generally takes at least 1 hour. The battery can be administered "by anyone who has had a basic introduction to measurement" (Hager, 1985, p. 694), and a procedure for learning to administer the battery is provided in the manual. However, interpretation of the scores requires a good understanding of psychometrics, as well as familiarity with the content of each subtest and experience in the interpretation of standardized tests.

SCORING AND INTERPRETATION

Each item is scored as either correct or incorrect. For some items there is only one acceptable response. For others the examiner must determine the acceptability of the response by using guidelines that give examples of responses that are correct, incorrect, or require further elaboration. Guidelines are fairly comprehensive and clear.

For most subtests calculation of the raw score involves counting the number of correct responses, including those below the basal level. For the Visual-Auditory Learning test the raw score is based on the number of errors. For the Visual-Auditory Learning, Analysis-Synthesis, and Concept Formation tests, the examiner must refer to charts within the test booklet to determine raw scores if the test is discontinued before all items are completed.

The procedure for calculating various scores for each Cluster is fairly involved and, as a result, is subject to error if the examiner is not extremely careful. Using a set of tables, raw scores are converted to "Part Scores," which are summed, resulting in a Cluster Score. Another set of tables is used to convert Cluster Scores to grade-equivalent scores and age-equivalent scores for each Cluster. (For the Scholastic Aptitude Clusters, the examiner computes "Expected Grade Scores" instead of grade-equivalent scores. In addition, "Expected Achievement Cluster Scores" are calculated, which can be compared with actual Cluster Scores from the Tests of Academic Achievement [Part II of the Woodcock-Johnson Psycho-Educational Battery], if they are administered.) The examiner then uses another set of tables to determine the Average Cluster Score for age or grade level and subtracts the Cluster Score obtained from the Average Cluster Score, resulting in a "Cluster Difference Score." Another set of tables allows the examiner to convert the Cluster Difference Scores to Percentile Scores, based on comparison with individuals of the same age or grade level. The tables also provide a "Percentile Rank Range," which gives a confidence band for the Percentile Score, based on the standard error of measurement. A Relative Performance Index can be calculated, which is "a predictive score that provides an indication of the *quality* of the subject's performance rather than the *relative level* of performance . . ." (Hessler, 1982, p. 156). This score theoretically represents the percentage mastery that would be expected from the student on tasks that are similar to the ones tested and that would be performed with 90% mastery by the average student. Finally, Percentile Scores can be converted to standard scores that have a mean of 100 and a standard deviation of 15. A Functioning Level, ranging from "severe deficit" to "very superior" can also be determined. A chart for graphing the Subtest Profile is provided on the back of the test booklet. Using a separately purchased publication (Marston & Ysseldyke, 1980), the examiner can also calculate grade-equivalent, age-equivalent, percentile, and standard scores for individual subtests. Computerized scoring packages are available to reduce scoring time and the likelihood of errors.

The Subtest Profile allows the examiner to estimate which subtest scores are significantly above or below the mean of all of the subtest scores. Using this profile, along with understanding of the content of each subtest, the examiner can make hypotheses regarding specific cognitive strengths or weaknesses. A separate publication, *Use and Interpretation of the Woodcock-Johnson Psycho-Educational Battery* (Hessler, 1982), provides extensive information regarding the interpretive process, as well as many informative case studies and suggestions regarding the use of the tests for educational programming.

TECHNICAL QUALITY

Norms

The standardization sample for the Woodcock-Johnson Psycho-Educational Battery included 555 preschoolers 3 to 5 years of age, 3,577 children between 6 and 17 years, and 600 adults aged 18 to 65 and older. The sample was matched to the U.S. population (according to the 1970 census) on sex, race, occupational status, geographic region, and type of community (urban, nonurban). The sample included handicapped children who were in regular classrooms, but not those with severe handicaps.

The norming sample can be considered adequate for school-age children. For the preschool group, the standardization sample was unrepresentative of the total population on several variables. Although a procedure was used to give more weight to scores from underrepresented segments of the population, the small number of children representing certain groups makes the adequacy of the preschool norms somewhat questionable. The standardization sample for adult norms is quite small, thus resulting in greater sampling error and less confidence regarding the adequacy of the norms for this group.

Reliability

Measures of internal reliability for the Full Scale Cluster (based on all 12 subtests) are excellent, with coefficients ranging from .96 to .98 across age levels from first grade on. The median reliability coefficients for the four cognitive factors are as follows: Verbal .90, Reasoning .87, Perceptual Speed .70, and Memory .85. Only the Perceptual Speed factor is somewhat suspect in regard to internal consistency. Subtest reliabilities are also excellent, with median coefficients ranging from .89 to .95, except for the timed Visual Matching subtest and for some subtests for preschool children. Test-retest data are not provided in the manual, except for the timed subtests, Spatial Relations and Visual Matching.

Validity

Concurrent validity was established by comparing scores from the Tests of Cognitive Ability with those from the Stanford-Binet, the WISC-R, and the WAIS. The Woodcock-Johnson Preschool Scale (based on six of the Cognitive Ability subtests) correlated .83 with the Stanford-Binet at age 4. The Full Scale Cluster Score correlated .79 with the WISC-R Full Scale IQ at both grades 3 and 5, and .83 with the WAIS Full Scale IQ at grade 12.

Predictive validity data are sparse in the technical manual, but are supportive. Cognitive scores at the end of kindergarten were found to predict scores on the Reading and Knowledge Clusters of the Woodcock-Johnson Psycho-Educational Battery Tests of Achievement at the end of first grade, with coefficients of .67 and .75, respectively.

Construct validity was evaluated primarily by cluster analysis. Using this approach, the test developers found moderate support for the choice and composition of clusters, "but there are still many findings at odds" with the Woodcock-Johnson factors (Kaufman, 1985, p. 1764). For example, Picture Vocabulary and Quantitative Concepts clustered more closely with achievement than with cognitive variables. Examination of both the validity data and the content of the various clusters provides adequate reason to question the validity of the Tests of Cognitive Ability as a true measure of cognitive ability, as will be discussed in the next section.

OTHER CONSIDERATIONS

Kaufman (1985) considers the strengths of the Woodcock-Johnson Psycho-Educational Battery to be the originality of many tasks, the technical expertise and sophistication regarding test construction, and the psychometric properties of the battery. Another strength involves the fact that the Woodcock-Johnson Psycho-Educational Battery provides a test of cognitive ability and a test of academic achievement that are normed on the same population. This strength is not fully realized, however, because of the limited nature of the Tests of Cognitive Ability, especially for learning-disabled students, as will be noted in the next paragraphs.

Kaufman (1985) considers a major weakness of the Battery to include the complexity of the scoring, the cumbersomeness of profile interpretation, and the nature of the clusters. The most serious criticism that must be considered by practitioners who might wish to include the Woodcock-Johnson Tests of Cognitive Ability in their repertoire involves the very nature of the abilities tapped by the tests. It can be easily argued that several of the tests (especially Blending) tap skills that would be more appropriate for a test of academic achievement than for a test of cognitive ability. Although developers of other recent tests, especially the K-ABC, have made efforts to intentionally avoid tasks that are dependent on environmental stimulation, the Woodcock-Johnson includes many subtests—especially Picture Vocabulary, Quantitative Concepts, and Antonyms-Synonyms—that measure verbal skills highly influenced by environmental stimulation.

The use of the Tests of Cognitive Ability cannot, therefore, be recommended as a measure of intelligence or cognitive development among children who might be environmentally deprived, as scores will undoubtedly underestimate their intelligence. Furthermore, because the Tests of Cognitive Ability are designed to measure "verbal cognition that specifically relates to academic achievement," their use cannot be recommended as a measure of intelligence for learning-disabled students. Most research has found scores from this test to be lower than WISC-R IQs for learning-disabled children. In fact, the Tests of Cognitive Ability have been found to yield overall standard scores .5 to 1 standard deviation below the WISC-R Full Scale IQ (Kaufman, 1985) for this population. It can be assumed, therefore, that the Tests of Cognitive Ability will often underestimate to some degree the learning-disabled child's cognitive abilities, which may in turn diminish the amount of discrepancy between the child's measured cognitive skills and academic abilities. If the discrepancy is diminished, criteria for the diagnosis of learning disability may not be met, and the child with a true learning disability may not qualify for special education services.

SUMMARY

Although the Tests of Cognitive Ability of the Woodcock-Johnson Psycho-Educational Battery can be considered to be technically excellent, at least for the school-age population, the practitioner must seriously consider the nature of the tasks included by the test developers as measures of cognitive ability. The Tests of Cognitive Ability have been widely criticized because of their tendency to emphasize abilities that are highly related to academic training and are dependent on environmental stimulation. Because the rationale underlying the Tests of Cognitive Ability was "to develop measures of cognition . . . that accurately predict academic achievement specifically" (Hessler, 1982, p. 348), the inclusion of tasks related to academic training is not unreasonable. Furthermore, the developers of the Tests of Cognitive Ability do not refer to their instrument as an intelligence test. Therefore, if one wishes a true measure of cognitive ability or intelligence, especially for children who are learning disabled or who are from impoverished environments, the Woodcock-Johnson Psycho-Educational Battery Tests of Cognitive Abilities cannot be recommended. However, if scores from the Tests of Cognitive Ability are interpreted as the test developers intended (i.e., as a predictor of academic achievement), they can be considered reliable and valid, at least for the school-age population.

MCCARTHY SCALES OF CHILDREN'S ABILITIES (MSCA)

Dorothea McCarthy

The Psychological Corporation
555 Academic Court
San Antonio, Texas   78204-2498

PURPOSE

The McCarthy Scales of Children's Abilities (MSCA), published in 1972, were designed to determine general intellectual level of young children, as well as their strengths and weaknesses in important abilities. The test is appropriate for children from 2½ through 8½ years of age.

DESCRIPTION OF TEST AND ADMINISTRATION

The MSCA contains 18 separate tests that are grouped into six Scales: Verbal, Perceptual-Performance, Quantitative, General Cognitive, Memory, and Motor. Figure 4-3 presents the six Scales and the tests that make up each one. The 18 subtests are described as follows:

Pictorial Memory requires the child to recall names of objects pictured on cards.

Word Knowledge, Part I, requires the child to point to pictures of common objects named by the examiner. Part II requires the child to give oral definitions of words.

Verbal Memory, Part I, requires the child to repeat word series and sentences. Part II requires the child to retell a story read by the examiner.

Verbal Fluency requires the child to name as many articles as possible in a given category within 20 seconds.

Opposite Analogies requires the child to complete sentences by providing "opposites" (e.g., "The sun is hot, and ice is _____ ").

4. Other Multi-Scale Tests of Intelligence and Cognitive Development

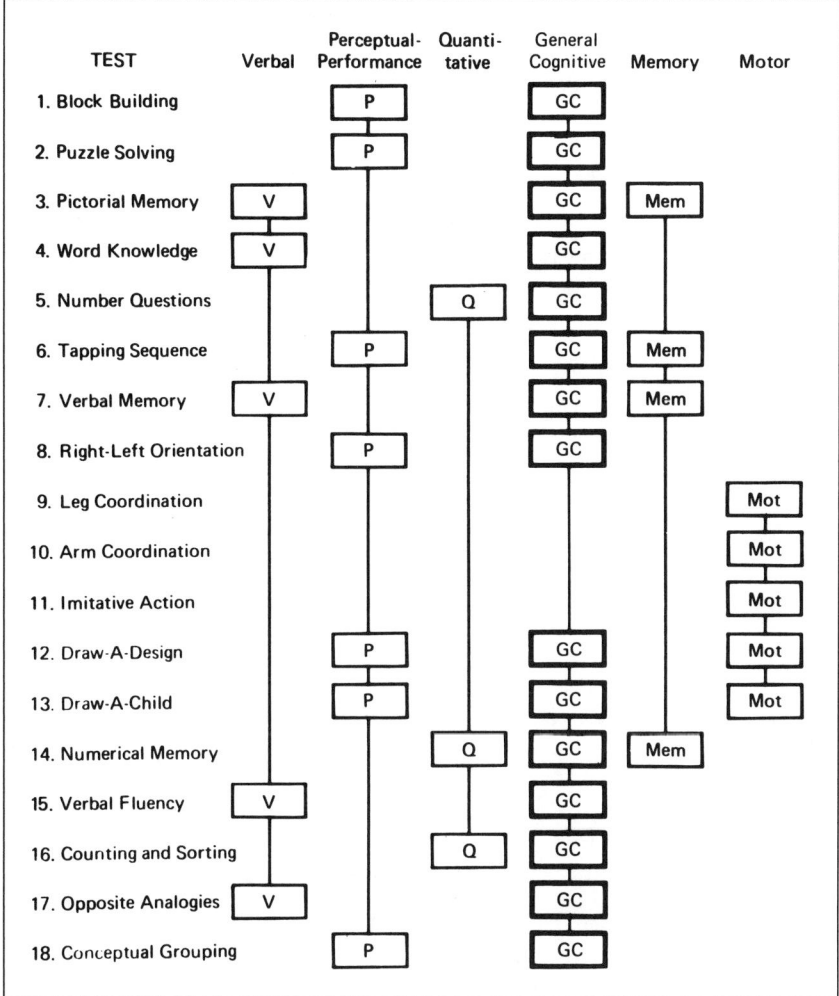

Source: From The McCarthy Scales of Children's Abilities. Copyright © 1972 by The Psychological Corporation. Reproduced by permission. All rights reserved.

Figure 4-3. Six scales of the McCarthy Scales of Children's Abilities and the subtests that are used to obtain them.

Block Building requires the child to copy block structures built by the examiner.

Puzzle Solving requires the child to assemble picture puzzles of common animals or foods.

Tapping Sequence requires the child to imitate sequences of notes on a xylophone, as demonstrated by the examiner.

Right-Left Orientation requires the child to demonstrate knowledge of right and left.

Draw-A-Design requires the child to draw geometrical designs, as presented in a model.

Draw-A-Child requires the child to draw a picture of a child of the same sex.

Conceptual Grouping requires the child to classify blocks on the basis of size, color, and shape.

Number Questions requires the child to answer orally presented questions involving number information or basic arithmetical computation.

Numerical Memory, Part I, requires the child to repeat series of digits exactly as presented by the examiner. Part II requires that digit series be repeated in exact reverse order.

Counting and Sorting requires the child to count blocks and then to sort them into equal groups.

Leg Coordination requires the child to perform motor tasks that involve lower extremities such as walking backward or standing on one foot.

Arm Coordination, Part I, requires the child to bounce a ball. Part II requires the child to catch a beanbag, and Part III requires the child to throw a beanbag at a target.

Imitative Action requires the child to copy simple movements, such as folding his hands or looking through a tube.

All tests are administered to all children, with the following exceptions: Right-Left Orientation is given only to children 5 years of age and older, Draw-A-Child is given only if the child scored at least 1 point on Draw-A-Design, and Counting and Sorting is given only if the child scored below 9 points on Number Questions. Some of the tests have starting points other than the first item for children older than 5 years of age. On most of the tests, however, all examinees begin with the first item, and there is no basal level. Most tests are discontinued after a prescribed number of consecutive failures.

Time limits are imposed for items on Puzzle Solving, Pictorial Memory, and Verbal Fluency. Some of the Leg Coordination tasks are timed for duration. The entire test administration takes approximately 45 to 50 minutes for children younger than 5 years of age, and 1 hour for children 5 years and older.

The examiner is required to observe the child's hand preference and eye preference on several tasks to determine whether dominance has been established.

Administration requires a fair amount of training and practice. Keith (1985) suggests that the MSCA is somewhat more difficult to learn to administer than are the WISC-R or K-ABC.

SCORING AND INTERPRETATION

The examiner scores each item as correct or incorrect for Pictorial Memory, Part I of Word Knowledge (Picture Vocabulary), Number Questions, Tapping Sequence, Right-Left Orientation, Imitative Action, Counting and Sorting, and Opposite Analogies. Scores for Block Building, Puzzle Solving, Part II of Word Knowledge (Oral Vocabulary), Verbal Memory, Leg Coordination, Arm Coordination, Draw-A-Design, Draw-A-Child, and Conceptual Grouping are assigned based on quality of the response. Scoring responses for several of the subtests, especially the two drawing tasks, requires at least some subjective judgment. The manual presents scoring criteria and many examples to minimize the amount of subjectivity involved. Bonus points are assigned for fast performance on some of the Puzzle Solving items. Numerical Memory scores are based on the number of trials needed for success at each level, and Verbal Fluency scores are based on the number of articles within a given category the child can name in 20 seconds.

Raw scores are calculated for each test or test part by adding scores for individual items. For Puzzle Solving and Verbal Memory–Part I, the examiner is instructed to multiply the raw score by one-half. For other tests (Number Questions, Numerical Memory–Part I, and Opposite Analogies), raw scores are multiplied by 2. For tests with more than one part, raw scores or weighted scores from the separate parts are summed to obtain a total raw score for the test. Instructions for these calculations are presented clearly on the record form.

Scores from certain combinations of the subtests are summed for Verbal, Perceptual-Performance, Quantitative, Memory, and Motor Scales, as presented in Figure 4-3. Scores from the Verbal, Perceptual-Performance, and Quantitative Scales are then summed to provide a total raw score for the General Cognitive Index (GCI). Total raw scores are converted to scaled scores, called Indexes, using the norms tables appropriate for the child's age. The GCI has a mean of 100 and standard deviation of 16. GCIs can range from 50 to 150. Ability classifications are as follows:

130 and above:	Very Superior
120–129:	Superior
110–129:	Bright Normal
90–109:	Average
80–89:	Dull Normal
70–79:	Borderline
69 and below:	Mentally Retarded

Indexes for the other five Scales have a mean of 50 and a standard deviation of 10. Scores for these five Scales can range from 22 to 78.

A profile can be drawn to summarize the six Indexes. Index scores can be converted to percentiles, and mental ages have been estimated for designated GCI ranges in each chronological age group. Instructions are also provided for assessing establishment of laterality, based on the child's eye and hand preference on several scales.

The manual provides good descriptions of the skills required by each subtest and each of the six scales. However, little further information is provided regarding interpretation of test scores. The manual does contain a table that presents the discrepancy between two Indexes necessary for significance (averaged across ages). Practitioners are cautioned against comparing scores from Verbal with those from Memory, Perceptual-Performance with Motor, and Quantitative with Memory. Practitioners are urged to consult Kaufman and Kaufman's (1977) text on the test's development, use, and interpretation.

TECHNICAL QUALITY

Norms

The standardization sample consisted of 1,032 children, evenly divided into 10 age groups, spaced at 6-month intervals between 2½ and 5½ years and at yearly intervals for 6½ through 8½ years. Within each age group, children were matched with the U.S. population on sex, "color," geographic region, and father's occupational group. Some attempt was made to select with consideration for accurate representation of children from urban versus rural residence. Institutionalized children, those with severe behavioral or emotional problems, those with known brain impairment, and those with obvious physical defects were excluded from the sample. In general, the norming sample appears to be adequate, although the norms, based on data collected in 1970 and 1971, are by now becoming obsolete.

Separate norms tables are provided at 3-month age range intervals for 2½ through 8½ years.

Reliability

Internal consistency reliability coefficients for the five Scales ranged from .60 to .92, with averages (across ages) of .88 for Verbal, .84 for Perceptual-Performance, .81 for Quantitative, and .79 for Motor. (Test-retest method was used for determining reliability of the Memory Scale, resulting in a coefficient of .79). Internal consistency reliability coefficients for the GCI ranged across ages from .90 to .96, with a mean of .93. Average standard errors of measurement were 3.4 for Verbal, 4.0 for Perceptual-Performance, 4.3 for Quantitative, 4.5 for Memory, 4.7 for Motor, and 4.1 for the GCI.

Stability of the MSCA was assessed by correlating test scores from 125 children at six age levels with scores obtained on the test after a 1-month interval. The GCI had an average test-retest reliability coefficient of .90. Correlations for the four other cognitive scales ranged from .75 to .89. Stability for the Motor Scale was somewhat poorer, with coefficients ranging from .69 to .78, with poorer reliabilities at older ages.

In general, reliability for the GCI and the four cognitive scales is adequate, especially considering the preschool population. The Motor Scale Index should be interpreted cautiously, however, especially for older children.

Validity

Concurrent validity was studied on a small group of first graders (N = 35), who were given the MSCA, the Stanford-Binet Intelligence Scale (Form L-M), and the WPPSI. The GCI correlated .81 with the Stanford-Binet IQ and .71 with the WPPSI Full Scale IQ. The MSCA Verbal, Perceptual-Performance, Quantitative, and Memory Scale Indexes correlated .41 to .70 with the Stanford-Binet IQ and from .27 to .61 with the WPPSI IQs. In general, correlations between MSCA Scale Indexes and the WPPSI and Stanford-Binet IQs were higher for the Verbal and Perceptual-Performance Indexes, ranging from .54 to .70. The Memory and Quantitative Scales were less highly correlated to the other two IQ scores.

Predictive validity was studied on 31 of the 35 children who participated in the concurrent validity study. These children were administered the Metropolitan Achievement Tests four months after administration of the MSCA. The GCI correlated significantly with most achievement scores, as did the Perceptual-Performance and Quantitative Indexes. It is interesting to note that correlations between the Verbal Scale Index and achievement test scores ranged from .06 to .27, whereas one would generally expect verbal skills to correlate much better with early academic skills.

In general, the validity data presented in the manual are too sparse and are based on samples that are too small to allow any definite conclusions.

OTHER CONSIDERATIONS

Keith (1985) reports that a major strength of the MSCA, aside from its strong technical qualities, is its attractiveness and ability to maintain interest among young children. Keith (1985) believes that one of the major weaknesses of the MSCA is its lack of items to assess social comprehension, judgment, and verbal abstract reasoning. In addition, McCarthy (1972) notes that the battery does not have a high enough ceiling for very superior children (GCI over 129) at 6, 7, or 8 years of age. For these reasons, the WISC-R or Stanford-Binet would be considered better tests for the school-age population. For practitioners who are not particularly interested in assessing verbal abstract reasoning, the K-ABC might be considered preferable to the MSCA, simply because the MSCA norms, based on data collected in 1970 and 1971, are becoming obsolete. Although it does not assess verbal abstract reasoning, MSCA does contain more verbal tasks than does the K-ABC. With the introduction of the WPPSI-R, the MSCA will probably be less widely used with preschool children aged 3 years and older.

SUMMARY

The MSCA is a well-developed and well-standardized test of general cognitive functioning for children between 2½ and 8½ years of age. The strengths and weaknesses of the MSCA, in comparison with other tests, are outlined in the previous pages and must be considered in test selection. There are several newer tests, with more recent norms and with strengths similar to those of the MSCA, that might be selected in place of the MSCA. Practitioners who have access to scores from the MSCA should be able to rely on them, except for older gifted children. Indexes from the four cognitive scales (Verbal, Perceptual-Performance, Quantitative, and Memory) should be considered fairly reliable. Validity of the scales for various purposes will require review of individual studies involving situations similar to those for which the test is being considered.

HISKEY-NEBRASKA TEST OF LEARNING APTITUDE

Marshall S. Hiskey

Marshall S. Hiskey
5640 Baldwin Avenue
Lincoln, Nebraska   68507

PURPOSE

The Hiskey-Nebraska Test, first published in 1941, is a revision and restandardization of the "Nebraska Test of Learning Aptitude for Young

Deaf Children," a test originally designed as a measure of learning ability for deaf children. The Hiskey-Nebraska Test was subsequently standardized on hearing children in 1955 to provide a measure of intelligence for children who would be at a disadvantage on highly verbal tests of ability. The test is suitable for children between 3 and 18 years of age.

DESCRIPTION OF TEST AND ADMINISTRATION

There are 12 subtests, described as follows:

Bead Patterns, when administered to children younger than age 5, begins by having the child string as many beads as possible in 1 minute. More difficult items require the child to reproduce a string of beads, matching the pattern of round, square, and rectangular beads. The most difficult items require reproduction of bead patterns from memory.

Memory for Color requires the child to select from memory one or more color chips that match the color chip(s) presented by the examiner.

Picture Identification requires the child to choose which of several pictures exactly matches a target picture.

Picture Association requires the child to select from four alternatives the picture that "goes with" a pair of pictures presented by the examiner.

Paper Folding requires the child to imitate from memory the examiner's procedure in folding a piece of paper into various shapes.

Visual Attention Span requires the child to reproduce a series of pictures from memory by sequencing one to seven pictures, selected from between 6 and 18 alternatives.

Block Patterns requires the child to reproduce block constructions, as presented by the examiner or as pictured.

Completion of Drawings requires the child to draw the missing parts of eight visual stimuli, including geometric forms and pictures of objects.

Memory for Digits requires the child to reproduce from memory a series of visually presented numerals, using black plastic numerals.

Puzzle Blocks requires the child to put together puzzle pieces to make a cube.

Picture Analogies requires the child to complete a visually presented analogy by pointing to which of five alternatives is related to a given stimulus in the same way that two other stimuli are related.

Spatial Reasoning requires the child to identify from four alternatives the group of geometric figures that could be assembled to form a target stimulus figure.

All tasks are presented to children between 3 and 10 years of age except for Memory for Digits, Puzzle Blocks, Picture Analogies, and Spatial Reasoning. Children aged 11 years and older are given Block Patterns and Completion of Drawings, in addition to the four tests just mentioned. For Picture Association, Completion of Drawings, Picture Analogies, and Spatial Reasoning, all items are given. Tests are discontinued after three consecutive failures for Paper Folding, Block Patterns, and Puzzle Blocks. All other tests are discontinued after two consecutive failures.

The manual clearly states how the examiner is to present instructions for each task. Instructions for each task may be presented orally or using pantomime, depending on the child's hearing acuity. Time limits for individual items are specified for Bead Memory, Block Patterns, and Puzzle Blocks. Testing time is estimated to be 45 to 50 minutes.

SCORING AND INTERPRETATION

Scoring criteria for each test are objective and clearly stated, but somewhat difficult to master because of the variability of scoring procedures among the tests. One point is awarded for each correct response for Memory for Color, Picture Identification, Picture Association, Paper Folding, Completion of Drawings, Picture Analogies, and Spatial Reasoning. For Bead Patterns, 1 point is given for each bead pattern reproduced, except for children who are unable to reproduce any items, in which case the score is based on the number of beads strung in 1 minute. For Visual Attention Span and Memory for Digits, 1 point per item is awarded for correct selection of pictures or digits and another point is awarded if pictures or digits are ordered correctly. For Block Patterns,

1 point is given for correct responses, with 1 or 2 additional points given, depending on speed of performance. For Puzzle Blocks, 1 point is given for correct construction, with an extra point given for fast performance and 1 point given if cubes are completed with the correct color.

Raw scores for each test are converted to "Learning Ages" (LA), based on tables of norms for either deaf or hearing children. (The deaf norms are to be used whenever the directions have been pantomimed.) Learning Ages range from 3 years 0 months through 18 years 6 months. The child's overall test performance is based on the *median* of the Learning Ages obtained on the subtests given. Hiskey (1966) claims that deaf children often tend to score poorly on initial items of a task because of their failure to grasp completely what is expected of them. He proposes that the median rating is preferable to a total score or mean score for deaf children because it allows some compensation for this tendency. The median Learning Age is converted to a deviation IQ (with a mean of 100 and standard deviation of 16) for hearing children, using tables provided. For deaf students, however, no conversion tables are provided, and the examiner is instructed to calculate a "Learning Quotient" (LQ), using the formula LQ = LA/CA × 100, with a minor correction for older children.

TECHNICAL QUALITY

Norms

Norms for deaf children were based on a standardization sample of 1,079 deaf children and 1,074 hearing children, ranging in age from 2 years 6 months to 17 years 5 months. The children in both samples came from 10 widely separated states. The majority of deaf children attended schools for the deaf. A fairly successful attempt was made to match the hearing sample to the U.S. population on the basis of parental occupational group (as defined by the 1960 U.S. Census). Both samples included representatives from minority racial groups, although no statistics are provided to indicate in what proportion. Hiskey (1966) notes that the norms for both groups of children are somewhat less reliable for very young deaf children (3 to 4 years) because of relatively small samples. Norms for individuals older than 17 years are based on extrapolations and, therefore, cannot be considered reliable. Separate norms are provided for each 6-month age-range interval between 3 years 0 months and 18 years 6 months.

4. Other Multi-Scale Tests of Intelligence and Cognitive Development

Sample size for each age range is fairly small. The lack of further information regarding the sample makes it impossible to assess its representativeness. Regardless, because of their age, the norms must be considered obsolete.

Reliability

Split-half reliability coefficients ranged from .918 to .947 for the deaf group and from .904 to .933 for the hearing group. These coefficients are adequate. However, information regarding other types of reliability is not presented in the manual.

Validity

Concurrent validity of the test for hearing children was assessed by correlating overall scores from the Hiskey-Nebraska Test with those from the Stanford-Binet (Form L-M) and WISC. Coefficients ranged from .78 to .86, leading Hiskey to conclude that the scale "can be used with confidence as a measure of intelligence with hearing children." Although these coefficients are sufficiently high, the criteria are outdated and do not, therefore, reflect on the validity of the test for a contemporary population.

Discussion of predictive validity is based on a study that correlated Hiskey-Nebraska scores with scores from the Stanford Achievement Test, the Metropolitan Achievement Test, the Gates Reading Test, and a Teacher Rating Scale. Subjects were 225 deaf students ranging in age from 7 to 17. Correlation coefficients were reasonable at lower and upper grades, but were relatively low for middle grades.

SUMMARY

Because the standardization sample's representativeness is questionable and because of the age of the norms, there does not appear to be any justification for using the Hiskey-Nebraska as a measure of nonverbal intelligence for hearing children. Other tests are available for this purpose that are as easy and fast to administer, have more recent norms, have standardization samples that are more representative, and use more sophisticated procedures for deriving scores. The K-ABC (which includes a Nonverbal Scale) is probably the best test for this purpose, although the WISC-R Performance subtests or the Stanford-Binet Abstract/Visual Reasoning Scale could also be used. The Hiskey-Nebraska is the only major test of ability that provides separate norms for children who are given the test with pantomimed instructions. However, Kaufman and Kaufman (1983) claim that the Nonverbal Processing Scale of the K-ABC can be administered with pantomimed instructions without violating the norms and recommend its use with deaf students.

In general, scores from the Hiskey-Nebraska should be interpreted cautiously. Unless more updated norms are made available for the Hiskey-Nebraska, its use cannot be recommended for decision-making purposes.

CHAPTER 5

SINGLE SCALE TESTS OF INTELLIGENCE AND COGNITIVE DEVELOPMENT

So far in this book, the instruments discussed have been fairly comprehensive, using a variety of methods to assess skills in more than one area of cognitive functioning and providing separate scores that reflect abilities in each of these areas. For example, the WISC-R uses 12 different tasks to assess cognitive skills and provides separate subtest scores for each of these tasks, as well as composite scores reflecting verbal, nonverbal, and overall intellectual functioning. The tests included in this chapter provide only a single measure of cognitive functioning. Some of the tests presented in this chapter measure functioning in only one area (e.g., receptive vocabulary, visual-spatial reasoning), whereas others tap several cognitive areas to arrive at a single score of cognitive functioning. Most of the tests discussed in the following pages are less time consuming and require less skill to administer and score than do the comprehensive intelligence tests. When using data from the tests described in this chapter, it is important to keep in mind the range of cognitive abilities being assessed. Practitioners who are interested in obtaining an accurate assessment of general cognitive functioning should not be tempted to substitute a brief measure for any of the broad-range instruments discussed in the previous chapters.

SLOSSON INTELLIGENCE TEST (SIT)

Richard L. Slosson

*Slosson Educational Publications, Inc.
P.O. Box 280
East Aurora, New York   14052*

PURPOSE

The SIT, originally published in 1961, was designed to "provide a measure which required little specialized training to administer; took only about 20 minutes to administer and score; and yielded IQ scores which were close approximates to the [Stanford-Binet] IQ which would have been obtained had that instrument been administered instead" (Armstrong & Jensen, 1981, p. 1). The test was revised and renormed in 1981 by Armstrong and Jensen. Norms for preschoolers were added in a 1985 publication. The SIT is designed for use with infants through adults, although norms are available only for ages 2 through 18 years.

DESCRIPTION OF TEST AND ADMINISTRATION

The SIT consists of 194 items, most of which are similar to those found in the Stanford-Binet (Form L-M), the test on which the SIT was modeled. There are no subtests. At the youngest age levels, items involve observation of the child's activities (e.g., "Lifts head when lying on stomach for short 10-second interval") or response to some type of stimulation (e.g., "When rattle is held in front of infant, he reaches for it with one hand, grabs, and is able to shake it."). Although not specifically stated in the manual, it is presumed that a parents' report of the infant's abilities must be obtained for certain items (e.g., "Feeds self with spoon, though may spill" or "When hungry asks for food, when thirsty asks for drink. Asks to go to toilet."). On many other items, it is not clear whether the examiner must observe the behavior or can rely on the parents' report (e.g., "Can walk up and down stairs alone" or "Uses 'me' and 'you' and refers to self by name"). Because infants are usually much more reticent when in the company of a stranger, the scores obtained for them on verbal items will be especially discrepant depending on whether or not the examiner accepts the parents' report.

The SIT contains many more items at the younger ages than at the older ages. For example, 23 items were devised for the age level between birth and 1 year, whereas 4 items were devised for the 16- to 26-year age levels. This suggests that sensitivity will be greater for younger children than for older individuals. Although some materials are needed for testing infants (e.g., a rattle, rubber ball, blocks), these materials must be provided by the examiner, resulting in the possibility of administration that differs significantly from standardized procedure.

For preschool children, items involve such tasks as identifying body parts, copying geometric shapes, counting objects, completing simple analogies (e.g., "An elephant is big, a mouse is _____ "), repeating series of digits, and answering simple comprehension items (e.g., "Why do we have beds?"). For older children and adults, items include tasks such as defining words, solving analogies, explaining how two concepts are alike and different, repeating series of digits forward and backward, answering factual questions in a variety of areas, and solving problems that require application of math concepts.

The test is designed so that it can be administered, scored, and interpreted by teachers, psychologists, social workers, or "other responsible persons" (Slosson, 1982, p. 1). Instructions for administration that are included in the manual are fairly informal, leaving much to the discretion of the examiner. Administration time varies from about 10 to 15 minutes for the average person, but can take up to 20 or 30 minutes. None of the items is timed.

The examiner is instructed to begin the test at the level where the child is felt to be able to pass 10 consecutive items. Each item is assigned an age level, and the examiner generally starts with the item that matches the child's chronological age. Questions are administered and, if necessary, the examiner goes back to easier items in order to establish the basal level of 10 consecutive successes. The test is discontinued after 10 consecutive failures.

SCORING AND INTERPRETATION

The examiner is instructed to score items as they are administered. Correct responses are given in the test manual directly after each item. Most responses have only one correct answer and can easily be scored as passed or failed. Some items, however, require a verbal explanation or definition, and the scoring criteria are sometimes too vague.

After testing is completed, the examiner calculates a Mental Age (MA). To do this, the examiner counts the number of questions passed above the basal age (the highest item in 10 consecutive successes). For items between 0 and 2 years, each success is credited with a half-month. One month's credit is given per success on items between 2 and 5 years, 2 months' credit per success between 5 and 16 years, and 3 months' credit per success from 16 years on. The examiner uses tables of norms to convert the MA to a deviation IQ, which has a mean of 100 and a standard deviation of 16. Tables are also provided for converting scores to percentiles, normal curve equivalents, stanines, and T-scores.

No information is provided in the manual regarding interpretation of test results, except for a one-page discussion of the "meaning and importance of accurate IQ's" (Slosson, 1982, p. 28).

TECHNICAL QUALITY

Norms

The 1982 renorming involved 1,109 New England residents, ranging in age from 27 to 216 months and in Stanford-Binet Mental Age from 31 to 271 months. These individuals, tested between 1968 and 1977, were administered both the SIT and the Stanford-Binet (L-M). Of course, the size of this norming sample is woefully inadequate for establishing norms, given the wide age range covered. Furthermore, the population can in no way be considered representative of the U.S. population on many important variables. In addition, the nine-year period of data collection suggests that some of the norming data were reaching obsolescence before the revised norms were even published!

To make matters worse, instead of using a typical norming procedure, the test developers used an "equipercentile method." Using this method mental ages were generated for each subject on both the SIT and Stanford-Binet. The 1972 Stanford-Binet norms were then established as the "anchor" in generating the 1981 SIT norms. Basically, a subject's Stanford-Binet IQ was assigned to that combination of Chronological Age and SIT Mental Age that was obtained by the subject. An elaborate system was then used to account for the curvilinear relationship between Stanford-Binet and SIT mental ages within certain age ranges. Smoothing of the SIT tables was then done, and some "final alterations" in the tables were made, particularly at the extremes. Finally, extrapolation was used to estimate SIT IQs for mental ages that surpassed mental ages possible on the Stanford Binet.

This unorthodox norming procedure, which is based on Armstrong and Jensen's (1981) inaccurate claim that the SIT is a "parallel form" of the Stanford-Binet, considered together with the inadequacy of the standardization sample, leads one to seriously question the accuracy of the norms.

Reliability

Slosson (1982) presents a stability coefficient of .97, based on 139 individuals from 4 to 50 years of age and a test-retest interval of 2 months. Although not stated, it is assumed that this study used the 1981 norms. The standard error of measurement was found to be 4.3. Slosson (1982) wisely asserts that any IQs obtained for children younger than 4 years of age must be considered tentative in view of the low reliability correlations shown by so many studies.

Validity

Slosson (1982) provides summary tables giving correlations between the SIT and Stanford-Binet (Form L-M) in a large group of independent studies. Coefficients range from .60 to .96. Similar tables summarize correlations between SIT and WISC scores, resulting in coefficients that range from .44 to .94 for the Full Scale IQ and from .52 to .94 for the VIQ. (The SIT consistently correlates more highly with Wechsler VIQs than with PIQs.) These studies were all done before the 1981 renorming. Slosson (1982) claims that the renorming method, "has vicariously adopted the sampling characteristics of the [Stanford-Binet] norms," and that the new SIT norms therefore "have the same degree of generalizability as do the [Stanford-Binet] norms" (p. 43). Support for these claims is inadequate. Furthermore, if Slosson bases his claims for reliability and validity on the Stanford-Binet's reliability and validity, it would seem that support for the SIT is seriously undermined by the decision of the Stanford-Binet authors to completely overhaul their test, as was done in 1986.

SUMMARY

Despite claims for high correlation with the Stanford-Binet, the SIT is plagued by many inadequacies that prevent its recommendation, even as a screening instrument. Indeed, as Reynolds (1985) notes, "one gets the impression that the primary use of the SIT is for masters' theses and doctoral research" (p. 1403). Instructions for administration are so vague that standardized administration is impossible. Norms are based on inaccurate assumptions, unorthodox methods, and an inadequate sample. This instrument's primary strength, its ease of administration, makes the SIT vulnerable to use by unsophisticated and untrained test users who lack the necessary background to adequately interpret IQs.

COLUMBIA MENTAL MATURITY SCALE (CMMS)

B. Burgemeister, L. Blum, and I. Lorge

Western Psychological Services
12031 Wilshire Boulevard
Los Angeles, California   90025

PURPOSE

The CMMS, originally published in 1954 and most recently revised in 1972, was designed to yield "an estimate of the general reasoning ability of children aged 3 years 6 months through 9 years 11 months" (Burgemeister, Blum, & Lorge, 1972). Because it is a nonverbal test, the developers claim it can be used with children who have cerebral palsy or other brain damage, mental retardation, visual handicaps, speech impairment, hearing loss, or lack of proficiency with English.

DESCRIPTION OF TEST AND ADMINISTRATION

The CMMS contains 92 items of identical format, which are arranged in a series of eight overlapping levels. The items are sequenced in order of difficulty, with each level consisting of between 51 and 65 items. Each level is associated with an age range, and the examiner is instructed to begin testing at the level corresponding to the child's chronological age. If the child has fewer than 10 correct responses at the level corresponding to the chronological age, the examiner is instructed to administer the items from the next lower level. If a child has four or fewer errors, additional items from the next higher level are administered.

Each item consists of a series of from three to five drawings of common objects, printed on a 6- × 19-inch card. The child is asked to look at the drawings on each card and to point to the one that is different from, or unrelated to the others. The target drawing may be different from the others on the basis of such elementary features as size, color, or shape. For more difficult items, the feature that distinguishes one drawing from the others may involve subtle relationships in pairs of pictures so as to exclude the target drawing from the series. Instructions are given verbally. There are three sample items, which the examiner uses to further demonstrate the nature of the task by explaining how the correct response on each of these items differs from the other drawings. A Spanish version of the instructions is provided.

There are no time limits for any items. Administration takes approximately 15 to 20 minutes. There is no specific list of examiner qualifications, and the test developers suggest that with some practice and supervision, classroom teachers can learn to administer the CMMS.

SCORING AND INTERPRETATION

The examiner marks the student's response to each item on a test form. Each item is scored as correct or incorrect. The examiner uses a set of tables to convert the raw score to an Age Deviation Score (ADS), which has a mean of 100 and a standard deviation of 16. ADSs can range from 50 to 150 and can be converted to percentile scores and stanines. A "Maturity Index" (MI), which is similar to an age-equivalent score, can also be calculated. This index indicates the standardization age group most similar to that of the child in terms of test performance.

TECHNICAL QUALITY

Norms

Standardization of the CMMS, conducted in 1970, involved 2,600 children between the ages of 3 years 6 months and 9 years 11 months. Two hundred subjects were selected for each 6-month age range. The sample was matched to the U.S. population according to geographic region, race, ethnic group, and parental occupation group. The sample was half male and half female. Separate norms are provided for 1-month age-range intervals between 3 years 6 months and 4 years 5 months, at 2-month age-range intervals between 4 years 6 months and 7 years 11 months, and at 3-month age range intervals between 8 years 0 months and 9 years 11 months. The norming sample appears to be adequate.

Reliability

The median split-half reliability coefficient across all age levels was .88. Test-retest reliability coefficients were determined for three different age groups, with a 7- to 10-day test-retest interval. A mean coefficient of .85 was found. The standard error of measurement is 5 points for ages 3½ through 5½, and 6 points for 6 through 9½ years. Although the information provided in the manual is somewhat sparse, it suggests reasonable reliability for the CMMS.

Validity

Concurrent validity was assessed by correlating scores on the CMMS with scores on the Otis-Lennon Mental Ability Test and on the Stanford-Binet (Form L-M). Correlations of .69 and .62 between CMMS and Otis-Lennon scores were obtained for two different samples of children in grades 1 through 3. The mean CMMS score was 10 to 12 points higher than the Otis-Lennon score. CMMS scores correlated .67 with Stanford-Binet scores for a group of preschool and first-grade students, with the mean CMMS score being approximately 4 points lower than the mean Stanford-Binet score.

Predictive validity was evaluated through correlations between the CMMS and the Stanford Achievement Test (SAT) for children in first and second grade. Correlations ranged from .31 to .61 for the various achievement subtests, with mean correlations of .57 for first graders and .47 for second graders. These coefficients are typical for correlations between measures of cognitive ability and academic ability.

Although the test developers do not discuss construct validity, they do provide a 51-item annotated bibliography of studies that have used the CMMS.

SUMMARY

The CMMS is an easily administered test of "general reasoning ability." This test can be used if a screening instrument is necessary, or when a nonverbal measure of reasoning is needed to supplement other test results. Scores from this test should certainly not be substituted for the more expansive information available through a broad-range test of intelligence, especially in cases where educational decisions are to be based on the test results. As with other "quick" tests whose administration requires little technical expertise, the CMMS is vulnerable to misuse and misinterpretation.

PEABODY PICTURE VOCABULARY TEST–REVISED (PPVT-R)

L. Dunn and L. Dunn

American Guidance Service
Publishers' Building
Circle Pines, Minnesota   55014-1796

PURPOSE

The PPVT-R, published in 1981, is a revision of the PPVT, originally published in 1959. It is designed to measure a child's receptive vocabulary for Standard American English and to provide a quick estimate of a major aspect of verbal abilities for children who have grown up in Standard English-speaking environments. The test developers stress that it is *not* a comprehensive test of general intelligence. The test is designed for individuals from 2½ through 40 years.

DESCRIPTION OF TEST AND ADMINISTRATION

The PPVT-R consists of two forms, each containing 175 items. Each item is presented on one page of an "Easel Book." On each page are four black and white drawings. The examiner pronounces a word, and the student is asked to point to the picture (or say the number of the picture) that best "tells the meaning of the word." Sample items are provided that the examiner can use to further demonstrate the nature of the task. Recommended starting points for each chronological age are listed on the test form. Examiners can choose different starting points if they estimate the child's verbal ability to be significantly above or below average. The examiner must establish a basal rate of eight consecutive correct responses and may need to work backward if the starting point is too high. A ceiling level is reached when the child makes six errors within eight consecutive responses.

No specific examiner qualifications are indicated except for thorough familiarity with the test materials and manual. Formal training in psychometrics is recommended for the person responsible for the test's interpretation.

There are no time limits for any items. The test takes approximately 10 to 20 minutes to administer. There are two forms of the test, L and M, which can be used interchangeably.

SCORING AND INTERPRETATION

The examiner scores each item as correct or incorrect while administering the test. The raw score is calculated by subtracting errors from the ceiling item. Tables are provided for converting raw scores to standard scores for each age group. The standard score has a mean of 100 and a standard deviation of 15. Tables are also provided for converting scores to percentiles, stanines, or age-equivalent scores.

TECHNICAL QUALITY

Norms

Standardization for the PPVT-R occurred in 1979 and involved 4,200 children and adolescents and 828 adults. For the sample of children and adolescents, subjects ranged in age from 2 years 6 months through 18 years, with a total of 100 males and 100 females in each of 21 age groups. The sample was matched to the U.S. population according to geographic region, parents' occupational group, ethnic group, and community size. Half of the subjects were administered each form. For the adult standardization sample, at least 200 subjects in each of four age groups were tested, with equal representation of males and females. The adult group was matched to the U.S. population fairly closely on occupational representation. An attempt was made to have the sample match the population on geographic region, but this was somewhat unsuccessful. No data were gathered on ethnic representation or community size for the adults. Adults were tested as a group using slides of the test plates. In general, the norming sample for the children and adolescents appears to be adequate. Results based on norms for the adult group should be interpreted cautiously.

Separate norms are provided for each 2-month age range interval for ages 2 years 6 months through 6 years 11 months and for each 3-month age range interval for 7 years 0 months through 19 years 0 months. Norms for adults are provided for four age ranges, each spanning 5 or 6 years. Separate norms are provided for Form L and Form M.

Reliability

Split-half reliability coefficients for the children and youth sample ranged from .68 to .86 on Form L and from .61 to .86 on Form M. The median split-half reliability coefficient for the adult groups was .82. Alternate-forms reliability was based on standard scores from a sample of 642 subjects, yielding coefficients ranging from .71 to .89. Test-retest reliability was determined by administering Forms L and M to a sample of 962 subjects, with a test-retest interval of 9 to 31 days. The test-retest coefficients for standard scores ranged from .54 to .90, with a median of .77. Overall, indices of reliability are somewhat lower than would be desired.

The standard error of measurement is 7, ranging from 4 to 8 across ages. Values for each form at each age level are presented in the manual. The standard error of measurement is approximately twice as large as that of several of the comprehensive tests of intelligence.

Validity

Content validity appears to be adequate, based on the test developers' thorough review of the process used to select items. The manual presents a fair amount of information substantiating the validity of the original version of the PPVT, but none for the PPVT-R.

SUMMARY

The PPVT-R is an easily administered test that assesses a child's receptive single-word vocabulary. The test manual supplies a great deal of information indicating the care with which test items were developed and selected. The standardization procedure, at least for individuals younger than 19 years, appears to be quite adequate. The reliability information provided in the manual suggests that the test results are not as stable as might be desired. The lack of validity data for the PPVT-R is also a drawback for this test. Practitioners are warned to use PPVT-R data cautiously, especially for decision-making purposes. It should never be substituted for one of the comprehensive intelligence tests when decisions regarding an individual student are at stake. The PPVT-R is often used in research studies to document that subjects are within the normal range of intellectual functioning. The PPVT-R appears to be adequate for this purpose.

STANDARD PROGRESSIVE MATRICES (SPM), ADVANCED PROGRESSIVE MATRICES (APM), AND COLOURED PROGRESSIVE MATRICES (CPM)

J.C. Raven

The Psychological Corporation
555 Academic Court
San Antonio, Texas   78204-2498

PURPOSE

Raven's Progressive Matrices (RPM) include the Standard Progressive Matrices (SPM), first published in 1938 and most recently revised in 1956, the Coloured Progressive Matrices (CPM), originally published in 1947 and revised in 1956, and the Advanced Progressive Matrices (APM), prepared initially in 1943 and most recently revised in 1962. The RPM were designed "to provide measures of ability to educe relationships and correlates" (Raven, Court, & Raven, 1986a, p. G2). The SPM is designed to cover ages 6 through adult. The CPM is an additional set of problems that was constructed to provide more detailed assessment for young children, the mentally retarded, and for elderly individuals who have experienced intellectual decline. The APM is designed for use with individuals of above average intelligence, but in many cases is a more suitable test for adults than is the SPM (Vernon, 1984a). Raven et al. (1986a) do not view the tests as measures of "general intelligence," but suggest that they be used in conjunction with a vocabulary test to provide "an index of reproductive ability" (p. G2). Because they are nonverbal tests, the RPM can be used with individuals who have hearing or language deficits or who are not proficient with English. Jensen (1980) considers the RPM as one of the most "culture-reduced" tests, suggesting that it may be useful for culturally disadvantaged or culturally different individuals.

The most recent and complete information regarding the RPM is presented in the *Manual for Raven's Progressive Matrices and Vocabulary Scales,* which is purchased separately from the test materials. This volume includes the most recent manuals for the SPM (Raven, Court, & Raven, 1983a), the CPM (Raven, Court, & Raven, 1986b), the APM (Raven, Court, & Raven, 1983b), Mill Hill Vocabulary Scale (Raven, Court, & Raven, 1977), the Crichton Vocabulary Scale (Raven, Court, & Raven, 1988), a lengthy table summarizing all known research pertaining to the reliability and validity of these instruments, and several research supplements. *Research Supplement No. 3* (Raven, 1986), included in the *Manual*, presents data relevant to norms for the United States. Practitioners who wish to use the RPM should avail themselves of these publications.

DESCRIPTION OF TESTS AND ADMINISTRATION

Standard Progressive Matrices

The SPM consists of 60 items, divided into five sets (A through E) of 12 items each. Sets are of overlapping levels of difficulty, but get progressively harder. Each item is presented on a separate page and depicts a figure with a piece missing. Below the figure are six or eight alternatives from which the examinee must select to complete the figure. The principles involved in selecting the correct response are completion of a pattern in a continuous figure, figural analogy in a 2×2 matrix, systematic alteration of a pattern in a 3×3 matrix, and systematic decomposition and synthesis of figural parts in a 3×3 matrix (Llabre, 1985). The test can be administered individually, to a group, or can be self-administered. When administered individually, the examinee can point to the correct response. In group or self-administration, the examinees must record their responses on a response sheet. No special training is required for test administration. There are no time limits for the SPM, and administration usually takes less than 45 minutes.

Advance Progressive Matrices

The APM was designed for individuals older than 11 years of age and of average or greater intellectual ability. The test consists of Set I, containing 12 problems, and Set II, containing 36 problems. Set I is used to quickly indicate whether the examinee is "dull," "average," or "bright." Set II is administered only to those who are average or above. Items are similar to the SPM items, but are more difficult and include eight alternatives from which the examinee must choose. The APM can be administered individually or in a group, and can be given under untimed or timed conditions. If timed, a limit of 40 minutes is usually used. If untimed, administration generally takes 60 to 90 minutes.

Coloured Progressive Matrices

The CPM was designed to assess "a person's present clarity of observation and level of intellectual development" (Raven et al., 1986b, p. CPM4). It is used with children younger than age 11, elderly people whose cognitive skills have deteriorated, individuals who cannot understand or speak English, and those who are intellectually below normal. The CPM consists of 36 items, divided into sets A, Ab, and B. As with the APM and SPM, sets are of overlapping difficulty levels that become progressively harder. The test can be presented in a book, as are the APM and SPM, or in a board form. The board form must, however, be constructed by the examiner according to directions provided in the manual, and this appears to be a fairly time-consuming task. Raven et al. (1986b) claim that the book and board forms of the test "give practically the same results" (p. CPM9), although no data are provided to support this claim. The board form may be easier to administer to very young children, mentally retarded individuals, or people with poor proficiency in English, as the nature of the task can be demonstrated quite clearly. The book form can be administered individually, as a group test, or as a self-administered test with children older than 8 years of age. There are no time limits. Administration generally takes 15 to 30 minutes.

SCORING

For all forms, each item is scored objectively as correct or incorrect, and the number of correct items is summed. The total raw score is converted to a percentile score using the norms tables that are provided. The test developers suggest that scores be interpreted by categorizing examinees as "intellectually superior" (95th percentile or above), "definitely above the average in intellectual capacity" (75th to 95th percentiles), "average in intellectual capacity" (25th to 75th percentiles), "definitely below the average in intellectual capacity" (5th to 25th percentiles), or "intellectually impaired" (below the 5th percentile). Raven (1986) discourages conversion of percentile scores to IQs, although a table is provided for this purpose.

TECHNICAL QUALITY

Norms

Standard Progressive Matrices. The latest manual for the SPM provides norms for several different standardization samples. These include British children between 6 and 16 years, Irish children between 6 and 12 years, Colchester children between 6 and 14 years, Colchester adults between 20 and 65 years, Hong Kong children between 5 and 16 years, and deaf British children, 15 to 16 years of age. All norming data were collected in the 1970s and 1980s except for the Colchester children and the adult samples, which were obtained in the 1940s and are, of course, obsolete. Norms from standardization samples around the world are available in the literature. However, investigators generally did not attempt to make these samples representative of an entire population.

Research Supplement No. 3 provides norms based on recent administration of the SPM to several samples of children and adolescents in the United States. Although most of the samples included a reasonable number of subjects across age spans of several years, they are restricted to single school districts or counties. Furthermore, it is not stated when the norms were obtained for every sample. The test developers present the norms from each study separately, as well as a table based on a compilation of the norms from all these U.S. studies. It is not clear how this compilation was achieved. Because the samples used to compile the table may not be representative, practitioners should be very cautious in interpreting scores based on these norms.

Advanced Progressive Matrices. Norms provided in the manual (Raven et al., 1983b) for the 1962 version are "estimated" from "existing data," and no further information is provided regarding the norming sample. Norms allow conversion of raw scores to percentile scores, but only for the 50th, 75th, 90th, and 95th percentiles. Raven (1986) states that it does not make sense to administer the APM to a random sample of individuals in order to obtain norms, as the APM is intended to identify adults of above average ability. A table of norms based on 300 University of California students is presented (Raven, 1986). These norms cannot, of course, be considered adequate as a basis of comparison for most individuals.

Coloured Progressive Matrices. The 1986 edition of the CPM manual provides several sets of norms obtained from communities around the world. Each set is based on a sample from a very restricted geographical area. Little information is provided regarding the demographics of these samples, and it is often not clear when the data were gathered. For each sample, the norms table allows conversion of raw scores to percentiles, but only for the 5th, 10th, 25th, 50th, 75th, 90th, and 95th percentiles. *Research Supplement No. 3* presents tables of norms obtained from several communities in the United States and a table based on a compilation of these data. As with the U.S. norms for the SPM, those for the CPM must be used with great caution, as they cannot be assumed to be based on a representative sample.

Reliability

Standard Progressive Matrices. Studies of split-half reliability for the SPM have generally revealed correlations of at least .90. From original studies on the SPM, test-retest reliability varies with age from .83 to .93 (Raven et al., 1983a). Later studies, also presented by Raven et al. (1983a), found test-retest reliabilities in the .80s except for studies that employed intertest intervals exceeding 1 year. Thus, the majority of data presented support both internal consistency and consistency over time for the SPM.

Advanced Progressive Matrices. Reliability data for the APM are based on the 1947 edition. Test-retest reliability coefficients for this version range from .76 (for age 10½ years) to .91 (for adult students) across ages, with an intertest interval of 6 to 8 weeks. Reliabilities were greater for groups older than 12½ years of age than for younger individuals, and the test developers recommend that the test not be used with children younger than 11 years. The 1962 version could be expected to have similar reliability, but no information is provided in the manual.

Coloured Progressive Matrices. Jensen (1974) found a split-half reliability estimate of .90 from a group of 1,662 children in kindergarten through sixth grade. Other studies have revealed lower split-half reliabilities when the samples included only younger children (Raven et al., 1986b).

Raven et al. (1986b) state that both the board and book forms of the CPM have low retest reliability "in the neighborhood of .65" for children younger than 7 years of age. The sample for this study is not described, and the interval between the two testings is not specified. Approximately 200 9-year-olds were given the CPM twice, with a 6-week intertest interval, resulting in a test-retest reliability coefficient of .80. Raven et al. (1986b) state that over the whole range of development for which the test is constructed, the CPM has a retest reliability "in the neighbourhood of 0.9" (p. CPM17). In another study of 25 normal and 29 emotionally disturbed children between 6½ and 12½ years of age, the CPM was administered three times with intertest intervals of 3 months. Correlations between scores from the three testings ranged from .85 to .92. Although samples used for the test-restest studies are not well defined, the reported data suggest that the CPM has adequate test-retest reliability only for children older than 7 years of age.

Validity

Part Three of the *Manual for Raven's Progressive Matrices and Vocabulary Scales* briefly outlines results from more than 50 reliability studies and more than 100 validity studies involving the RPM. Many more studies are outlined in *Research Supplement No. 4* (Raven & Court, 1989). As with the normative studies discussed previously, the reliability and validity studies come from many countries, with each study based on a fairly limited population (e.g., from a specific community, a specific occupational group, or a group with a specific disability). It is impossible in a review such as this to meaningfully summarize all of the data from these studies. Those individuals who are considering using the RPM may want to refer to Part Three of the *Manual* in order to review specific studies that are based on populations similar to the one for whom they wish to use the test. The validity data discussed in the following sections are presented in the most recent versions of the SPM, CPM, and APM manuals.

Standard Progressive Matrices. Raven et al. (1983a) report that the correlations between scores on the SPM and those on the Binet and Wechsler scales range from .54 to .86 for English-speaking students. As would be expected, SPM scores generally correlate higher with scores from the nonverbal intelligence tests than with those from tests of verbal skills. Correlations between SPM scores and performance on achievement tests or other measures of academic achievement are generally lower than correlations with tests of intelligence, "ranging from negligible . . . to very high" (Raven et al., 1983a, p. SPM9). Studies of predictive validity have shown the SPM to be somewhat successful in predicting childrens' academic performance, with coefficients ranging up to .70, and in predicting adults' occupational levels. Factorial studies have generally found SPM items to load quite highly on a factor of general intellectual functioning (up to .94 for adults), with "no loading on verbal-educative and numerical ability factors" (Raven et al., 1983a, p. SPM11).

Advanced Progressive Matrices. Validity data for the APM are much more sparse than for the SPM and CPM. Because of the limited nature of the samples employed in most of these studies, it is impossible to draw any definite conclusions regarding the validity of the APM for most individuals.

Coloured Progressive Matrices. Several factor analytic studies have revealed three factors for the CPM: simple pattern completion, pattern completion through identity and closure, and abstract reasoning by analogy. These factors are very similar to those described when the test was originally constructed. Many cross-cultural studies have been conducted using the CPM. In general, these studies have found that the CPM measures the same construct for all cultural and ethnic groups.

OTHER CONSIDERATIONS

The *Manual for Raven's Progressive Matrices and Vocabulary Scales* contains an extraordinary amount of information regarding the RPM that has been gathered from many countries across several decades, involving older as well as current versions of the test. The manual's layout makes it somewhat cumbersome to use. The material is often redundant from one section to the next, and it is difficult to efficiently find answers to specific questions. Verbatim instructions are provided, but some of the language sounds a bit awkward for children in the United States.

SUMMARY

The SPM, CPM, and APM are quick and easily administered instruments that claim to yield an estimation of the examinee's capacity for "observation and clear thinking." The RPM have been used extensively throughout the world for several decades, suggesting that psychologists, educators, and researchers have found the tests to be useful, or at least intriguing. The major problem with the RPM, at least for use in the United States, is the lack of norms based on an adequately representative sample. An examiner wishing to use the RPM would have to carefully examine the characteristics of the many small norming samples described in the manuals to determine which, if any, would be comparable to the population with which he or she wanted to use the test. Unfortunately, the information provided in the manual is often inadequate to allow this careful examination. Although there is an abundance of research involving the RPM, most of it is not relevant for U.S. populations because of the limited nature of the study samples or because the data are obsolete. Thus, it is quite difficult to make judgments about the reliability and validity of the RPM for particular groups other than those on which the research was conducted. It is probably not justifiable to use the RPM as a norm-referenced test for most children, and it is not recommended that scores from the test be used for decision-making purposes. However, the long history of the RPM, along with abundant cross-cultural research, suggests that the test does assess nonverbal reasoning ability. It appears reasonable, therefore, that these tests might be used cautiously by an examiner who is interested in obtaining a subjective impression of an individual's approach to visual problem-solving tasks or for research studies that do not require normative information.

BAYLEY SCALES OF INFANT DEVELOPMENT (MENTAL SCALE)

Nancy Bayley

The Psychological Corporation
555 Academic Court
San Antonio, Texas 78204-2498

Unlike most of the other tests reviewed in this chapter, the Bayley Mental Scale is not a "quick test" and is not limited to one aspect of cognitive functioning. Indeed, it is generally considered one of the best measurements, if not the best, of cognitive development for children younger than 2½ years.

PURPOSE

The Bayley Scales of Infant Development consist of three scales: The Mental Scale, which will be discussed here; The Motor Scale, which was designed to provide a measure of body control, coordination of large muscles and fine motor skills of the hands and fingers; and The Infant Behavior Record, which helps the clinician assess the child's "social and objective orientations toward his environment" (Bayley, 1969, p. 4).

The Bayley Mental Scale was designed to

> assess sensory-perceptual acuities, discriminations, and ability to respond to these; the early acquisition of 'object constancy' and memory, learning and problem-solving ability; vocalizations and the beginnings of verbal communication; and early evidence of the ability to form generalizations and classifications, which is the basis of abstract thinking (Bayley, 1969, p. 3).

Bayley states that the Mental Scale has limited value in predicting later abilities. Its primary value is in assessment of the child's *current* status, and the extent of any deviation from normal expectancy (Bayley, 1969). The Mental Scale is appropriate for infants from 2 to 30 months of age.

DESCRIPTION OF TEST AND ADMINISTRATION

The Mental Scale contains 163 items, each requiring the examiner to observe a spontaneous behavior (e.g., "vocalizes two different sounds"), the infant's response to a particular stimulus (e.g., "smiles at mirror image"), imitation of the examiner's behavior (e.g., imitating a scribble), response to a request from the examiner (e.g., pointing to pictures named by the examiner), or correct manipulation of test stimuli (e.g., solving formboards and pegboards). Items are arranged in order of age placement (the age at which 50% of the children tested passed a given item). The age placement is indicated for each item, along with an age range estimating the ages at which each item is passed by 5% and 95% of children in the standardization sample. Age-placement values below 2 months were estimated, based on a very small sample of newborns. There are no subtests.

Test stimuli include approximately 35 objects that are supplied in the test kit. These include such things as cubes, cups, a mirror, ball, crayons, book, toy clock, scissors, toy car, bell, and rattle. Very few items (e.g., paper, facial tissue) are supplied by the examiner. Usually a test material is used for several different items, each at a different age. For example, the bell is used to observe the child's response to sound, interest in detail of the bell, and purposeful ringing of the bell. Because items are arranged according to difficulty, the examiner must either repeatedly take test materials in and out of the kit, or more appropriately, learn all of the items that require use of each material and administer together those items that are appropriate for the child's ability level. This task is facilitated by "situation codes" printed on the test form that allow the examiner to tell at a glance what items should be administered together. A fair amount of practice is required, however, to learn to administer the test smoothly.

The examiner usually begins administering items at a level 1 month below the child's chronological age, unless there is indication that the child is functioning at a much lower level. Although criteria for establishing basal and ceiling levels are not strictly prescribed, the examiner can usually be safe in using a criterion of 10 successive items passed or failed to establish basal and ceiling levels. (The exception to this is observed in cases when verbal skills are significantly above or below the level of nonverbal problem-solving skills.)

Average testing time for both the Mental and Motor Scales is approximately 45 minutes. The author has found that administration of the Mental Scale alone usually takes approximately 30 minutes.

In testing infants and very young children, it is often necessary to use procedures different from those used with school-age children. For example, a parent or parent-substitute remains present during the test administration and is sometimes asked to participate in eliciting responses from the child. Particular attention is given to the child's state (e.g., tired, hungry) at the time of testing, and efforts must be made to test at a time when the infant is awake and content. Breaks may be necessary for such tasks as nursing, changing diapers, or rest. If the child is not content and alert, test results will not reflect true levels of ability. The examiner must be particularly alert and sensitive in establishing rapport with the infant. Bayley (1969) clearly indicates that examiners should have some background in theory of measurement and the interpretation of test results. A suggested training strategy for mastering administration is provided.

SCORING

Scoring criteria for each item are presented in the test manual. Many items require a certain amount of examiner judgment, and scoring criteria sometimes leave room for a fair amount of subjectivity. However, with experience, it is generally fairly easy to determine whether or not criteria have or have not been met. In addition, a recent manual supplement (Rhodes, Bayley, & Yow, 1984) clarifies administration and scoring of some of the more ambiguous items.

The raw score is the total number of items passed, including all items below the basal level, whether administered or not. The examiner uses the norms tables to convert the raw score to a Mental Development Index (MDI), which has a mean of 100 and standard deviation of 16. The minimum score that can be obtained is 50, and the maximum is 150. The minimum score of 50 is somewhat problematic, as many children younger than 30 months who are referred for testing are significantly delayed. For these children, the examiner can determine a mental age, based on the age level at which the child's raw score would correspond to an MDI of 100. Bayley (1969) firmly warns that an intelligence quotient should *not* be computed by dividing the mental age by the child's chronological age, as there is no evidence to support this interpretation.

TECHNICAL QUALITY

Norms

The norming sample was composed of 1,262 children between 2 and 30 months of age. Eighty-three to 95 children were tested at each of 14 age levels. The sample was matched to the U.S. population (according to the 1960 census) for sex, race, urban versus rural residence, and education of the head of household. The sample slightly underrepresented children from rural areas and children whose parents were more poorly educated. Only "normal" children living at home were included in the sample. Bayley (1969) notes that the standardization sample must be considered somewhat biased, as participation in testing was voluntary on the part of parents. In general, though, the standardization sample appears adequate. However, the norms derived from this sample are now fairly old and may not reflect current developmental abilities of a contemporary population. The age of the norms may not be as much of a problem for the Bayley Mental Scale as for tests designed for older children, however, as increases in cognitive and academic skills that have been influenced by early preschool activity and exposure through television will not be as relevant for infants.

Separate norms are provided at half-month age range intervals for infants 2 through 6 months, and at 1-month age range intervals for infants 6 through 30 months, making a total of 32 age ranges for which norms are provided. Bayley (1969) indicates that standard score equivalents are based on the scores obtained from the children in each of the 14 age groups sampled. Norms for the intermediate age groups (those falling between the ages actually sampled) are based on extrapolation. For each age group, the standard scores were generally found to range between 55 and 145. Values were extrapolated at the extremes to provide standard scores covering the full range from 50 to 150. Thus, scores at the extremes are less reliable than scores closer to the mean, as is the case with most tests.

Reliability

Split-half reliability coefficients for each of the 14 age groups in the standardization sample ranged from .81 to .93, with a median of .88. The standard errors of measurement range across ages from 4.2 to 6.9. Inter-rater reliability is especially important for a test such as the Mental Scale, as criteria for scoring items involve some subjective judgment, and the examiner's ability to establish good rapport must be considered critical in obtaining the child's best performance. Using the immediate predecessor of the current Mental Scale (whose administration and content are very similar to those of the current scale), ninety 8-month-old infants were tested, while a second examiner observed through a one-way mirror. The examiner's scoring agreed on 89% of the items, averaged across all cases. Twenty-eight infants from this same group were retested 1 week later, with agreement across time for 76% of items. Correlation coefficients for interobserver reliability and test-retest reliability would be desirable for each age range.

Validity

Concurrent validity was assessed by correlating scores obtained from the Mental Scale with IQs from the Stanford-Binet (presumably Form L-M). One hundred children, ranging in age from 24 to 30 months, earned basal scores on the Stanford-Binet. Correlation coefficients ranged across age from .47 to .64, with a mean of .57. As Bayley (1969) notes, the correlations can be considered somewhat low, given the restricted nature of the sample (i.e., limited to only those bright children who could reach basal level on the Stanford-Binet).

OTHER CONSIDERATIONS

Little specific information is presented regarding interpretation of scores. Some mention of item analysis for individual examinees might be useful, as many children referred for testing show specific delays (e.g., in expressive language). The MDI, which represents *overall* cognitive development, is not particularly useful in evaluating these children. The manual does provide information regarding the differences between MDIs and PDIs (the Psychomotor Development Index obtained on the Motor Scale) that are required for statistical significance. Discussion of correlations between MDIs and PDIs is also presented. However, the *clinical* significance of comparing MDIs with PDIs is not clear.

SUMMARY

The Bayley Mental Scale is generally considered the best standardized instrument for measuring cognitive development in children younger than 30 months of age. The major advantage of the Mental Scale over other tests of infant cognitive development is the provision of norms based on a large representative sample. A major drawback is the lack of any subtest scores reflecting development in various areas of cognition. Despite its wide use, practitioners must be cautioned regarding the low correlation between MDIs and future IQs. The purpose of the test, as clearly outlined by its author, is to assess *current* level of cognitive development, and the test should be interpreted only in this way. Practitioners must also be cautioned that validity and reliability of an individual score depend a great deal on the infant's state at the time of testing. If the infant is not alert and cooperative, test results will, of course, not reflect the infant's best abilities. The Mental Scale is probably best used for early identification of children with significant delays, and it is generally considered appropriate for this purpose. Its value for children closer to the average range or above is not as well established.

LEITER INTERNATIONAL PERFORMANCE SCALE (LIPS)

Russell G. Leiter

Western Psychological Services
12031 Wilshire Boulevard
Los Angeles, California   90025

PURPOSE

The LIPS is a test of nonverbal intelligence designed for use with individuals from 2 through 17 years of age. (Norms are available, however, only through age 13.) The test was developed by Russell Leiter in 1930 and has been revised several times, with the most recent edition being published in 1948. According to Levine (1982), the scale was "originally conceived as an instrument for assessing adaptability to one's environment" (p. 1). Although the test was originally intended as a culturally fair test for normal children of all races, it is now most commonly used with hearing-impaired children or children with severe speech or language abilities.

DESCRIPTION OF TEST AND ADMINISTRATION

The LIPS consists of 54 items, divided into 13 age levels between 2 years and 17 years. Levels are at 1-year intervals for ages 2 through 10 years, and at 2-year intervals between 12 and 18 years. Each level contains four items, except for the 18-year level, which contains six items.

Items are all of the same format. Each item consists of four to 25 wooden blocks, each with a geometric form or picture on one side, and a paper strip with four to eight forms or pictures arranged in a line. Also included in the test kit is a wooden frame that has eight square notches or "stalls." Above the stalls is a sliding metal frame in which the examiner places the paper strip for each test item. Each form or picture on the paper strip is directly above one of the stalls. For each item the child is required to place blocks in the stalls by determining the relationship between the forms or pictures on the blocks and the forms or pictures on the paper strip. For example, for one of the very easiest items, the paper strip shows five squares of different colors. The child is given five blocks of different colors, and must match the colors of the blocks with the colors on the paper strip. At higher levels, the relationship between the forms on the blocks and the paper strip might involve matching of faces, classifying animals (e.g., a butterfly is matched with a bee and a dog with a tiger), or matching numerals with the numbers of cubes used in elaborate three-dimensional block constructions. For some items the child does not use every block, but must choose which ones are related to the forms or pictures on the paper strip. A few items have more than one part, and the child must execute all parts correctly to receive credit.

The test items are considered to test both perceptual and conceptual skills (Matey, 1985). Perceptual items include tasks involving matching of shapes and colors, construction of block designs, and visual closure. Conceptual items include tasks requiring the child to deduce underlying relationships, categories, and classes, demonstrate understanding of visual-spatial relationships, and demonstrate understanding of numerical processes (Matey, 1985).

Testing is begun at the level approximately 2 years below the child's estimated mental age. A basal level is established at the level where all items are solved correctly. The test is discontinued when all items are failed at two consecutive levels.

The test manual instructs the examiner to administer the test with as little verbalization as possible. Essentially no verbal explanation is given regarding the nature of the tasks. Leiter recommends that testing begin approximately 2 years below the child's estimated mental age in order to provide the child with some practice with easy items so that the nature of the tasks will be evident. Demonstration and teaching are permissible on some of the items at the lowest levels. Except for four block-design items, none of the items is timed. The entire test generally takes 30 to 90 minutes to administer.

The LIPS is to be administered by a professional with training in administration and interpretation of individually administered intelligence tests.

A commonly used version of the LIPS, the Arthur Adaption, was devised for children between 3 and 7 years of age. The same materials are used, but items above the 12-year level are omitted. Unlike the standard administration of the LIPS, the Arthur Adaption allows the examiner to correct errors on some of the items, to provide the child with additional structure for completing some of the tasks (e.g., pointing to the next stall to be filled), and to discontinue block design items if the previous block design item was failed. Separate norms are provided by Levine (1982) for the Arthur Adaptation.

SCORING AND INTERPRETATION

All items are scored objectively as passed or failed, with little or no need for subjective judgment. Like the old Stanford-Binet (Form L-M), the examiner adds up the months of credit earned for each item passed beyond the basal age, and adds that sum of months to the basal age, thus obtaining a mental age. Items at age levels 2 though 10 years are each credited with 3 months and items between levels 12 and 16 years are each credited with 6 months. A ratio IQ is obtained from a table in the manual. Values in this table were calculated by dividing mental age by chronological age and multiplying by 100. Because scores that are obtained through this method were found to have a mean of 95, Leiter (1979) instructs the examiner to add 5 points to the IQ derived from the table. The mental age is then adjusted to take into account the additional 5 points. Tables of norms in *Leiter International Performance Scale: A Handbook* (Levine, 1982) allow the examiner to obtain scores directly without calculating a mental age or making the 5-point adjustment. Levine (1982) claims that the adjusted norms make the LIPS comparable to other measures of intelligence with mean scores of 100 and a standard deviation of 16. No empirical data are provided, however, to substantiate this mean and standard deviation.

No information is presented in the manual regarding interpretation of the LIPS score. Levine (1982) presents an "interpretive profile form" that categorizes the 54 LIPS items according to the skills needed to solve each problem. The categories include concretistic matching, symbolic transformation, quantitative discriminations, spatial imagery, genus matching, progression discriminations, immediate recall, and speed. Levine reports that the profile has only "face validity" and should therefore be "considered only *suggestive* of possible interpretation of Leiter results" (p. 72).

TECHNICAL QUALITY

Norms

Although Levine (1982) provides tables of norms for both the standard administration and the Arthur Adaptation, the scores presented are not based on the actual performance of a normative sample. They are simply calculations of mental age (obtained from the test) divided by chronological age and multiplied by 100, with a correction of 5 points. These scores should, therefore, be used quite cautiously and should not be assumed to be necessarily equivalent to IQs obtained through more conventional techniques. The LIPS items were designed and revised several times in an attempt to have the level of each item correspond appropriately to the average performance of children at that same age level. That is, the objective was to design items at the 4-year level, for example, that were passed by half of 4-year-old children. Previous versions of the LIPS were administered to large samples of children to test the adequacy of this correspondence between item levels and chronological age. Although average chronological ages were approximately equal to average mental ages, it must be kept in mind that the sample of children was not selected to be representative of the total population. Furthermore, most of these studies were conducted in the 1930s and 1940s, so that the results cannot be considered to accurately reflect today's population. Thus, the assumption that mental ages from the LIPS correspond to the average intellectual performance of a child at that chronological age is questionable. For these reasons, it is recommended that scores from the LIPS not be used for decision making.

Reliability

Levine (1982) reports results from four studies regarding the internal consistency of the current version of the LIPS. Correlation coefficients ranged from .75 to .97, with three of the four studies indicating acceptable internal consistency. Results of six test-retest studies, all conducted with handicapped children, revealed correlations ranging from .36 to .92 (Levine, 1982). The lowest test-retest correlation was obtained on a group of preschool deaf children, with a test-retest interval of 2 to 3 years. Four of the other studies used test-retest intervals of approximately 6 months. Correlation coefficients for these studies ranged from .64 to .92, which is somewhat lower than would be desired. (Some of these studies used the Arthur Adaptation of the LIPS.)

A standard error of measurement of 3.3 points obtained by Smith (1976) was reported by Levine (1982).

Validity

The LIPS manual contains no information regarding validity of the instrument. Levine (1982) presents results of many studies, all of which are relevant to concurrent validity. Twelve of the studies reported by Levine involve comparison of scores from the LIPS and the Stanford-Binet (Form L-M). Some of the studies were conducted with normal children and some with children who have various mental handicaps. Correlations ranged from .38 to .89, with a median correlation (for both IQ and mental age) of .77.

Comparisons of Full Scale IQs on the WISC with LIPS IQs resulted in correlations ranging from .55 to .86, with correlations from five of the six studies presented at .77 or above (Levine, 1982). In general, the LIPS was more highly correlated with WISC Full Scale IQs than with either VIQs or PIQs, and more highly with PIQs than with VIQs. Correlations between the LIPS and the PPVT were moderate (ranging from .37 to .62) in six studies reported by Levine (1982). In studies involving teacher ratings, a median correlation of .76 was found when LIPS scores were compared with teacher ratings of intelligence and a median correlation of .60 when LIPS scores are compared with teacher ratings of achievement.

In general, studies have shown moderate correlations between scores from the LIPS and other measures of intelligence. Thus, concurrent validity for the LIPS, for both normal and handicapped children, has been established, at least to a moderate extent. The lack of more information regarding predictive and construct validity, however, limits the extent to which scores can be used and interpreted confidently.

SUMMARY

Although the LIPS has a "rich clinical history" (Matey, 1985, p. 419) and consists of items that appear to tap nonverbal intelligence, the test's lack of appropriate standardization and its technical unsophistication prevent it from being the test of choice, even for children with hearing or language deficits. With the advent of the technically excellent K-ABC, which includes a Nonverbal Scale, use of the LIPS cannot be justified. Primarily because of the outdated method for obtaining IQs and the obsolescence of the sample against which mental ages were originally tested, scores from the LIPS should not be used to make decisions about individual children.

CHAPTER 6

TESTS OF VISUAL-SPATIAL AND VISUAL-MOTOR SKILLS

This chapter will present information regarding tests of visual-spatial processing and visual-motor integration. Unlike some of the tests presented in the previous chapters that purport to measure intelligence through nonverbal tasks (e.g., Progressive Matrices Tests and the Leiter International Performance Scale), the tests included in this chapter are designed specifically to determine levels of competence in various areas of visual-spatial functioning. They are used primarily in attempts to diagnose specific problems that might interfere with learning.

DEVELOPMENTAL TEST OF VISUAL-MOTOR INTEGRATION (VMI)

Keith E. Beery

Modern Curriculum Press
13900 Prospect Road
Cleveland, Ohio   44136

PURPOSE

The VMI was "designed primarily to serve as a regular classroom screening instrument that helps prevent learning and behavioral disorders through early identification of difficulties" (Beery, 1982, p. 13). Originally published in 1967 and revised in 1982 and 1989, the VMI is based on Beery's observation of significant correlations between children's abilities to copy geometric forms and their academic achievement. More specifically, the VMI assesses the child's ability to integrate visual-spatial perception with fine-motor output. The VMI can be used with preschool children through adults, although norms are provided only through 17 years 11 months.

DESCRIPTION OF TEST AND ADMINISTRATION

The test booklet contains 24 drawings of geometric designs, presented three to a page. Under each drawing is a box in which the child is to copy the drawing. The forms are copied in order, starting with the first item. The child is given only one attempt for each item, and erasing is not allowed. The test is discontinued after three consecutive failures. The VMI can be administered individually or in a group setting. Individual administration is advised for children younger than 4 years of age. No special training is required for the administration or scoring of the VMI, except for familiarity with the manual and scoring criteria. Total testing time generally ranges from 10 to 15 minutes. There are no time limits for items.

SCORING AND INTERPRETATION

Each item is scored as passed or failed. Specific scoring criteria, accompanied by examples, are presented for each drawing. Scoring criteria are outlined as clearly as possible, and many of the ambiguities of the scoring criteria in the 1982 manual have been clarified in the 1989 manual. Items that are failed are assigned 0 points. Items that are passed may earn 1, 2, 3, or 4 points, with higher point values assigned to more difficult designs.

Scores for each item are totalled. Tables of norms for each age level are used to convert total raw scores to standard scores, which have a mean of 100 and a standard deviation of 15. Tables are also provided for converting standard scores to percentiles, normal curve equivalents (NCEs; mean = 50, standard deviation = 21.06), T-scores (mean = 50, standard deviation = 10), and scaled scores (mean = 10, standard deviation = 3). The examiner can also compute an age-equivalent score, ranging from 2 years 11 months through 18 years 0 months.

TECHNICAL QUALITY

Norms

Test norms are provided for individuals 4 years 0 months through 17 years 11 months. They are based on data from three samples, including 1,030 children tested in 1964, 2,060 children tested in 1981, and 2,734 children tested in 1988. The 1964 sample was composed entirely of children in urban, suburban, and rural Illinois, and the 1981 sample included children from various ethnic and income groups in California. The 1988 sample was more representative, including children from several eastern, northern, and southern states. Beery (1989) reports that results from the three groups were not significantly different.

Children in the norming sample ranged in age from 2 years 6 months through 19 years 0 months, but were not evenly divided across the range. For example, ages 3, 15, 16, 17, and 18 years were each represented by less than 100 children. Other age levels, each spanning 1 year, included 198 to 828 children. The manual gives figures regarding the percentage of the sample representing various racial, economic, and residence groups, and Beery (1989) claims that the VMI norming sample is "reasonably representative" of the U.S. population, as reported in the 1980 census. Approximately half of the sample was male. Although norming was done in a less than optimal fashion, the norms are probably acceptable for ages 4 through 14 years. Norms are provided for each 3-month age range interval from age 4 years 0 months through 17 years 11 months.

Reliability

Because of the nature of scoring, inter-rater reliability is particularly important in assessing the value of the VMI. Beery (1982) reports inter-rater reliability coefficients for the 1981 scoring system ranging from .58 to .99, with a median correlation of .93. Inter-rater reliability coefficients increased in cases where scorers received training from psychologists or resource teachers. It is suspected that inter-rater reliabilities would be higher using the 1989 scoring system, as many of the scoring criteria have been clarified.

Beery reports several studies of test-retest reliability conducted by himself and others. Using the 1982 version, correlation coefficients ranged from .92 for a 2-week test-retest interval to .63 for a 7-month interval, with a median correlation of .81. Coefficients reflecting internal consistency for the 1989 version range from .76 to .91, with a median of .85. Information regarding the reliability studies is quite sparse in the manual. Available data suggest, however, that reliability is adequate, assuming that examiners have sufficient training and experience in applying the scoring criteria.

Standard errors of measurement (for the standard scores), based on the norming sample, range from 4.50 to 7.35 across age ranges, with a median of 5.81.

Validity

Concurrent validity was assessed by correlating VMI scores with measures of visual perception, visual-motor integration, and handwriting. Correlations between the VMI and scores from the Bender Visual Motor Gestalt Test, another figure-copying task, have ranged from .29 to .93, with a median of .56. The VMI has been found to correlate .80 with the Frostig Test of Visual Perception. The average correlation between VMI scores and scores from a measure of handwriting was .42. Although these correlations are not particularly impressive, they do lend some support for concurrent validity.

Correlations between the VMI and mental age on the Primary Mental Abilities tests ranged from .37 to .59 across age levels. VMI scores correlated .50 with Slosson IQs, .49 with WISC-R Verbal IQs, .56 for Performance IQs, and .56 for Full Scale IQs. It is not clear, however, to what extent the test should be expected to correlate with overall intelligence. Correlations between the VMI and readiness tests have averaged about .50. Correlations with measures of academic achievement in reading and other areas have tended to be higher for younger children than for older children.

Studies of predictive validity have found that combined use of scores from the VMI and a test of auditory-vocal association was the best predictor of first-grade achievement among a battery of prekindergarten test scores. VMI scores at the beginning of kindergarten were found to be significantly correlated with SRA Reading, Language Arts, and Mathematics scores at the end of first grade. VMI scores in kindergarten have also been found to correlate with classification of reading as severe problem, mild problem, average, or superior in sixth grade.

Although Beery (1982, 1989) provides some information regarding the validity of the VMI in the manual, the discussion of validation studies is too sparse to allow the test user to determine the studies' adequacy without personally reviewing each of them. For example, for most studies reported in the manual, Beery fails to provide size of the sample, ages of children involved, or any background information. For this reason it is difficult to judge the validity of the VMI for specific purposes. In general, however, it appears that the VMI is a better predictor of academic achievement, and specifically of handwriting, for preschool and early elementary children than for older children.

OTHER CONSIDERATIONS

VMI scoring criteria are more specific and more complete than those for the Bender Visual Motor Gestalt Test. In addition, the structured format of the VMI makes the task easier for very young children, and facilitates scoring.

The value of administering the VMI should be questioned when other figure-copying tasks have been administered in one of the multi-scale tests of intelligence (e.g., WPPSI, WPPSI-R, or Stanford-Binet).

The VMI manual contains information and examples regarding developmental trends in the copying of each figure. A section is also included in the manual regarding instruction in visual-motor integration, although the effectiveness of this training in improving academic skills is unproven.

SUMMARY

The VMI is a well-structured test of visual-motor integration that is appropriate for children between 4 and 18 years of age. A major advantage of the VMI, in comparison with many other figure-copying tasks, is the specificity and clarity of its scoring criteria. The structure provided by the test format makes the VMI easier for small children to understand and follow than less structured tests such as the Bender Visual Motor Gestalt Test. The increased range of ages covered by the norms in the 1989 manual makes the VMI a more useful test with older children, although predictive validity of tests of visual-motor integration generally tends to be better with younger than with older children. Because the norming sample may not be totally representative of the U.S. population, examiners should review data about characteristics of the sample to determine whether scores are meaningful for individual children or specific groups of children. Particular caution should be used in interpreting scores for children older than 14 because of the limited norming samples at these ages.

In general, the VMI can be considered a useful tool in identifying difficulties in visual-motor integration, which are often associated with handwriting problems and *may* signal later academic problems. The VMI, like other brief tests, should never be used in isolation to make decisions regarding individual children.

MOTOR-FREE VISUAL PERCEPTION TEST

Ronald P. Colarusso and Donald D. Hammill

Academic Therapy Publications
20 Commercial Boulevard
Novato, California 94947

PURPOSE

The Motor-Free Visual Perception Test (MVPT), copyrighted in 1972, was designed to test visual perceptual skills in a way that avoids motor involvement and is practical for screening, diagnostic, and research purposes. As Colarusso and Hammill (1972) observe, many tests of visual perceptual skills require the child to copy a drawing or reproduce a figure. Because motor abilities and visual perceptual abilities are quite distinct, the test developers perceived a need for a test that measures visual perceptual skills in such a way that would not penalize the child with poor motor coordination. The MVPT is appropriate for children between the ages of 4 and 8 years.

DESCRIPTION OF TEST AND ADMINISTRATION

The MVPT is composed of 36 multiple-choice items, each of which requires the child to point to the correct answer among four alternatives.

The test developers include items that measure five categories of "prominent theoretical constructs of visual perception," which are derived from the literature and other tests of visual perception: spatial relationships, visual discrimination, figure-ground, visual closure, visual memory. Separate scores are not derived for each type of item, however.

The first four test items require the child to identify which of four alternatives is identical to a simultaneously presented model. The next four items also require the child to identify which of four alternatives matches the model, but in these items the figure is "hidden" among extra irrelevant lines. The next set of items again requires the child to find the model stimulus figure among four choices, but is told that it "might be smaller, bigger, darker, or turned on its side." The next group of items requires the child to look at a model stimulus for 5 seconds and then to select from memory which of the four alternatives is an identical match. The next set asks the child to look at a completed model stimulus and to identify which of the four incomplete alternatives would look like the model "if we finished drawing these figures." The final group of items requires the child to identify which of four alternatives is different from the rest. Sample items are provided for each set.

All items are administered to every child. No basal or ceiling levels are established, although the test developers warn against interpretation of raw scores of less than 10. None of the items is timed, and average administration takes less than 10 minutes.

SCORING AND INTERPRETATION

Each item is scored as either correct or incorrect. The total raw score is the number of items answered correctly. Raw scores can be transformed to Perceptual Ages (PAs) or Perceptual Quotients (PQs). PQs have a mean of 100 and standard deviation of 15. Standard errors of measurement are provided for each of these scores.

Little information is provided regarding interpretation of test results. Colarusso and Hammill (1972) suggest that a PQ of 85 or less be the "criterion for inadequacy on the test," and recommend that the teacher verify this conclusion by evaluating the child's classroom performance. The test developers are careful to avoid any claims regarding the relationship of test performance to intelligence, reading ability, or any other school skills.

TECHNICAL QUALITY

Norms

The MVPT was standardized on a sample of 881 normal children, ages 4 through 8 years. Although the manual states that children in the norming sample resided in 22 states and included all races, economic levels and residential areas (urban, suburban, rural), no information is included regarding the representativeness of the sample on these variables. The sample was not equally representative of each age group. Norms are provided for each 6-month age range interval between 5 years 0 months through 8 years 11 months; only one set of norms is provided for children between 4 years 0 months and 4 years 11 months.

Reliability

A study of test-retest reliability, involving 162 children and a 20-day interval between the two administrations, resulted in an overall reliability coefficient of .81. Split-half reliability was based on data from the entire standardization sample, and resulted in an average coefficient of .88 for the total sample. The test developers conclude that the MVPT shows adequate reliability for ages 5 through 8 years, but accurately note that because of the small size of the sample of 4-year-olds, scores from this age group should be interpreted cautiously.

Validity

Content validity is reflected by the test's sampling of five visual-perceptual skill areas, which the developers claim are "the most prominent theoretical constructs of visual perception reported in the current literature . . ." (Colarusso and Hammill, 1972, p. 2). To the extent that one agrees with the developer's interpretation of visual-perceptual skills, the content validity appears adequate.

Establishment of construct validity was based primarily on correlations of the MVPT with tests of intelligence, academic achievement, and visual-motor skills. The test developers predicted that the MVPT would correlate higher with tests of visual-motor abilities than with the intelligence or achievement tests, and this is what was found. A correlation of .73 was found between the MVPT and the Frostig test, a test of visual perception, suggesting some overlap in the constructs measured by these two tests. Colarusso and Hammill suggest that this correlation would probably be lower if the sample had included children with motor impairments, as the Frostig includes items requiring fine motor performance. Although the amount of validity data is sparse and is based on small samples, the available data suggest adequate validity for this type of instrument.

SUMMARY

The MVPT is designed to assess visual-spatial perception in such a way that results are not confounded by poor motor coordination. The attempt to distinguish visual-spatial perceptual skills from visual-motor integration is important, as consequences of deficits in these areas can be significantly different and warrant different management and treatment strategies. However, the technical qualities of the MVPT are not sufficient for confident use of scores. Data on reliability and validity are promising, but too little information is presented in the manual to make any definite conclusions regarding their adequacy. Similarly, the norming sample is too poorly described to allow users to determine how representative norms are for certain populations. Until more adequate information is presented, practitioners should use the MVPT only in conjunction with other tests of visual-spatial perception such as the Performance subtests of the WISC-R or WPPSI-R that do not require paper and pencil skills or manipulation of materials.

BENDER VISUAL MOTOR GESTALT TEST

Lauretta Bender

American Orthopsychiatry Association
1775 Broadway
New York, New York   10019

PURPOSE

The Bender Visual Motor Gestalt Test (also known as the Bender Gestalt Test) was originally developed by Lauretta Bender in 1938. Since that time the test has continued to be used extensively in the evaluation of children and adults. The scoring system most often used with children is the Developmental Scoring System, developed by Elizabeth Koppitz and described thoroughly in *The Bender Gestalt Test for Young Children,* published as two volumes in 1964 and 1975. Although test stimuli are available from many test distributors, Koppitz's books are generally considered to be the "manual" for using the instrument with children. The Bender Test, according to Koppitz (1975), assesses visual-motor integration skills. The Developmental Scoring System provides normative data for children between the ages of 5 and 11 years.

DESCRIPTION OF TEST AND ADMINISTRATION

The Bender Test consists of nine test cards, each presenting an abstract design. The child is shown the cards, one at a time, and asked to copy the design onto a blank sheet of paper. Erasing is allowed, and the child is allowed to rework the drawing as much as desired. There is no time limit. Koppitz (1975) reports that most elementary school children are able to complete the drawings in less than 10 minutes.

The Bender Test has traditionally been administered individually. Koppitz (1975) describes several techniques that have been used successfully to administer the Bender Test to groups of students. Group administration takes approximately 15 to 20 minutes. Koppitz (1975) reports correlations between scores obtained from individual and group administrations range from .75 to .87. Although not specifically stated, it is assumed that the 1974 norms were based on individual administration of the test. Therefore, the extent to which these norms are appropriate for group administration is questionable.

SCORING AND INTERPRETATION

Koppitz's (1963, 1975) Developmental Scoring System provides a standardized method for evaluating drawings for children between 5 and 11 years of age. According to this system, each of the nine drawings is scored, where appropriate, for distortion of shape, rotation of the whole design or part of it, failure to integrate parts of the design, and perseveration. Thirty such errors are outlined for the entire nine-drawing protocol, and 1 point is assigned to each of the errors observed. Thus, a higher score on the Bender Test indicates poorer performance. It is unusual for a child to produce a protocol with more than 20 errors, as some types of errors necessarily preclude other types. Koppitz does not consider the scoring system to be useful for 5-year-olds who are immature or developmentally disabled, as their protocols often contain too much distortion to allow accurate scoring.

Raw scores can be converted to age-equivalent scores or percentile scores, according to norms provided by Koppitz (1975). Koppitz states that these scores are most meaningful for children younger than the age of 8, as many children older than this age produce perfect protocols and thus skew the distribution. Other investigators have attempted to calculate standard scores based on the number of copying errors (Hartlage & Lucas, 1971; Furr, 1970), but Koppitz does not advocate using these systems.

Interpretation of test scores should consider the child's cultural background, and Koppitz (1975) provides a fair amount of information comparing scores of children from different ethnic groups and from disadvantaged versus advantaged backgrounds. Extensive discussion is also provided regarding the use of the Bender Test as a tool for diagnosis of brain injury, minimal brain dysfunction and emotional disturbance, and for early screening to predict school achievement.

In addition to the formal scoring system, Koppitz (1975) stresses the importance of subjectively evaluating the child's approach to the task. For example, clinicians should look for signs of impulsivity, low tolerance for frustration, obsessive or perfectionist tendencies, poor ability to organize the drawings on the sheet of paper, or difficulty staying on task.

TECHNICAL QUALITY

Norms

The norms provided by Koppitz (1975) are based on a sample of 975 elementary school students, aged 5 to 11 years. Most of the students were from the Northeast, although the West and South were represented. Eighty-six percent of the students were white, with the remainder including black, Mexican-American, Puerto Rican, and Asian-American students. Students were from large cities, small towns, suburbs, and rural areas, although it is not clear whether representation matched the proportions for the U.S. population. Because the norming sample is not well defined and does not appear to be well matched to the U.S. population, scores based on these norms should be interpreted cautiously.

Reliability

Koppitz (1975) reports the results of 23 studies of inter-rater reliability for the Developmental Scoring System of the Bender Test. Correlations between scores obtained by different raters range from .79 to .99, with most correlations being above .90, indicating that scoring criteria are sufficient to allow trained scorers to obtain similar results.

Koppitz (1975) reports the results of nine studies of test-retest reliability. Children in these studies ranged in age from kindergarten to sixth-grade level. The inter-test interval ranged from less than a day to 8 months. Test-retest reliability coefficients ranged from .50 to .90. Almost half of the coefficients were below .70, suggesting some reason for concern about the reliability of the test. Correlations were not consistently higher or lower for older children or for longer inter-test intervals, making it impossible to determine the source for the lack of reliability. Koppitz (1975) states that "erratic, inconsistent progress on the Bender Test reflects a child's unstable functioning and is not due to unreliability on the part of the Bender Test scoring system" (p. 30). No convincing data are presented, however, to support this conclusion.

Validity

Koppitz (1975) reports results of studies that correlated scores on the Bender Test with those from several other tests of visual perception and visual-motor integration. A correlation of .82 was found between scores from mentally retarded children on the Bender Test and the Beery Developmental Test of Visual-Motor Integration, another figure-copying test. Correlations with scores from the Frostig Test (which assesses both visual-spatial perception and visual-motor integration) ranged from .39 to .52 for children in kindergarten through age 12 years. Coefficients of .58 and .69 were found in two studies correlating scores on the Bender Test and the Progressive Matrices, a test of visual perception and nonverbal reasoning. Thus, the Bender Test appears to correlate fairly highly with other tests of visual-motor integration and less highly with tests of visual perception, as would be predicted.

Koppitz reports that scores from the Bender Test are significantly correlated with IQs for children of average and below-average mental ability, but not significantly correlated for children of superior intelligence. As would be predicted, Bender Test scores are more highly correlated with Performance IQs than with Verbal IQs. Koppitz (1963) states that "the Bender Gestalt Test can be used with some degree of confidence as a short nonverbal intelligence test for young children, particularly for screening purposes" (p. 50). Such use of the test does not appear to be justifiable, especially considering the availability of more effective screening instruments.

Koppitz (1975) presents results from 54 studies that have investigated the relationship between Bender Test scores and academic achievement for children in kindergarten through sixth grade. Although most studies found statistically significant correlations between scores on the Bender Test and tests of reading and arithmetic (with coefficients ranging from .13 to .58), and between Bender scores and teacher ratings, the coefficients are too low to justify using Bender Test scores as predictors of school success for individual children. Bender Test scores are generally more highly correlated with arithmetic than with reading achievement for children in first through third grades.

Koppitz (1975) reports results from a 10-year study of more than 500 learning-disabled children, which demonstrates convincingly that learning-disabled children, as a group, show delays in the development of visual-motor integration skills, as measured by the Bender Gestalt. Thus, it may be justifiable to use the Bender Gestalt as part of a screening battery, and to provide more thorough testing for children who show significant discrepancies between intellectual ability and visual-motor integration skills.

OTHER CONSIDERATIONS

The Bender Test and the VMI both provide measures of visual-motor integration skills for school-age children. Some of the advantages of the VMI were noted in the section on this test. It should be noted that both tests have fairly good inter-rater reliability, but the VMI appears to have somewhat better test-retest reliability. As noted previously, the scoring criteria for the VMI are somewhat more clearly described than those for the Bender Test. In addition, the structured format of the VMI makes it easier for young children and facilitates scoring. The drawings presented in the VMI have a wider range of difficulty than those in the Bender Test, specifically providing some very easy drawings for young children (e.g., horizontal and vertical lines, circle, triangle). Thus, the VMI must be considered the test of choice for children younger than 5 years of age. Both the VMI and the Bender Test are more sensitive for younger children (younger than 8 years of age) than for older children.

The Bender Test's unstructured format allows clinical observation of some important performance characteristics that are not allowed by the VMI. For example, the examiner can learn something about the child's planning ability if the sheet of paper is filled after the first few drawings, or if the drawings overlap one another. The child who engages in much erasing may be demonstrating excessive anxiety. The Bender Test's long history has allowed practitioners to develop detailed descriptions of test performance and "emotional indicators" that may be observed in the protocols.

SUMMARY

The Bender Visual Motor Gestalt Test, developed in 1938, has been widely used as both a developmental measure for children and a clinical measure for adults with suspected brain dysfunction. Koppitz's Developmental Scoring System (1963, 1975) is the most widely used approach to interpretation of the Bender Test for children. The test appears to have adequate inter-rater reliability, but test-retest reliability is not as good as would be desired. The adequacy of the standardization sample is questionable. Scores based on the norms should, therefore, be interpreted cautiously.

Koppitz considers the test to be a measure of visual-motor integration ability for children, and this use appears to be valid. Although some research indicates that Bender Test results can adequately discriminate between groups of children with average versus low intelligence, good versus poor academic achievement, or emotional disturbance versus no disturbance, evidence does not justify the use of the test for diagnosis of individual children on these factors. The Bender Test's unstructured format does, however, provide the experienced examiner with the opportunity for clinical observations that may be helpful in directing further testing.

CHAPTER 7

TESTS OF ADAPTIVE BEHAVIOR

The term "adaptive behavior" was introduced and defined by the American Association on Mental Deficiency (AAMD) (now the American Association on Mental Retardation) in 1959, and refers primarily to "the effectiveness of an individual in coping with the natural and social demands of his or her environment" (Nihira, Foster, Shellhaas & Leland, 1975, p. 5). In the past, mental retardation was diagnosed exclusively on the basis of intelligence test results. The AAMD viewed this practice as inadequate, primarily because test results are not valid for certain populations (e.g., those with little exposure to the predominant culture) and because of the error of measurement inherent in such instruments. In the AAMD's *Manual on Terminology and Classification in Mental Retardation* (Grossman, 1977), mental retardation was redefined to designate those individuals who have "significantly subaverage general intellectual functioning existing concurrently with deficits in adaptive behavior which are manifested during the developmental period" (p. 5). Thus, in order to make a diagnosis of mental retardation, professionals must now document the individual's level of adaptive functioning as well as IQ. The tests described in this chapter are designed to assist in this documentation.

AAMD ADAPTIVE BEHAVIOR SCALE

Kazuo Nihira
Ray Foster
Max Shellhaas
Henry Leland

PRO-ED, Inc.
8700 Shoal Creek Boulevard
Austin, Texas 78758

PURPOSE

The AAMD Adaptive Behavior Scale (ABS) is designed to provide objective description and evaluation of the adaptive behavior of mentally retarded, emotionally maladjusted, and developmentally disabled children and adults. The ABS is composed of two parts, with Part I designed to evaluate an individual's skills and habits in behavior domains "considered important to the development of personal independence in daily living" (Nihira et al., 1975, p. 6). Part II is designed to assess "maladaptive behavior related to personality and behavior disorders" (Nihira et al., 1975, p. 7).

DESCRIPTION OF TEST AND ADMINISTRATION

The ABS is a structured interview that is administered to one or more persons who are familiar with the day-to-day behavior and abilities of the individual being assessed. Part I of the ABS contains 66 items that address behaviors in 10 behavior domains and 21 subdomains (see Table 7-1). Each subdomain contains several items. For example, the Eating subdomain includes items regarding use of table utensils, eating in public, drinking, and table manners.

Items can be of two types. The first type requires the respondent to select from a list of developmentally ordered statements the one that best describes the *most difficult* task the individual can usually manage. For example, the item "Room Cleaning" requires the respondent to select among the options "Does not clean room at all," "Cleans room but not thoroughly," or "Cleans room well, e.g., sweeping, dusting, and tidying." Points are assigned, depending on the option chosen, with higher points reflecting more advanced levels of functioning.

The second type of item requires the respondent to select from a list of options *all* that describe the individual's typical behavior. For example, the item "Cleanliness" requires the respondent to identify which of the following behaviors are typically performed by the individual: "Washes hands with soap," "Washes face with soap," "Washes hands and face with water," "Dries hands and face." For most of these items, the number of options selected is totalled to obtain the score for the item. For a few items, however, the options listed are *negative*, and the score is obtained by subtracting the number of options chosen from the total number of options. For example, the item "Persistence" lists the options "Becomes easily discouraged," "Fails to carry out tasks," "Jumps from one activity to another," and "Needs constant encouragement to complete task." The number of options selected is subtracted from 4, resulting in a higher score for fewer negative behaviors.

Instructions for completing the scoring are clearly presented on the test form. If the individual being assessed has no opportunity to perform the behavior indicated, the respondent is asked to judge whether the individual could perform the behavior without additional training.

Table 7-1. Domains and subdomains of the Adaptive Behavior Scale (Part I)

I. Independent functioning
   A. Eating
   B. Toilet use
   C. Cleanliness
   D. Appearance
   E. Care of clothing
   F. Dressing and undressing
   G. Travel
   H. General independent functioning
II. Physical development
   A. Sensory development
   B. Motor development
III. Economic activity
   A. Money handling and budgeting
   B. Shopping skills
IV. Language development
   A. Expression
   B. Comprehension
   C. Social language development
V. Numbers and time
VI. Domestic activity
   A. Cleaning
   B. Kitchen duties
   C. Other domestic activities
VII. Vocational activity
VIII. Self-direction
   A. Initiative
   B. Perseverance
   C. Leisure time
IX. Responsibility
X. Socialization

Source: From K. Nihira, R. Foster, M. Shellhaas, and H. Leland, *AAMD Adaptive Behavior Scale Manual*, American Association on Mental Retardation, 1975, p. 6. Reprinted by permission.

Part II includes 44 items that address maladaptive behaviors in 14 domains (see Table 7-2). Each item includes a list of statements related to a particular maladaptive behavior. The respondent is asked to select all of the statements that are true of the individual and assess whether the behavior occurs occasionally or frequently. Those that are identified as occurring frequently are assigned 2 points, those that occur occasionally are assigned 1 point, and those not selected are assigned 0 points. The number of points for each item is summed, with a higher score indicating a greater degree of maladaptive behavior.

Table 7-2. Maladaptive behavior domains of the Adaptive Behavior Scale (Part II)

  I. Violent and destructive behavior
  II. Antisocial behavior
  III. Rebellious behavior
  IV. Untrustworthy behavior
  V. Withdrawal
  VI. Stereotyped behavior and odd mannerisms
  VII. Inappropriate interpersonal manners
  VIII. Unacceptable or eccentric habits
  IX. Unacceptable vocal habits
  X. Self-abusive behavior
  XI. Hyperactive tendencies
  XII. Sexually aberrant behavior
  XIII. Psychological disturbances
  XIV. Use of medications

Source: From K. Nihira, R. Foster, M. Shellhaas, and H. Leland, *AAMD Adaptive Behavior Scale Manual,* American Association on Mental Retardation, 1975, p. 7.

The ABS can be administered by professionals or individuals who do not have a great deal of special training. The manual describes three possible methods for administration. The first involves evaluation by a professional who is familiar enough with the individual's behavior to complete each item of the scale himself or herself. The second method involves administration of each item, one by one, to the respondent. It may sometimes be necessary to involve several respondents, such as parents, residential staff, and teachers, to obtain all of the information needed. The third method uses a less formal interview approach whereby each subdomain is addressed with a question specific to that subdomain. For example, instead of directly asking about each item in the Eating subdomain, the interviewer might ask the respondent to "tell me about your child's eating skills and habits." Follow-up questions are asked to obtain any additional information necessary for scoring each of the items. The third method requires approximately 15 to 20 minutes to complete. No information is provided regarding the equivalency of these administration methods.

SCORING AND INTERPRETATION

Each item is assigned a raw score, as described in the previous sections. Raw scores are totalled for each subdomain and domain. Raw scores for each domain can be converted to a percentile score, based on norms for various age groups. These percentile scores can then be plotted on a Profile Summary that provides a visual summary of the individual's strengths and weaknesses, as compared with other institutionalized mentally retarded individuals of the same age. Brief information is provided regarding general interpretation of profiles, and suggestions are made for using the scale in program planning and design, resource allocation, administrative control, and program evaluation.

TECHNICAL QUALITY

Norms

Norms are based on a sample of approximately 4,000 residents in 68 facilities in the United States. Norms are provided at 1-year intervals for children between 3 and 5 years of age, at 2-year intervals for ages 6 to 9 years, and at 3-year intervals for ages 10 to 18 years. In addition, separate tables are presented for ages 19 to 29 years, 30 to 49 years, and 50 to 69 years. The norming sample included individuals of both sexes in the mild, moderate, severe, and profound ranges of mental retardation. Average IQs ranged from 28.1 for the 3-year-olds to 45.8 for the 16- to 18-year-olds. Sample size for each age group ranged from 97 for the 3-year-olds to 528 for the 10- to 12-year-olds. No further information regarding the norming samples is provided in the manual. Thus, it is not possible to determine the representativeness of the groups from which the norms were derived. Furthermore, because of the relatively large differences in mean IQs for the samples at different age levels, it would be difficult to confidently compare scores for individuals of different ages or to follow a single individual's development in adaptive behavior over time.

Reliability

Inter-rater reliability was established by correlating scores obtained from two different ward personnel for each of 133 residents at three state training schools. Reliabilities for Part I domains ranged from .71 for Self-Direction to .93 for Physical Development, with a mean reliability for all domains in Part I of .86. Part II reliabilities ranged from .37 for Unacceptable Vocal Habits to .77 for Use of Medications, with a mean reliability for all domains in Part II of .57. Thus, inter-rater reliability for many of the domains in Part II is too low to allow confident use of the scores.

Validity

Factor analysis of domain scores yielded three major dimensions: Personal Independence, Social Maladaptation, and Personal Maladaptation. It is not clear to what extent these findings support the test developer's approach to measuring adaptive behavior.

Results from four studies of predictive validity are presented in the manual, albeit with very little detail. One study of 41 institutionalized retarded children between 10 and 13 years found that Part I domain scores discriminated significantly between those who had previously been classified at different levels of adaptive behavior by clinical judgment. Another study involving 531 institutionalized retarded adults indicated that all of Part I domain scores and some of Part II domain scores significantly discriminated among individuals who have been placed in five homogeneous administrative units. A third study found significant changes between pretest and posttest administration of the ABS for 41 retarded children and adolescents who participated in an intensive operant program, as compared with a nonoperant control group. Finally, the manual reports results from a study demonstrating that six domain scores from Part II significantly discriminated between "impairment groups" of 260 IQ-matched retarded adults with psychiatric impairment.

SUMMARY

The ABS is a structured interview and questionnaire designed to assess adaptive functioning and maladaptive behaviors in retarded adults and children. Although it appears that the ABS items can be valuable in obtaining a great deal of information regarding an individual's adaptive functioning, the lack of adequate description of the norming sample, the apparent weaknesses in reliability, and the sparseness of data on other aspects of technical quality prevent confident use of scores from the ABS. Use of the ABS is hard to justify, given the availability of the Vineland Adaptive Behavior Scales, which is designed with a format similar to that of the ABS and is technically a much sounder instrument.

VINELAND ADAPTIVE BEHAVIOR SCALES

Sara S. Sparrow
David A. Balla
Domenic V. Cicchetti

American Guidance Service
Publishers' Building
Circle Pines, Minnesota   55014-1796

PURPOSE

The Vineland Adaptive Behavior Scales, published in 1984, are a revision of the Vineland Social Maturity Scale, developed by Edgar Doll in 1935 and revised in 1965. The Scales are designed to "assess personal and social sufficiency" of handicapped or nonhandicapped individuals from birth to adulthood. The Scales are administered to a respondent who is familiar with the abilities and behavior of the individual being assessed.

DESCRIPTION OF TEST AND ADMINISTRATION

The Vineland consists of three forms that differ in number of items and method of administration: the Interview Edition, Survey Form; the Interview Edition, Expanded Form; and the Classroom Edition. Each version assesses adaptive behavior in four areas: Communication, Daily Living Skills, Socialization, and Motor Skills. The Survey and Expanded forms also include an optional scale of Maladaptive Behavior.

Survey Form

The Survey Form is administered as a semistructured interview to the parent or caregiver of a child, aged 0 to 19 years, or of a low-functioning adult. It is to be administered by a psychologist, social worker, or other professional with training and experience in individual assessment and test interpretation. The respondent should be the adult most familiar with the social and adaptive functioning of the individual who is being evaluated.

The Survey Form includes 261 items that assess Adaptive Behavior and 36 items that assess Maladaptive Behavior. The Adaptive Behavior portion consists of four sections, each containing items about a particular domain of adaptive functioning: (1) The Communication domain is represented by 67 items, each assessing skills in either the Receptive, Expressive, or Written Communication "subdomains." (2) The Daily Living Skills domain includes 92 items, each assessing abilities in either the Personal, Domestic, or Community subdomains. (3) There are 66 items within the Socialization domain, and these are divided into the Interpersonal Relationships, Play and Leisure Time, and Coping Skills subdomains. (4) The final domain, assessing Motor Skills, consists of 36 items that comprise the Fine Motor and Gross Motor subdomains. Items in the Motor Skills Domain are administered only for children younger than 6 years of age or for older individuals with motor impairment.

Within each of the Adaptive Behavior domains, items are ordered according to developmental level, permitting the establishment of basal and ceiling levels and obviating the need to complete every item on the form for each individual. Suggested starting points for each age (or estimated mental age) level are provided.

The Maladaptive Behavior portion of the Survey Form contains 36 items that assess the presence of minor maladaptive behaviors (e.g., sucking thumb or fingers) in Part I and the presence and severity of more serious maladaptive behaviors (e.g., using bizarre speech) in Part II. Each item is administered individually by describing the behavior and asking the respondent to tell whether the individual usually, sometimes, or rarely engages in the activity. In Part II, the respondent is also asked to rate the intensity of the behavior as either moderate or severe. The Maladaptive Behavior portion is only administered when the individual being evaluated is 5 years of age or older.

The items are not administered by asking direct questions of the respondent. Instead, the respondent is asked to describe the individual's skills in general areas. For example, the interviewer might ask "What is Jack doing in school in terms of reading and writing?" Based on this description, items assessing Written Communication would be scored by the interviewer. When necessary, the interviewer probes with more specific questions or asks for examples or clarification until he or she has the specific information needed to score each item. Although this conversational approach prevents absolutely standardized administration and is somewhat cumbersome for the interviewer to master, the test developers claim that it is more efficient, enhances rapport, and yields more useful data.

The Survey Form takes approximately 20 to 60 minutes to administer, and should be completed in one session. A Spanish translation of the Survey Form is available.

Expanded Form

The Expanded Form of the Vineland Interview Edition contains 577 items, 297 of which are from the Survey Form. According to the manual, "The Expanded Form offers a more comprehensive assessment of adaptive behavior and, most important, a systematic basis for preparing individual educational, habilitative, or treatment programs" (Sparrow, Balla, & Cicchetti, 1984a, p. 1). Domains and subdomains are the same as for the Survey Edition. The Expanded Form includes 133 items in the Communication domain, 201 items in the Daily Living Skills domain, 134 items in the Socialization domain, and 73 items in the Motor Skills Domain. The Maladaptive Behavior Composite is identical for the Survey and Expanded Forms. Unlike the Survey Form, the Interview Form groups items within each subdomain separately. Items within each subdomain are further subdivided into "clusters." For example, the Gross Motor subdomain of the Motor Skills domain includes clusters that cover sitting, beginning mobility, walking, running, jumping, and others. Items within clusters are sequenced in developmental order. Method of administration is the same as for the Survey Form, and administration time is generally 60 to 90 minutes.

Classroom Edition

The Classroom Edition "provides an assessment of adaptive behavior in the classroom" (Sparrow et al., 1984a, p. 2). Some items are identical to those in the Survey and Expanded forms, whereas others are directly related to academic functioning. The Classroom Edition covers the same domains and subdomains as the other versions. There are 244 items, with 63 assessing the Communication domain, 99 assessing Daily Living Skills, 53 assessing the Socialization Domain, and 29 assessing Motor Skills. There are no items representing the Maladaptive Behavior domain. The Classroom Edition is designed for administration to teachers of children between 3 and 13 years of age. It is administered as a questionnaire that is independently completed by the teacher. Completion takes approximately 20 minutes.

SCORING AND INTERPRETATION

For the Survey and Expanded Forms, the examiner uses the information obtained from the open-ended interview to score each item in the Adaptive Behavior portion as either 2 (for activities that are usually performed), 1 (for those performed sometimes or with partial success), 0 (for those never performed), N (for those not performed because of limiting external circumstances), or DK (for those about which the respondent has no knowledge of the individual's performance). Scoring criteria for each item are provided in the manual, and the administrator must be familiar with these criteria in order for the interview to proceed smoothly. For the Classroom Edition, teachers are instructed to score each item as 2, 1, or 0, using the same criteria as the other forms. In addition, the teacher is asked to indicate whether the score is based on "observed performance" or "estimated performance."

For the Survey Form, basal level is defined as the lowest seven consecutive items earning scores of 2, and ceiling level is the highest seven consecutive items scored 0. For the Expanded Form, basal level is established when all items in two consecutive clusters are scored 2; no ceiling is established. All items below basal level are assigned 2 points and all items above ceiling level (for the Survey Form) are assigned 0 points. Basal and ceiling levels are not established for the Classroom Edition. Items from the Motor Skills Domain are not scored on the Classroom Edition if the child is older than 6 years and without motor impairment.

Regardless of the form being used, the sum of all 2s, 1s, and 0s is obtained for each subdomain individually and then for each of the Adaptive Behavior domains (Communication, Daily Living Skills, Socialization, Motor Skills). For the Survey and Expanded Forms, N and DK responses are also assigned 1 point, and these points are included in the totals.

For each of the four Adaptive Behavior domains, a standard score is obtained (mean = 100, standard deviation = 15) from the tables of norms. The total of these standard scores is used to obtain an Adaptive Behavior Composite (mean = 100, standard deviation = 15). (If one of the domains is unscorable, or if the Motor Skills domain has not been administered because of the individual's age, the Adaptive Behavior Composite is prorated.) For each of the four Adaptive Behavior domains and for the Adaptive Behavior Composite, it is also possible to obtain confidence bands for the standard score, percentile rankings, stanines, adaptive levels (High, Moderately High, Adequate, Moderately Low, or Low), and age-equivalent scores. Supplementary percentile rankings and adaptive levels can be calculated, based on norms for any of several special populations (ambulatory and nonambulatory mentally retarded adults in residential facilities, mentally retarded adults in nonresidential facilities, emotionally disturbed, visually handicapped, or hearing-impaired children in residential facilities). Adaptive levels and age-equivalent scores are available for each of the subdomains.

The Maladaptive Behavior items of the Survey and Expanded forms are also scored as 2 (the individual usually engages in the behavior), 1 (the individual sometimes engages in the behavior), 0 (the individual never or very seldom engages in the behavior), N (no opportunity), or DK (respondent does not know). The Maladaptive items are not presented in any particular order, and there are no basal or ceiling levels.

The 2s, 1s, and 0s are summed separately for Parts I and II of the Maladaptive domain and are then totalled. A high score on the Maladaptive Behavior portion reveals greater behavioral difficulty, whereas a high score on the Adaptive Behavior portion reveals greater adaptive competence. "Maladaptive levels" (Nonsignificant, Intermediate, or Significant) are available for Part I of the Maladaptive Behavior domain. Maladaptive levels based on supplementary norm groups can be obtained for Part I or for Parts I and II combined.

Scoring is not complicated, but is rather time consuming if all possible scores are calculated. Software packages for scoring are available.

The manual presents three methods for identifying strengths and weaknesses, based on differences between domain standard scores. For each method, the test developers have wisely discussed interdomain differences that are *statistically* significant (i.e., probably not the result of chance), as well as interdomain differences that are *unusual*, based on the proportion of the norming sample demonstrating differences of various magnitudes. As Kaufman (1979) discusses in regard to the WISC-R, many individuals demonstrate statistically significant differences among subtest scores. It is only when these differences are unusual for the population that they should be considered "abnormal."

The manual also provides a fair amount of information regarding the interpretation of the scores from the Vineland. Included is a discussion regarding the use of the Vineland in conjunction with the K-ABC and instructions for direct comparison of scores from these two instruments. As mentioned in the introduction to this chapter, evaluation of adaptive functioning is essential for making the diagnosis of mental retardation.

7. Tests of Adaptive Behavior

The ability to integrate scores from a test of intelligence and a test of adaptive functioning is very helpful in documenting this diagnosis, as well as in planning for the management of the individual.

The Expanded Form includes Program Planning Profiles that allow the individual's performance in each cluster to be plotted. The purpose of these profiles is "to pinpoint the clusters that describe activities that should be included in an individual program plan, or those activities that the individual should be performing but is not" (Sparrow, Balla, & Cicchetti, 1984b, p. 104). Specific information on the use of these profiles is included in the Expanded Form manual. The manuals for both the Expanded and Survey Editions provide several case studies that demonstrate interpretation of the test results. A form is available for reporting results of the Vineland to parents, and discussion of this report is included in the manual.

TECHNICAL QUALITY

Norms

Survey and Expanded Forms. Norms for the Survey and Expanded Forms are based on a national sample of 3,000 individuals, with about 100 individuals in each of 30 age groups between birth and 19 years. Based on data from the 1980 U.S. Census, the sample was stratified on the variables of sex, race or ethnic group, community size, region of the country, and parents' level of education. Many of the children in the norming sample also participated in the standardization of the K-ABC. Review of the data indicates that the nonhandicapped norming sample is quite adequate in its size and representativeness.

In addition to the sample of nonhandicapped individuals, seven samples of handicapped individuals also participated in the norming process for the Survey and Expanded Forms. These samples contained between 100 and 1,050 individuals each. Although it is difficult to determine to what extent the handicapped norming samples reflect the populations they represent, the test developers are commended for including data against which the adaptive functioning of a handicapped individual can be compared.

It is important to note that norms for the Survey and Expanded Forms are based on administration of the Survey Form *only* (i.e., the Expanded

Form was not administered to the norming sample). Before the standardization procedure, a national tryout of all items for both the Survey and Expanded Forms was carried out. This tryout provided data that allowed the difficulty level of each item of the Expanded Form to be ascertained. This, in turn, allowed each item on the Expanded Form to be linked with items of similar difficulty level on the Survey Form, resulting in a common scale for the two Forms. Based on this common scale, it was determined what raw scores for each domain and subdomain on the Survey Form were equivalent to what raw scores for each domain and subdomain on the Expanded Form. Although this procedure is theoretically sound, it is not possible to determine to what extent the norms for the Expanded Form would mirror norms obtained if the Expanded Form had been actually administered to the norming sample.

Norms are provided at 1-month age intervals for infants between birth and 24 months, at 2-month age intervals for children aged 2 through 5 years, at 3-month intervals for children aged 6 through 8 years, and at 4-month intervals for children aged 9 through 18 years.

Classroom Edition. A sample of approximately 3,000 students, aged 3 through 12 years, provided norms for the Classroom Edition. A rather unorthodox method, which the authors do not justify, was used to select the norming sample for the Classroom Edition. School districts, parochial school systems, and preschools that did not participate in the standardization of the Interview Edition were contacted and asked to submit names of elementary schools that would participate in the Classroom Edition standardization. Teachers in each of these elementary schools were asked to randomly select six students to whom parental permission letters were given. The teacher then completed a standardization form of the Classroom Edition on two students from whom permission was obtained. The authors report that this selection process did not result in as close a match with the U.S. Census data as did the method used to select subjects for the Interview Edition, but consider the sample to be "an adequate representation." The major areas that might be considered problematic are overrepresentation of children whose parents are better educated, overrepresentation of children from large cities as opposed to small towns and rural areas, and slight underrepresentation of racial and ethnic minorities.

Teachers did not respond to the entire Classroom Edition questionnaire for the students in the norming sample. To decrease the number of items to which each teacher had to respond, the Classroom Edition items were split into eight forms with an overlapping set of items that appeared on all of the forms. Considering that teachers who would eventually use the form would be required to respond to the entire set of items, it is not clear why it was believed to be necessary to use the shorter versions for standardization. The set of items that overlapped for the eight forms permitted the authors to equate the raw scores on the eight forms and to generate estimated domain and subdomain raw scores for the final Classroom Edition. As with the Expanded Form, it is not clear to what extent the norms derived for the Classroom Edition would mirror the norms that would have been obtained if a more orthodox standardization procedure had been used.

Norms for the Classroom Edition are provided at 2-month intervals for children aged 3 through 5 years, at 3-month intervals for children between 6 and 8 years, and at 4-month intervals for children between 9 and 12 years.

Reliability

Survey and Expanded Forms. Most of the reliability data reported in the manual are based on analysis of data from the standardization sample. Because the Survey Form and not the Expanded Form was used during the standardization, the reliability data can be assumed to be accurate only for the Survey Form. Unless otherwise stated, the information that follows was based on the Survey Form only.

Split-half reliability coefficients for the various age groups within the standardization sample ranged from .89 to .98 for the Adaptive Behavior Composite and from .77 to .88 for the Maladaptive Behavior domain. These appear to be quite adequate. Median split-half coefficients from the various age groups for the four adaptive behavior domains ranged from .83 for Motor Skills to .90 for Daily Living Skills, suggesting good internal consistency for the items within each domain. Split-half reliability coefficients for the Expanded Form were estimated, and because of the increased number of items, are somewhat higher than for the Survey Form.

Test-retest reliability coefficients are based on administration of the instrument to parents or caregivers of 484 individuals from the age of 6 months to 19 years. The interval between the two administrations was 2 to 4 weeks. The average test-retest reliability coefficients across age groups for the Adaptive Behavior Composite and for the four Adaptive Behavior domains were in the .80s for standard scores and .90s for raw scores. Test-retest reliabilities for Maladaptive Behavior Domain raw scores were also quite high, with an average of .88 across ages.

To establish inter-rater reliability, 160 individuals were interviewed separately by two different interviewers, with an interval of 1 to 14 days between the two administrations. Correlations between the standard scores obtained by the two interviewers were in the .70s for all domains except Socialization, which was somewhat low, with a correlation of .62. The relatively low inter-rater reliability coefficients may be due, at least in part, to the nonstandardized interview method.

Standard errors of measurement for the four adaptive behavior domains, averaged across age groups, range from 5.0 to 6.1, whereas the Adaptive Behavior Composite has an average standard error of measurement of 3.6. These errors of measurement are not much higher than those found for the WISC-R Full Scale IQ, PIQ, and VIQ, and allow the examiner to be confident that "true" scores will not deviate much from the obtained scores. For individual age groups, however, standard errors of measurement were a bit high for children older than 12 years in the Communication domain and for children older than 4 years in the Motor Skills domain. Thus, these scores should be interpreted a bit more cautiously.

Standard errors of measurement were estimated for the Expanded Form, based on the standard deviation and the estimated split-half reliabilities. Because of the increased length of the Expanded Form, estimated standard errors of measurement are somewhat lower than for the Survey Form.

Classroom Edition. Coefficient alpha (a measure of internal consistency among items) was computed for nine age groups ranging from 3 to 12 years of age. The median coefficients were .93 for Communication, .95 for Daily Living Skills, .94 for Socialization, .80 for Motor Skills (based only on children younger than 6 years), and .98 for Adaptive Behavior Composite. Except for Motor Skills, all correlations for all age groups were above .88, indicating good internal consistency. Median coefficient alpha reliabilities for subdomains were all above .88 except for Play and Leisure Time (.78), Gross Motor Skills (.68), and Fine Motor Skills (.72). Thus, internal consistency is generally adequate for the Adaptive Behavior Composite and for the domain scores for the Classroom Edition. However, information regarding other important types of test reliability is not provided for the Classroom Edition.

Standard errors of measurement, averaged across ages, were 4.0 for Communication, 3.4 for Daily Living Skills, 3.8 for Socialization, 6.6 for Motor Skills, and 2.4 for Adaptive Behavior Composite.

Validity

Content validity of the Vineland was assured through careful review of other adaptive behavior scales (including Doll's original version of the Vineland) and literature concerning child development. Thorough item analysis and a national tryout of 529 initial items were conducted to assure that items were of appropriate difficulty level, were sequenced in correct developmental order, and had adequate discriminative ability.

Criterion-related validity was studied by correlating scores from the Survey Form with those from the original Vineland Social Maturity Scale (Doll, 1935, 1965). Correlation between the new version's Adaptive Behavior Composite standard score and the older version's Deviation Social Quotient resulted in a coefficient of .55. Although this suggests only a moderate degree of relationship between the two scales, the test developers claim that higher correlation was not expected because of the many differences in content and standardization. Higher correlations between the two versions of the Vineland were found with samples of mentally retarded adults and hearing-impaired children.

Domain and Adaptive Behavior Composite Standard Scores from the Survey Form were correlated with the same scores from the Classroom Edition. Coefficients ranged from .31 to .54, indicating only a moderate degree of correlation between scores from these two instruments. The test developers claim that the two editions "yield relatively discrete measures, and the moderate correlations support the use of *both* instruments when evaluating a child's adaptive behavior" (Harrison, 1985, p. 31). Even lower correlations between the Classroom Edition and the Survey Form were found for a group of preschool children in a Head Start Program, whereas relatively high correlations (ranging from .73 to .88) were reported for a group of mentally retarded students. Considering the substantial overlap among items on the Classroom Edition and Survey Form, the relatively low correlations raise the issue of why children are apparently perceived so differently by parents and teachers. Perhaps the difference lies in the objectivity of the respondent or in the format of the administration (interview vs. questionnaire), but the possibility must be raised that adaptive behavior is a construct that may not necessarily remain stable across environments (i.e., school and home). Furthermore, it is possible that adaptive behavior is a construct that is meaningful primarily in the context of mental subnormality, and its use should perhaps be restricted to this population. More attention to these issues from the test developers would be desirable.

Scores from both the Survey Form and the Classroom Edition were compared to scores from other measures of adaptive functioning. A correlation of .58 was found between the Survey Form Adaptive Behavior Composite and the Adaptive Behavior Inventory for Children (Mercer & Lewis, 1978) for a sample of 39 handicapped children. Correlations between raw scores from the four adaptive behavior domains of the Survey Form and raw scores from the subdomains of the AAMD Adaptive Behavior Scale for a group of retarded adults fell primarily in the .40 to .70 range. For a group of developmentally handicapped children, Ronka (1984) found only a .08 correlation between the Survey Form Adaptive Behavior Composite score and comparison scores from the AAMD Adaptive Behavior Scale.

The test manual reports several studies that have investigated the correlations between scores from the Classroom Edition (domain and Adaptive Behavior Composites) and the AAMD Adaptive Behavior Scale–School Edition. Correlations ranged from .18 to .51 for a sample of nonhandicapped children and from .62 to .92 for a group of mentally retarded students. One study (Ronka, 1984), found only a .16 correlation between the Classroom Edition Adaptive Behavior Composite standard score and the score on the AAMD–School Edition.

Scores from both the Classroom Edition and the Survey Form were correlated with scores from The Kaufman Assessment Battery for Children (K-ABC) and Peabody Picture Vocabulary Test–Revised (PPVT-R), both of which were administered to large groups of individuals from the standardization sample. Correlations between the adaptive behavior domains and the PPVT-R standard scores were positive but fairly low, with the highest correlations between the Communication Domain and the PPVT-R (.37 for the Survey Form and .45 for the Classroom Edition). Global Scale standard scores from the K-ABC were correlated with standard scores from the adaptive behavior domains and the Adaptive Behavior Composite. Correlations were generally low for the Survey Form (ranging from .07 to .52) and moderate for the Classroom Edition (ranging from .23 to .64), supporting the assumption that the Vineland's domains are measuring constructs somewhat related to, but different from, the constructs measured by tests of cognitive functioning.

Construct validity is supported by the progressive increases in mean raw scores with age. Additionally, principal components analyses for both the Classroom Edition and Survey Forms were conducted on domain standard scores. For each age level studied, only one significant factor emerged, and this factor accounted for 55 to 79% of the variance in domain standard scores, suggesting that the use of the Adaptive Behavior Composite as a reflection of overall adaptive skills is appropriate.

Other principal factor analyses were conducted for subdomain raw scores for the Survey Form and Classroom Edition. In general, the results from the Survey Form factor analysis supported the organization of the subdomains into their respective domains. Results from the Classroom Edition were less supportive of the theoretical framework.

In general, review of the technical data indicates that the Adaptive Behavior portion of the Survey Form is normed on an appropriately large and representative sample and has adequate reliability. Although information regarding validity is still somewhat sparse, the available data for the Survey Form are generally encouraging. Norms for the Expanded Form are statistically derived from norms for the Survey Form, and therefore may not be a true reflection of the actual norms that would have been obtained if the Expanded Form had been administered to the standardization sample. Assuming that norms are an accurate reflection, reliability and validity data can be expected to be as good or better for the Expanded Form as for the Survey Form, although no empirical data are presented to support this presumption.

Technical quality of the Maladaptive Behavior portion of the scale is not as well documented as that for the Adaptive Behavior portion, but it appears that the items from the Maladaptive Behavior domain may be quite useful in gathering information about the presence and severity of certain behavior problems.

Technical data regarding the Classroom Edition are less positive than those for the Survey Form. The procedure for selecting the standardization sample and dividing the form into several versions for administration to the standardization sample were unorthodox, and the effects of these procedures cannot be estimated. The reliability data available in the manual are based on measures of internal consistency only and thus do not permit evaluation of the instrument's stability over time. The factor analysis of subdomain scores is not particularly supportive of the theoretical framework for the Classroom Edition, and other measures of validity, particularly criterion-related validity, are also not particularly encouraging. Of particular concern are the low correlations between scores from the Classroom Edition and the Survey Form.

SUMMARY

The Vineland Adaptive Behavior Scales are composed of three forms: the Survey Form, the Expanded Form, and the Classroom Edition. The

Survey Form appears to be a well-constructed instrument that can provide essential data regarding the adaptive functioning of handicapped and nonhandicapped individuals. Although administration of the Survey Form is somewhat cumbersome at first, the interview method is fairly well described in the manual and criteria for scoring are clearly stated. Inter-rater reliability is somewhat lower than would be desired. The organization of the Survey Form according to domains and subdomains of adaptive functioning allows a good understanding of the individual's strengths and weaknesses. Results from the Adaptive Behavior portion of the Survey Form can be used with confidence and are valuable when used with IQ data to make diagnoses of mental retardation and to plan for training. Although the Maladaptive Behavior portion of the Survey and Expanded Forms may be less technically sound, data from this section may be useful in understanding specific behavior problems and planning for management.

Because the norms and technical data for the Expanded Form are derived from those for the Survey Form, it is not possible to directly assess the reliability and validity of this instrument. However, the available data would generally support the use of results from this instrument.

The Classroom Edition is less technically sound than the Survey Form. Additional information regarding reliability would be desirable. In addition, some discussion of the stability of the construct of adaptive functioning across environments might be useful in determining the reason for lack of correlation between scores from the Classroom Edition and the Survey Form and in determining the necessity of administering separate measures of adaptive functioning in different settings.

WOODCOCK-JOHNSON PSYCHO-EDUCATIONAL BATTERY SCALES OF INDEPENDENT BEHAVIOR

Robert Bruininks
Richard Woodcock
Richard Weatherman
Bradley Hill

DLM Teaching Resources
One DLM Park
Allen, Texas   75002

PURPOSE

As stated in Chapter 4, the Woodcock-Johnson Psycho-Educational Battery is composed of four sections: Tests of Cognitive Ability, Tests of Academic Achievement, Tests of Interest Level, and the Scales of Independent Behavior (SIB). The first three were originally published in 1977, whereas the SIB was first published in 1984. The authors state that the SIB is "a comprehensive measure of functional independence and adaptive behavior in motor skills, social and communication skills, personal living skills, and community living skills." It is appropriate for assessing these adaptive behaviors in handicapped and nonhandicapped individuals from infancy through adulthood.

DESCRIPTION OF TEST AND ADMINISTRATION

Like the other tests described in this chapter, the SIB provides measures of both adaptive and maladaptive behavior. The measure of adaptive behavior, called Broad Independence, is made up of four Clusters of Independence: Motor Skills, Social Interaction and Communication Skills, Personal Independence Skills, and Community Independence Skills. Each of these Clusters includes two to five subscales. (See Figure 7-1 for a diagram of the components of the SIB, including the 14 subscales.)

The 14 subscales that make up the four Clusters of Independence contain a total of 226 items. Each item states a task, and the subject's independent performance of the task is rated, with 0 points assigned if the subject "never or rarely performs the task (even if asked)," 1 point assigned if the subject "does the task but not well, or about one-fourth of the time (may need to be asked)," 2 points assigned if he or she "does the task fairly well, or about three-fourths of the time (may need to be asked)," and 3 points assigned if he or she "does the task very well always or almost always (without being asked)." When the respondent is unfamiliar with the individual's ability to perform a specific activity, or when the individual has no opportunity to perform it, the respondent is asked to estimate whether the individual *could* perform the task without assistance.

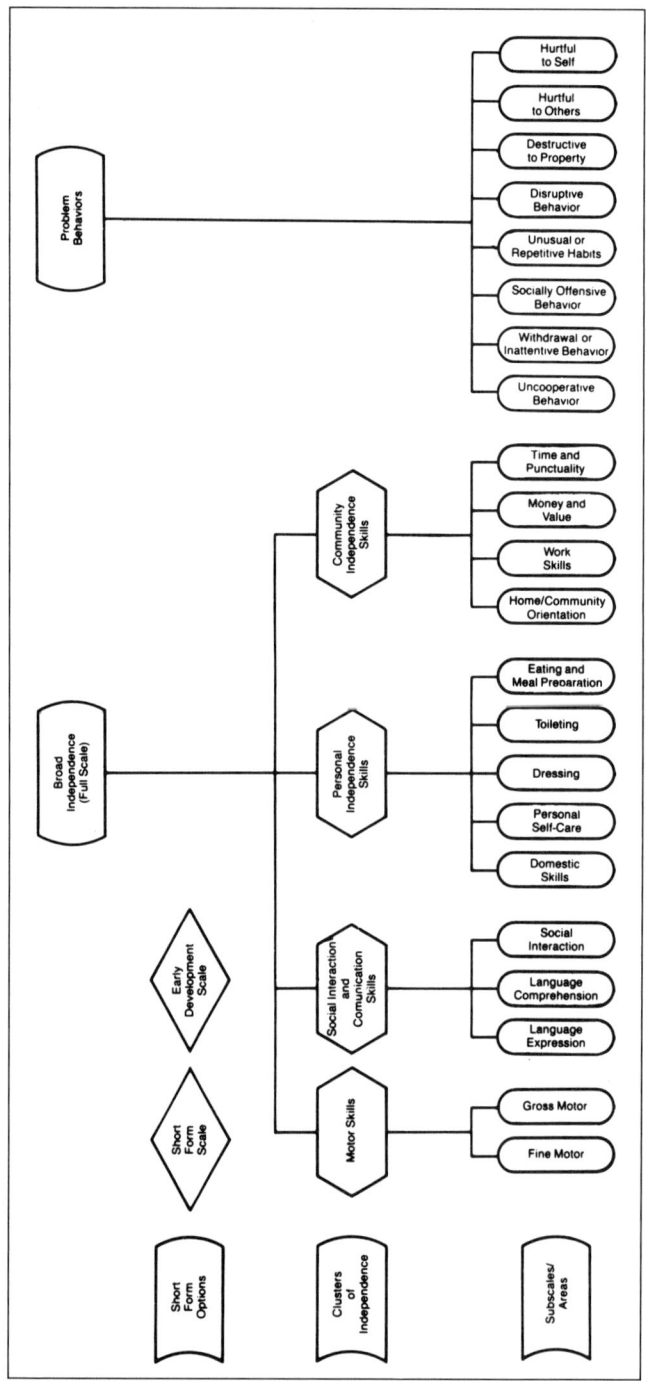

Source: From R. Bruininks, R. Woodcock, R. Weatherman, and B. Hill, 1984, p. 3.

Figure 7-1. Components of the Woodcock-Johnson Psycho-Educational Battery Scales of Independent Behavior.

The SIB provides the option of using a Short Form Scale for brief, overall screening or evaluation. This scale consists of 32 discriminating items selected from all 14 subscales and takes approximately 10 to 15 minutes to administer. There is also an Early Development Scale that is designed for assessing independent functioning for children from birth to 2 1/2 years or for severely handicapped children. This scale consists of 32 items and takes approximately 10 to 15 minutes to administer. The items in the Short Form Scale and the Early Development Scale are of the same format as those in the 14 subscales.

The items in the 14 subscales, Short Form Scale, and Early Development Scale are all arranged in developmental order, and starting points are indicated for each age level. For the Early Development and Short Form scales, basal level is established when all four items on a page are scored 3, and ceiling is established when all four items on a page are scored 0. For the 14 subscales, basal level is established when three or more items out of five are scored 3, and ceiling is reached when three or more items out of five are scored 0.

The measure of maladaptive behavior, the Problem Behaviors Scale, provides a summary of problem behaviors in eight categories (see Figure 7-1). Each category provides several examples of problem behaviors. The respondent indicates whether the individual being assessed demonstrates similar behavior problems and provides a description of one of the most serious problems related to that category. The behavior is then rated according to severity, on a 5-point scale ranging from "Not serious/not a problem" (0 points) to "Extremely serious/a critical problem" (4 points), and according to frequency of occurrence, on a 5-point scale ranging from "Less than once a month" (1 point) to "one or more times an hour" (5 points).

The SIB is generally administered to a respondent who is familiar with the day-to-day behavior and functioning of the individual being assessed. The SIB can, however, be administered to the individual being assessed, if his or her deficits are not severe. The SIB can also be completed by the interviewer if he or she is familiar enough with the subject. There are no specific qualifications necessary for administering the SIB. Practice with an experienced interviewer is recommended for those with little formal training in test administration.

Administration time for the 14 subscales and the Problem Behaviors Scale is, on average, about an hour or less.

SCORING AND INTERPRETATION

Each item is scored as it is administered. Each of the adaptive behavior items is scored as either 0, 1, 2, or 3. Scores are totalled for each subscale, with 3 points assigned for each item below basal level and 0 points assigned for each item above ceiling level. Scoring then proceeds in a manner similar to that described for the Woodcock-Johnson Psycho-Educational Battery Tests of Cognitive Ability, as described in Chapter 4. (Scoring for the Problem Behavior Scale is done differently from that of the adaptive behavior items, and is discussed later.)

Briefly, the subscale raw scores are converted to Part Scores, which are summed for each of the four adaptive behavior Clusters, resulting in Cluster scores. The Cluster scores are added and divided by 4, resulting in the cluster score for Broad Independence (the overall measure of adaptive functioning). The Cluster scores for the four clusters and for Broad Independence can then be converted to age-equivalent scores. The Average Cluster Score for the individual's age group is determined for each cluster and for Broad Independence. The Average Cluster Score is subtracted from the actual Cluster Score obtained for each cluster and for Broad Independence, resulting in Cluster Difference Scores. The Cluster Difference Scores are then used to determine percentile ranks, standard scores (with means of 100 and standard deviations of 15), normal curve equivalents (NCEs) (with means of 50 and standard deviations of 21.06), stanines, Relative Performance Indexes (RPIs), and functioning levels for each cluster and for Broad Independence. RPIs indicate the percentage of independence predicted for the individual on a set of tasks that a reference group could perform with 90% independence. Functioning levels are descriptive categories ranging from Severe Deficit to Very Superior. Standard errors of measurement can be determined for the percentiles, standard scores, and NCEs, allowing confidence bands to be established.

The examiner can also calculate Adjusted Scores, which allow comparison of the individual's adaptive behavior with that of other individuals of the same age and cognitive ability (as determined by the Woodcock-Johnson Tests of Cognitive Ability). Finally, scores can be plotted on five different profiles (two Percentile Rank Profiles, a Subscale Profile, a Training Implications Profile, and a Problem Behaviors Profile), allowing visual representation of the information contained in the various test scores.

Scoring for the Early Development and Short Form Scales is identical to that for the four adaptive behavior Clusters, except that there is no need to calculate Part Scores. For the Behavior Problems Scale the frequency and severity score for each of the eight items is converted separately to a stanine score, according to age-based tables of norms. If desired, four special maladaptive behavior indexes can be derived from the scores: the Internalized Maladaptive Index, the Asocial Maladaptive Index, the Externalized Maladaptive Index, and the General Maladaptive Index.

As with the other parts of the Woodcock-Johnson Psycho-Educational Battery, scoring of the SIB is somewhat complicated and time consuming, providing a fair amount of opportunity for errors. The manual does, however, provide very clear instructions and many examples for completing the scoring. Thorough descriptions of each Cluster and subscale facilitate interpretation of scores, although little specific information is provided directly regarding test interpretation.

TECHNICAL QUALITY

Norms

Standardization of the SIB was based on a sample of 1,700 subjects randomly selected from more than 40 communities. These communities were chosen on the basis of census data to closely approximate the U.S. population on community size, geographic location, ethnic composition, sex, and socioeconomic characteristics. Additional norms were based on a sample of more than 1,000 handicapped and nonhandicapped people including extensive samples of retarded, learning-disabled, behavior-disordered, and hearing-impaired subjects (Bruininks, Woodcock, Hill, & Weatherman, 1985).

Reliability

Split-half reliabilities were calculated for both the handicapped and nonhandicapped samples. For the nonhandicapped group, median composite reliabilities (across ages) ranged from .83 for the Motor Skills Cluster to .92 for Community Living Skills. The Broad Independence measure yielded a median composite reliability of .96. Median split-half reliabilities (across ages) ranged from .73 for the Toileting subscale to .86

for Domestic Skills. Some subtests had low split-half reliabilities for specific age groups (e.g., Toileting for adults, Money and Value for preschoolers), presumably because of the limited variability among individuals of these ages on these behaviors. Split-half reliabilities were also calculated for several different handicapped samples (moderately to severely retarded, mildly retarded, learning disabled, and behavior disorders). Coefficients for subtests, Clusters, and Broad Independence were generally in the .80s to .90s, with highest correlations reported for the more severely impaired groups. Overall, internal consistency for the Clusters appears to be adequate, although internal consistency for some subtests for some ages is lower than desirable.

Test-retest reliability was assessed with two samples of nonhandicapped children. Reliability coefficients for the Clusters, Broad Independence, the Short Form Scale and the four indexes of maladaptive behavior ranged from .71 to .96. Overall, reliability appears to be adequate.

Validity

Validity data for the SIB are somewhat sparse. Bruininks et al. (1985) report high correlations between age and SIB scores for a sample of children and adults, indicating that "SIB adaptive behavior scores are strong developmental measures of social developmental and adaptive behavior." Similarly, levels of performance were lowest among individuals considered to be the most severely handicapped. The Maladaptive Indexes did not show the same developmental trends, but did reflect more behavior problems in the behavior disordered sample than in the retarded, learning disabled, or normal samples. Scores from the four adaptive behavior clusters were found to correlate fairly highly with Woodcock-Johnson Broad Cognitive Ability scores for handicapped, but not nonhandicapped children and adults. Although sparse, available validity data support the SIB as a measure of adaptive and maladaptive behavior.

OTHER CONSIDERATIONS

The SIB is similar in content to the Vineland Adaptive Behavior Scales, and both are well-constructed instruments for assessing adaptive functioning and identifying certain maladaptive behaviors. Although item content is similar for the two instruments, the typical administration of items is done quite differently. The SIB requires the examiner to read each item to the respondent and requires the respondent to rate the individual's performance of that behavior on a 4-point scale. The Vineland is generally administered by asking open-ended questions about the particular subdomain of behavior being addressed and using the information obtained to score each item within that subdomain. It is presumed that the SIB administration, because of its more standardized approach, will lead to more reliable data than the Vineland. (Indeed, inter-rater reliabilities for some of the Vineland domains are lower than would be desired.) On the other hand, the Vineland approach is less tedious and may be easier for some respondents who are not accustomed to psychological instruments. Because of its open-ended format, the Vineland also encourages the respondent to provide more anecdotal data that may help the examiner obtain a fuller view of the individual's strengths, weaknesses, behavior problems, and relationship with the respondent. The test user should consider these possible strengths and weaknesses of the two instruments to determine which is most appropriate for his or her particular needs.

SUMMARY

The SIB appears to be a well-developed instrument for assessing functional independence and adaptive behavior. The 14 subscales and four clusters provide a meaningful framework in which to evaluate the individual's abilities. Administration is fairly easy, but scoring is fairly time consuming and complicated. Norms for the nonhandicapped sample appear to be adequate. It is difficult to assess the representativeness of the handicapped sample, but the test developers should be commended for providing data from several groups of individuals with different types of disabilities. Reliability appears to be adequate, but data are too sparse to draw conclusions about the instrument's validity.

References

American Psychological Association. (1974). *Standards for educational and psychological tests.* Washington, DC: Author.

Anastasi, A. (1982). *Psychological testing* (5th ed.). New York: Macmillan.

Armstrong, R., & Jensen, J. (1981). *Slosson intelligence test (SIT) for children and adults, 1981 norms tables application and development.* East Aurora, NY: Slosson Educational Publications.

Bayley, N. (1969). *Bayley scales of infant development.* San Antonio, TX: The Psychological Corporation.

Beery, K. (1982). *The developmental test of visual-motor integration* (rev. ed.). Cleveland: Modern Curriculum Press.

Beery, K. (1989). *The VMI (developmental test of visual-motor integration) administration, scoring, and teaching manual.* Cleveland: Modern Curriculum Press.

Berk, R. (1984). *Screening and diagnosis of children with learning disabilities.* Springfield, IL: Charles C. Thomas.

Bruininks, R., Woodcock, R., Hill, B., & Weatherman, R. (1985). *Technical summary for the scales of independent behavior.* Allen, TX: DLM Teaching Resources.

Bruininks, R., Woodcock, R., Weatherman, R., & Hill, B. (1984). *Woodcock-Johnson psycho-educational battery scales of independent behavior: Interviewer's manual.* Allen TX: DLM Teaching Resources.

Burgemeister, B., Blum, L., & Lorge, I. (1972). *Columbia mental maturity scale.* San Antonio: The Psychological Corporation.

Colarusso, R., & Hammill, D. (1972). *Motor-free visual perception test.* Novato, CA: Academic Therapy Publications.

Cronbach, L. (1970). *Essentials of psychological testing.* New York: Harper and Row.

Cummings, J. (1985). Review of Woodcock-Johnson psycho-educational battery. In J.V. Mitchell (Ed.), *The ninth mental measurements yearbook.* Lincoln, NE: Buros Institute of Mental Measurements.

Delaney, E., & Hopkins, T. (1987). *The Stanford-Binet intelligence scale: Fourth edition. Examiner's handbook.* Chicago: Riverside.

Doll, E. (1935). A genetic scale of social maturity. *The American Journal of Orthopsychiatry, 5,* 180–188.

Doll, E. (1965). *Vineland social maturity scale.* Circle Pines, MN: American Guidance Service.

Elbert, J., & Holden, E. (1985). Wechsler preschool and primary scale of intelligence. In D. Keyser & R. Sweetland (Eds.), *Test critiques: Volume III.* Austin, TX: PRO-ED.

Furr, K. (1970). Standard scores for the Koppitz developmental scoring system. *Journal of Clinical Psychology, 26,* 78–79.

Grossman, H. (Ed.). (1977). *A manual on terminology and classification in mental retardation,* (3rd ed.). Washington, DC: American Association on Mental Deficiency.

Hager, P. (1985). Woodcock-Johnson psycho-educational battery. In D. Keyser & R. Sweetland (Eds.), *Test critiques: Volume IV.* Austin, TX: PRO-ED.

Harrison, P. (1985). *Vineland adaptive behavior scales classroom edition manual.* Circle Pines, MN: American Guidance Service.

Hartlage, L., & Lucas, D. (1971). Scaled score transformations of Bender gestalt expectancy levels for young children. *Psychology in the Schools, 8,* 76–78.

Hessler, G. (1982). *Use and interpretation of the Woodcock-Johnson psycho-educational battery.* Allen, TX: DLM Teaching Resources.

Hiskey, M. (1966). *Hiskey-Nebraska test of learning aptitude.* Lincoln, NE: Author.

Jensen, A. (1974). How biased are culture-loaded tests? *Genetic Psychology Monographs, 90,* 185–244.

Jensen, A. (1980). *Bias in mental testing.* New York: The Free Press.

Kamphaus, R., Kaufman, A., & Kaufman, N. (1982). *A cross-validation study of sequential-simultaneous processing at ages 2½–12½ using the Kaufman assessment battery for children* (K-ABC). Paper presented at the meeting of the American Psychological Association, Washington, DC.

Kaufman, A. (1979). *Intelligent testing with the WISC-R.* New York: John Wiley & Sons.

Kaufman, A. (1983). Some questions and answers about the Kaufman assessment battery for children (K-ABC). *Journal of Psychoeducational Assessment, 4,* 205–218.

Kaufman, A. (1985). Review of the Woodcock-Johnson psycho-educational battery. In J.V. Mitchell, (Ed.), *The ninth mental measurements yearbook.* Lincoln, NE: Buros Institute of Mental Measurements.

Kaufman, A., & Doppelt, J. (1976). Analysis of WISC-R standardization data in terms of the stratification variables. *Child Development, 43,* 521–535.

Kaufman, A., & Kaufman, N. (1977). *Clinical evaluation of young children with the McCarthy scales.* New York: Grune & Stratton.

Kaufman, A., & Kaufman, N. (1983). *Kaufman assessment battery for children: Interpretive manual.* Circle Pines, MN: American Guidance Service.

Keith, T. (1985). McCarthy scales of children's abilities. In D. Keyser & R. Sweetland (Eds.), *Test critiques: Volume IV.* Austin, TX: PRO-ED.

Koppitz, E. (1963). *The Bender gestalt test for young children.* New York: Grune and Stratton.

Koppitz, E. (1975). *The Bender gestalt test for young children, Vol. II: Research and application, 1963-1973.* New York: Grune and Stratton.

Kviz, F., & Knafl, K. (1980). *Statistics for nurses: An introductory text.* Boston: Little, Brown.

Leiter, R. (1979). *Leiter international performance scale: Instruction manual.* Wood Dale, IL: Stoelting.

Levine, M. (1982). *Leiter international performance scale: A handbook.* Los Angeles: Western Psychological Services.

Llabre, M. (1985). Standard progressive matrices. In D. Keyser & R. Sweetland (Eds.), *Test critiques: Volume I.* Austin, TX: PRO-ED.

Marston, D., & Ysseldyke, J. (1980). *Derived subtest scores for the Woodcock-Johnson psycho-educational battery.* Allen, TX: DLM Teaching Resources.

Matey, C. (1985). Leiter international performance scale. In D. Keyser & R. Sweetland (Eds.), *Test critiques: Volume I.* Austin, TX: PRO-ED.

McCarthy, D. (1972). *McCarthy scales of children's abilities.* San Antonio, TX: The Psychological Corporation.

Mercer, J., & Lewis, J. (1978). *Adaptive behavior inventory for children.* San Antonio, TX: The Psychological Corporation.

Nihira, K., Foster, R., Shellhaas, M., & Leland, H. (1975). *AAMD adaptive behavior scale manual.* Austin, TX: PRO-ED.

Raven, J. (1986). *Manual for Raven's progressive matrices and vocabulary scales: Research supplement No. 3.* London: H.K. Lewis & Co.

Raven, J., & Court, J. (1989). *Manual for Raven's progressive matrices and vocabulary scales: Research supplement No. 4.* London: H.K. Lewis & Co.

Raven, J., Court, J., & Raven, J. (1977). *Manual for Raven's progressive matrices and vocabulary scales: The Mill Hill vocabulary.* London: H.K. Lewis & Co.

Raven, J., Court, J., & Raven, J. (1983a). *Manual for Raven's progressive matrices and vocabulary scales: Standard progressive matrices (1983 ed.).* London: H.K. Lewis & Co.

Raven, J., Court, J., & Raven, J. (1983b). *Manual for Raven's progressive matrices and vocabulary scales: Advanced progressive matrices sets I and II.* London: H.K. Lewis & Co.

Raven, J., Court, J., & Raven, J. (1986a). *Manual for Raven's progressive matrices and vocabulary scales: General overview.* London: H.K. Lewis & Co.

Raven, J., Court, J., & Raven, J. (1986b). *Manual for Raven's progressive matrices and vocabulary scales: The coloured progressive matrices (1986 ed., with U.S. norms).* London: H.K. Lewis & Co.

Raven, J., Court, J., & Raven, J. (1988). *Manual for Raven's progressive matrices and vocabulary scales: The Crichton vocabulary scale: 1988 revision.* H.K. Lewis & Co.

Reynolds, W. (1985). Review of Slosson Intelligence Test. In J.V. Mitchell, (ed.) *The ninth mental measurements yearbook.* Lincoln, NE: Buros Institute of Mental Measurements.

Reynolds, C., Chatman, S., & Willson, V. (1983). *Relationships between age and raw score increases on the K-ABC.* Paper presented at the meeting of the National Association of School Psychologists, Detroit, MI.

Rhodes, L., Bayley, N., & Yow, B. (1984). *Supplement to the manual for the Bayley scales of infant development.* San Antonio, TX: The Psychological Corporation.

Ronka, C. (1984). A comparison of adaptive behavior ratings: Revised Vineland and AAMD. ABS-SE. Unpublished doctoral dissertation, University of Cincinnati, Cincinnati.

Slosson, R. (1982). *Slosson intelligence test (SIT) and oral reading test (SORT).* East Aurora, NY: Slosson Educational Publications.

Smith, R. (1976). Standardization of the Leiter international performance scale (Doctoral dissertation, University of Southern California, 1975). *Dissertation Abstracts International, 36,* 11A.

Sparrow, S., Balla, D., & Cicchetti, D. (1984a). *Vineland adaptive behavior scales interview edition expanded form manual.* Circle Pines, MN: American Guidance Service.

Sparrow, S., Balla, D., & Cicchetti, D. (1984b). *Vineland adaptive behavior scales interview edition survey form manual.* Circle Pines, MN: American Guidance Service.

Spruill, J. (1987). Stanford-Binet intelligence scale, fourth edition. In D. Keyser & R. Sweetland (Eds.), *Test critiques: Volume VI.* Austin, TX: PRO-ED.

Thorndike, R., Hagen, E., & Sattler, J. (1986). *The Stanford-Binet intelligence scale: Fourth edition. Guide for administering and scoring*. Chicago: Riverside.

Tuma, J., & Applebaum, A. (1980). Reliability and practice effects of WISC-R IQ estimates in a normal population. *Educational and Psychological Measurement, 40,* 671–678.

Vance, H., Blixt, S., Ellis, R., & Debell, S. (1981). Stability of the WISC-R for a sample of exceptional children. *Journal of Clinical Psychology. 37,* 397–399.

Vernon, P. (1984a). Advanced progressive matrices. In D. Keyser & R. Sweetland (Eds.), *Test critiques: Volume I*. Austin, TX: PRO-ED.

Vernon, P. (1984b). Wechsler intelligence scale for children–revised. In D. Keyser & R. Sweetland (Eds.), *Test critiques: Volume I*. Austin, TX: PRO-ED.

Wechsler, D. (1974). *Manual for the Wechsler intelligence scale for children–revised*. San Antonio: The Psychological Corporation.

Wechsler, D. (1989). Wechsler preschool and primary scale of intelligence–revised. San Antonio: The Psychological Corporation.

Willson, V., Reynolds, C., Chatman, S., & Kaufman, A. (1983). *Confirmatory analysis of simultaneous, sequential, and achievement factors on the K-ABC*. Paper presented at the meeting of the National Association of School Psychologists, Detroit.

Woodcock, R., & Mather, N. (1989). WJ-R tests of cognitive ability—standard and supplemental batteries: Examiner's manual. In R. Woodcock & M. Johnson, *Woodcock-Johnson psycho-educational battery–revised*. Allen, TX: DLM Teaching Resources.

Index

AAMD. *See* American Association on Mental Deficiency
AAMD Adaptive Behavior Scale (ABS)
  behavior domains, 166–169
  description and administration, 167–169
  impairment groups, 171
  maladaptive behavior, 168
  medications, use of, 170
  negative options, 167
  norms, 170
  personal independence, 171
  personal maladaptation, 171
  physical development, 170
  profile summary, 170
  purpose, 166–167
  raw scores, 169
  reliability, 170–171
  scoring and interpretation, 169–170
  self-direction, 170
  social maladaptation, 171
  structured interview, 167, 171
  summary, 171
  unacceptable vocal habits, 170
  validity, 171
  and Vineland Adaptive Scales, 182
Abbreviated batteries for Stanford-Binet, 59
Abstract/visual reasoning subtests for Stanford-Binet, 49, 51–53, 55–59
Academic achievement, 39, 61, 63, 80, 99, 135
Achievement scale for K-ABC, 40
Achievement subtests for K-ABC, 61

Adaptive behavior
  composite on Vineland Test, 175, 180, 182–84
  defined, 166
  Inventory for Children, 182
  subtests on Vineland Test, 173, 180, 182
  tests, 166–191
Adaptive-testing format, 59, 63
Adjusted scores of WJ-SIB, 188
Advanced Progressive Matrices (APM)
  description and administration, 131
  norms, 132
  other considerations, 136
  purpose, 129–130
  reliability, 134
  scoring, 132
  subtests, 131
  validity, 134
Age-equivalent scores, 5–6, 8, 89, 99
Alternate-form reliability, 11–12
American Association on Mental Deficiency (AAMD), 166
American Association on Mental Retardation, 166
American Psychological Association, 9, 15, 17
Anastasi, A., 36–37
Anxiety, test, 25
APM. *See* Advanced Progressive Matrices
Applebaum, A., 37
Area Standard Age Scores (Area SASs) for Stanford-Binet, 53, 55–56

199

Armstrong, R., 118–119, 121
Arthur Adaptation, of LIPS, 144, 146
Average cluster score of WJ Part I, 99
Average cluster score of WJ-SIB, 188
Average score, 7
Avoidance behavior, 26

Balla, D., 174, 177
Basal level
   for Bayley Scales Test, 139
   for PPVT-R, 127
   for Stanford-Binet, 49
Bayley Mental Scale, 58, 137–142
Bayley, N., 137, 139–140
Bayley Scales of Infant Development
    (Mental Scale)
   basal level, 139
   description and administration, 138–139
   mental age, 139
   mental development index (MDI), 139
   mental scale, 58, 137–142
   motor scale, 138
   norms, 140
   other considerations, 142
   psychomotor development index
    (PDI), 141
   purpose, 137
   raw score, 139
   reliability, 140–141
   scoring, 139
   situation codes, 138
   summary, 142
   test stimuli, 138
   validity, 141
Beery Developmental Test of Visual-
    Motor Integration, 161
Beery, K., 150, 152–153
Behavior domains on ABS, 166–169
Behavior, during testing, 23–28
Behavioral disorders, 46, 150, 167
Bender Gestalt Test. *See* Bender Visual
    Motor Gestalt Test
Bender Gestalt Test for Young Children, The,
    159
Bender, L., 158
Bender Visual Motor Gestalt Test
   description and administration, 159
   norms, 160–161

   other considerations, 162–163
   performance IQ, 162
   purpose, 158–159
   reliability, 161
   scoring and interpretation, 159–160
   summary, 163
   test cards, 159
   validity, 161–162
   verbal IQ, 162
   and VMI Test, 153–154
Berk, R., 6, 9, 12–13, 16–17
Bias, test, 19–20
Blixt, S., 37
Blum, L., 123
Boehm Tests of Basic Concepts, 91
Bracken Basic Concepts Scale, 91
Broad cognitive ability on W-J Part I, 95–96
Broad independence clusters of WJ-SIB, 189
Bruininks, R., 184, 189–190
Burgemeister, B., 123

Ceiling level
   for PPVT-R, 127
   for Stanford-Binet, 49
Chatman, S., 45
Chronological age, 7, 36
Cicchetti, D., 174, 177
Classroom edition, of Vineland Test, 172, 174–175, 178–180
Cluster difference score on WJ Part I, 99
Cluster scores
   expected achievement on WJ Part I, 99
   full scale on WJ Part I, 101
   scholastic aptitude, on WJ Part I, 99
   of WJ Part I, 95, 99, 102
   of WJ-SIB, 188–189
CMMS. *See* Columbia Mental Maturity
    Scale
Coefficient alpha, 13
Cognitive Abilities Test, 46
Cognitive factors on WJ Part I, 95–96, 101
Cognitive tests. *See* Intelligence Tests
Colarusso, R., 155–157
Coloured Progressive Matrices (CPM)
   board form, 131
   book form, 131
   description and administration, 131

Index

ethnic groups, 135
norms, 133
other considerations, 136
purpose, 129–130
reliability, 134
scoring, 132
validity, 135
Columbia Mental Maturity Scale (CMMS)
description and administration, 123–124
norms, 124
purpose, 123
reliability, 125
scoring and interpretation, 124
summary, 125–126
validity, 125
Community living skills of WJ-SIB, 189
Composite SAS for Stanford-Binet, 53, 55–56, 60
Concurrent validity
defined, 16
on K-ABC, 46
on MSCA, 110
Confidence, during testing, 25
Confidence intervals, 43
Construct validity, 17, 45
Content validity, 15
Court, J., 129–136
Crichton Vocabulary Scale, 130
Criterion-related validity, 16
Cronbach, L., 2
Crystallized abilities on Stanford-Binet, 48–49
Cultural influence, 24
Cummings, J., 98

Deaf children. *See* Hearing impaired
Debell, S., 37
Delaney, E., 54
Developmental Scoring System, 159, 161, 163
Developmental Test of Visual-Motor Integration (VMI)
and Bender Test, 162–63
description and administration, 150–151
norms, 151–152
other considerations, 154
purpose, 150

reliability, 152–153
scoring and interpretation, 151
summary, 154–155
validity, 153–154
Deviation IQs, 7, 9
Deviation social quotient, on Vineland Test, 181
Distractibility, 23–24
Doll, E., 172, 181
Doppelt, J., 62
Dyslexic students, 46

Early development scale of WJ-SIB, 187
Easel book, for PPVT-R, 126
Easel kits, for K-ABC, 41
Elbert, J., 73
Ellis, R., 37
Entry level, on Stanford-Binet, 49, 59
Environment, for testing, 22–23
Environmentally deprived, 102
Equipercentile method, on SIT, 121
Equivalence, 10–12
Equivalent forms, 10
Estimated performance, on Vineland Test, 175
Ethnic differences, 46, 62, 114, 135
Examiner's Handbook, 49, 53–54, 56–57, 59
Exceptional children, 39, 46, 48, 61, 73, 103, 112, 123, 143, 166
Expected grade scores on WJ Part I, 99
Extended scores, 89

Fluid-analytic abilities on Stanford-Binet, 48–49
Foster, R., 166–169
Frostig Test of Visual Perception, 153, 157, 161
Frustration, during testing, 26
Full Scale IQ
on Stanford-Binet, 56
on WISC-R, 36–39
on WPPSI, 71–73
on WPPSI-R, 77, 79–81
Functioning level on WJ Part I, 100

Gates Reading Test, 115
General cognitive index (GCI) on MSCA, 108

General cognitive scale on MSCA, 105–106, 109–110
General reasoning factor on Stanford-Binet, 48
Gifted students, 46, 48, 61, 73, 92
Global scale score for K-ABC, 42, 44
Grade-equivalent scores, 5–6, 8, 89, 99
Grants for K-ABC, 45
Grossman, H., 166

Hagen, E., 47, 49
Hager, P., 99
Hammill, D., 155–157
Harrison, P., 181
Hartlage, L., 160
Head Start Program, 181
Health problems, 28
Hearing impaired, 26, 43, 46, 50, 62, 112, 114–115, 123, 143, 181
Hessler, G., 95, 97, 100, 103
High-risk preschoolers, 46
Hill, B., 184, 186, 189–190
Hiskey, M., 111, 114
Hiskey-Nebraska Test of Learning Aptitude
  description and administration, 112–113
  learning ages, 114
  learning quotient (LQ), 114
  norms, 114–115
  purpose, 111–112
  reliability, 115
  scoring and interpretation, 113–114
  subtests
    bead patterns, 112–113
    block patterns, 112–113
    completion of drawings, 112–113
    memory for color, 112–113
    memory for digits, 112–113
    paper folding, 112–113
    picture analogies, 112–113
    picture association, 112–113
    picture identification, 112–113
    puzzle blocks, 112–114
    spatial reasoning, 112–113
    visual attention span, 112–113
  summary, 115–116
  validity, 115
Holden, T., 73

Hopkins, T., 50, 53–54
Horn-Cattell theory, 83, 93

Impairment groups, on ABS, 171
Impulsive approach to testing, 24
Indexes, for MSCA, 108
Intelligence quotient, 7–8, 20, 36
Intelligence test, considerations, 60–65
Intelligence tests, multi-scale, 7–8, 32–65, 68–116, 118, 153–154, 158, 176, 182, 188
Intelligence tests, single scale, 118–147, 153, 182
Interclass correlation, 11
Internal consistency, 10, 12–13
Interobserver consistency, 11
Interscorer consistency, 11
Interview editions, of Vineland Test, 172–175, 177–180
IQ. See Intelligence quotient

Jensen, J., 118–119, 121, 130
Johnson, M., 82, 94, 102–103

K-ABC. See Kaufman Assessment Battery for Children
K-ABC Interpretive Manual, 43
Kamphaus, R., 45
Kaufman, A., 39–41, 45–46, 102, 108, 116
Kaufman, N., 40, 45–46, 108, 116
Kaufman Assessment Battery for Children (K-ABC)
  achievement scale, 40
  achievement subtests, 61
  concurrent validity, 46
  confidence intervals, 43
  construct validity, 45
  description and administration, 40–42
  easel-kits, 41
  global scale score, 42, 44
  grants, 45
  hearing impaired, 43
  and Hiskey-Nebraska, 115–116
  language disorders, 43
  mental processing composite, 42, 44
  mental processing global scales, 40–42, 44
  mental processing subtests, 61
  and MSCA, 110

Index

nonverbal scale, 62
norms, 43–44
other considerations, 46–47
predictive validity, 45–46
purpose, 40
raw score, 42
reliability, 44
scaled score, 42
scoring and interpretation, 42–43
selecting intelligence tests, 60–65
sequential processing subtests, 41, 44
  hand movements, 41
  number recall, 41
  word order, 41
simultaneous processing subtests, 41–42, 44
  face recognition, 41
  gestalt closure, 42
  magic window, 41
  matrix analogies, 42
  photo series, 42
  spatial memory, 42
  triangles, 42
speech disorders, 43
split-half reliability, 44
standard error of measurement, 44
and Stanford-Binet, 48, 56, 58
test-retest reliability, 44
true score, 43
validity, 45–46
and Vineland Adaptive, 176, 182
and Woodcock-Johnson, 91, 93–94
and WPPSI-R, 80
Keith, T., 107, 110
Koppitz, E., 159–163
Kraft, K., 8
Kuder-Richardson, 10, 13
Kviz, F., 8

Language abilities, 33–34
Language delays, 58
Language problems, 27, 43, 50, 58, 143
Learning ages, on Hiskey-Nebraska, 114
Learning disabilities, 39, 46, 48, 61, 92, 103, 123, 150
Learning quotient (LQ), on Hiskey-Nebraska, 114
Learning styles, 46, 48

Leiter International Performance Scale (LIPS)
  description and administration, 143–144
  norms, 145–146
  purpose, 142–143
  reliability, 146
  scoring and interpretation, 144–145
  summary, 147
  validity, 146–147
Leiter International Performance Scale: A Handbook, 145
Leiter, R., 142, 144–145
Leland, H., 166–169
Levine, M., 142, 144–147
Lewis, J., 182
LIPS. *See* Leiter International Performance Scale
Llabre, M., 130
Lorge, I., 123
Lucas, D., 160
Luria-Nebraska Children's Battery, 46

Maladaptive behavior, on ABS, 168
Maladaptive behavior indexes of WJ-SIB, 189
Maladaptive behavior subtests, on Vineland Test, 173, 182–184
Manual for Raven's Progressive Matrices and Vocabulary Scales, 130, 134–136
Manual on Terminology and Classification in Mental Retardation, 166
Marston, D., 100
Matey, C., 143–144, 147
Mather, N., 86
McCarthy, D., 104–105, 110
McCarthy Scales of Children's Abilities (MSCA)
  concurrent validity, 110
  description and administration, 104–107
  general cognitive index (GCI), 108
  general cognitive scale, 105–106, 109–110
  indexes, 108
  and K-ABC, 46
  memory scale, 104–105, 108–110
  motor scale, 104–105, 108–109
  motor scale index, 109

McCarthy Scales of Children's Abilities
(MSCA)—Continued
  norms, 109
  other considerations, 110–111
  perceptual performance scale, 104–105, 108–110
  predictive validity, 110
  purpose, 104
  quantitative scale, 104–105, 108–110
  raw scores, 107–108
  reliability, 109
  scoring and interpretation, 107–108
    summary, 111
  subtests
    arm coordination, 105–107
    block building, 105–107
    conceptual grouping, 105–107
    counting and sorting, 105–107
    draw-a-child, 105–107
    draw-a-design, 105–107
    imitative action, 105–107
    leg coordination, 105–107
    number questions, 105–108
    numerical memory, 105–108
    opposite analogies, 104–105, 107–108
    pictorial memory, 104–105, 107
    puzzle solving, 105–107
    right-left orientation, 105–107
    tapping sequence, 105–107
    validity, 110
    verbal fluency, 104–105, 107
    verbal memory, 104–105, 107
    word knowledge, 104–105, 107
  summary, 111
  verbal scale, 104–105, 108, 110
  and WPPSI-R, 80–81
Mean score, 7
Measured score, 14
Medications, and ABS, 170
Memory scale on MSCA, 104–105, 108–110
Mental age, 7, 36, 120, 139
Mental development index (MDI) on Bayley Test, 139
Mental processing
  composite for K-ABC, 42, 44
  global scales for K-ABC, 40–42, 44
  subtests for K-ABC, 61
Mental retardation, 39, 46, 48, 61, 73, 92, 131, 181

Mental scale on Bayley Test, 58, 137–142
Mercer, J., 182
Metropolitan Achievement Test, 110, 115
Mill Hill Vocabulary Scale, 130
Motor-Free Visual Perception Test (MVPT)
  description and administration, 155–156
  norms, 157
  perceptual ages (PAs), 156
  perceptual quotients (PQs), 156
  purpose, 155
  reliability, 157
  scoring and interpretation, 156–157
  summary, 158
  validity, 157–158
Motor scale
  on Bayley Test, 138
  index on MSCA, 109
  on MSCA, 104–105, 108–109
Motor skills cluster of WJ-SIB, 189
MSCA. *See* McCarthy Scales of Children's Abilities
Multi-scale tests, 68
  See also Intelligence test, multi-scale form
MVPT. *See* Motor-Free Visual Perception Test

Nebraska Test of Learning Aptitude for Young Deaf Children, 111–112
Negative options on ABS, 167
Nihira, K., 166–169
Non-English speaking, 43, 131
Nonverbal scale for K-ABC, 62
Normal curve, 7–8
Norming procedures, 18–19
Norming samples, 18–19

Observed performance, on Vineland Test, 175
Observing test behavior, 23–28
Obsessive approach to testing, 24–25
Optimal testing conditions, 22–23
Otis-Lennon Mental Ability Test, 125

Parallel forms, 10–12
Part scores on WJ Part I, 99

Peabody Picture Vocabulary Test (PPVT), 126, 128, 147
Peabody Picture Vocabulary Test—Revised (PPVT-R)
  basal level, 127
  ceiling level, 127
  description and administration, 126–127
  easel book, 126
  norms, 127–128
  purpose, 126
  reliability, 128
  scoring and interpretation, 127
  summary, 128–129
  validity, 128
  and Vineland Test, 182
Pencil grasp, during testing, 26
Percentile rank profiles
  of WJ Part I, 99
  of WJ-SIB, 188
Percentile scores
  defined, 4
  on WJ Part I, 100
Perceptual ages (PAs) on MVPT, 156
Perceptual performance scale on MSCA, 104–105, 108–110
Perceptual quotients (PQs) on MVPT, 156
Perceptual speed factors on WJ Part I, 101
Performance IQ
  on Bender Test, 162
  on WISC-R, 36–39
  on WPPSI, 71–73
  on WPPSI-R, 77–81
Performance subtests
  on WISC-R, 34–35, 62
  on WPPSI, 70–71
  on WPPSI-R, 75–77, 79, 82
Perseverance, taking tests, 26
Personal independence, on ABS, 171
Personal maladaptation, on ABS, 171
Personality characteristics, during testing, 27
Physical development, on ABS, 170
Physically impaired, 46
PPVT. *See* Peabody Picture Vocabulary Test
PPVT-R. *See* Peabody Picture Vocabulary Test-Revised

Predictive validity
  defined, 16
  and K-ABC, 45–46
  on MSCA, 110
Problem behaviors profile of WJ-SIB, 188
Problem behaviors scale of WJ-SIB, 187
Problem-solving skills, 41–42
Profile analysis chart on Stanford-Binet, 54
Profile summary, on ABS, 170
Psychological construct, 17
Psychomotor development index (PDI) on Bayley Test, 141

Quantitative reasoning subtests on Stanford-Binet, 49, 51, 53, 55–56, 58–59
Quantitative scale on MSCA, 104–105, 108–110

Racial differences, 62, 114
Rasch-Wright model, 44
Raven, J., 129–135
Raven's Progressive Matrices (RPM), 129–137, 161
  culture-reduced, 130
Raw scores
  on ABS, 169
  on Bayley Test, 139
  defined, 3, 5
  on K-ABC, 42
  on MSCA, 107–108
  on Stanford-Binet, 53
  on WPPSI-R, 77
Relative performance indexes (RPI)
  of WJ Part I, 100
  of WJ-SIB, 188
Reliability
  alternate form, 11–12
  defined, 9
  equivalence, 11–12
  test-retest, 11
  types of, 9–11
Research Supplement No. 3, 130, 132–133
Restlessness, taking tests, 24
Retarded children. *See* Exceptional children
Reynolds, C., 45

Reynolds, W., 9, 122
Rhodes, L., 139
Ronka, C., 182
RPM. *See* Raven's Progressive Matrices
Rushed approach, to testing, 24

SAT. *See* Stanford Achievement Test
Sattler, J., 47, 49
Scaled scores
   on K-ABC, 42
   on WISC-R, 38
   on WPPSI-R, 77
Scholastic aptitude on WJ Part I, 95
Scoring tests, 28
Selecting intelligence tests, 60–65
Self-direction, on ABS, 170
Sequential processing subtests on K-ABC, 41, 44
Sex differences, 46, 62
Shellhaas, M., 166–169
Short form scale of WJ-SIB, 187
Short-term memory, 83
Short-term memory subtests on Stanford-Binet, 48–49, 52–53, 55–58
Simultaneous processing subtests on K-ABC, 41–42, 44
SIT. *See* Slosson Intelligence Test
Situation codes, on Bayley Test, 138
Slosson, R., 120–122
Slosson Intelligence Test
   chronological age, 121
   description and administration, 119–120
   deviation IQ, 120
   equipercentile method, 121
   full scale IQ, 120
   mental age, 120
   norms, 121
   performance IQ, 122
   purpose, 118–119
   reliability, 121
   scoring and interpretation, 120
   and Stanford-Binet, 119, 121–122
   summary, 122
   validity, 122
   verbal IQ, 122
   and WISC, 122
Slow approach, to testing, 24–25

Smith, R., 146
Social maladaptation, on ABS, 171
Sociocultural norms, 62
Socioeconomic status, 46
Sparrow, S., 174, 177
Spearman-Brown formula, 10, 91
Speech problems, 27, 43, 50, 58, 63, 143
Speeded tests, 13
Split-half method
   defined, 10, 12
   and K-ABC, 44
SPM. *See* Standard Progressive Matrices
Spruill, J., 53, 56–58, 60
SRA Reading scores, 153
Stability, 10–12
Stability coefficient, 11
Standard age scores on Stanford-Binet, 53
Standard deviation, 7
Standard error of measurement
   defined, 9, 13–14
   on K-ABC, 44
Standard Progressive Matrices (SPM)
   academic achievement, 135
   description and administration, 130–131
   norms, 132
   other considerations, 136
   purpose, 129–130
   reliability, 133
   scoring, 132
   subtests
      completion of a pattern, 130
      figural analogy, 130
      systematic alteration, 130
      systematic decomposition, 130
   summary, 136–137
   validity, 135
Standard scores
   defined, 4, 7–9
   on WJ Part I, 100
Standardized procedures, 22
Standards for Educational and Psychological Tests, 15
Stanford Achievement Test (SAT), 115, 125
Stanford-Binet Intelligence Scale (Fourth Edition)
   abbreviated batteries, 59

Index 207

abstract/visual reasoning subtests, 53, 55
  copying, 49, 51–52, 56, 58
  matrices, 49, 51
  paper folding and cutting, 49, 52, 57
  pattern analysis, 49, 51, 58–59
adaptive testing format, 59, 63
Area Standard Age Scores (Area SASs), 53, 55–56
basal level, 49
ceiling level, 49
Composite SAS, 53, 55–56, 60
crystallized abilities, 48–49
description and administration, 48–52
entry level, 49
fluid-analytic abilities, 48–49
full scale IQ, 56
general reasoning factor, 48
and Hiskey-Nebraska, 116
and K-ABC, 45
and MSCA, 110
norms, 54
other considerations, 57–59
profile analysis chart, 54
purpose, 48
quantitative reasoning subtests, 53, 55
  equation building, 49, 51, 59
  number series, 49, 51, 59
  quantitative, 49, 51, 56, 58
raw scores, 53
reliability, 55–56
scoring and interpretation, 7–8, 52–54
selecting intelligence tests, 32, 60–65
short-term memory subtests, 48–49, 52–53, 55, 57
  bead memory, 52, 56, 58
  memory for digits, 52
  memory for objects, 52, 55
  memory for sentences, 52
standard age scores, 53
summary, 60
validity, 57
verbal reasoning subtests, 53, 55
  absurdities, 49–50, 52, 58
  comprehension, 49–50, 52, 56, 58
  verbal relations, 49–50, 52, 59
  vocabulary, 49–50, 52, 58
and VMI Test, 154
and Woodcock-Johnson, 91, 93, 101
and WPPSI-R, 80
Stanford-Binet Intelligence Scale: Form L-M, 48, 56, 110, 115, 119, 121–122, 125, 141, 144, 146, 154
and WISC-R, 38
Stanines, 8–9
Structured interview, on ABS, 167, 171
Subscale profile of WJ-SIB, 188
Subtests
  on Hiskey-Nebraska, 112–114
  on MSCA, 104–108, 110
  on W-J Part I, 95–102
Survey form, of Vineland Test, 172–180

Teacher Rating Scale, 115
Technical Manual, 53, 55–57
Test
  administration, 22
  ages on WISC-R, 36
  ages on WPPSI, 71
  ages on WPPSI-R, 78
  anxiety, 25
  behaviors, 23–28
  bias, 19–20
  cards, on Bender Test, 159
  criterion-referenced, 2–3
  defined, 2
  environment, 22–23
  norm-referenced, 2–3
  percentiles, 4
  reliability, 9–12
  scoring of, 3–8, 28
  stimuli, on Bayley Test, 138
Test-retest reliability
  defined, 10–11
  and K-ABC, 44
Test reviews
  AAMD Adaptive Behavior Scale, 166–171
  Advanced Progressive Matrices (APM), 129–137
  Bayley Scales of Infant Development (Mental Scale), 137–142
  Bender Visual Motor Gestalt Test, 158–163
  Coloured Progressive Matrices (CPM), 129–137
  Columbia Mental Maturity Scale (CMMS), 123–126

Test reviews—Continued
  Developmental Test of Visual-Motor Integration (VMI), 150–155
  Hiskey-Nebraska Test of Learning Aptitude, 111–116
  Kaufman Assessment Battery for Children (K-ABC), 40–48
  Leiter International Performance Scale (LIPS), 142–147
  McCarthy Scales of Children's Abilities (MSCA), 104–111
  Motor-Free Visual Perception Test (MVPT), 155–158
  Peabody Picture Vocabulary Test—Revised (PPVT-R), 126–129
  Slosson Intelligence Test (SIT), 118–122
  Standard Progressive Matrices (SPM), 129–137
  Stanford-Binet Intelligence Scale (Fourth Edition), 47–64
  Vineland Adaptive Behavior Scales, 171–184
  Wechsler Intelligence Scale for Children—Revised (WISC-R), 32–39
  Wechsler Preschool and Primary Scale of Intelligence (WPPSI), 68–74
  Wechsler Preschool and Primary Scale of Intelligence—Revised (WPPSI-R), 74–82
  Woodcock-Johnson Psycho-Educational Battery (Part I: Tests of Cognitive Ability), 94–103
  Woodcock-Johnson Psycho-Educational Battery—Revised (WJ-R COG), 82–94
  Woodcock-Johnson Psycho-Educational Battery Scales of Independent Behavior (SIB), 184–191
Thorndike, R., 47, 49, 57, 59
Training implication profile of WJ-SIB, 188
True score
  defined, 13–14
  on K-ABC, 43
  on WISC-R, 37
T scores, 7
Tuma, J., 37

Use and Interpretation of the Woodcock-Johnson Psycho-Educational Battery, 100

Validity
  concurrent, 16
  construct, 17
  content, 15
  criterion-related, 16
  defined, 14–15
  other considerations, 17–18
  predictive, 16
Vance, H., 37
Verbal IQ (VIQ)
  on Bender Test, 162
  on WISC-R, 36–38
  on WPPSI, 71–73
  on WPPSI-R, 77–81
Verbal reasoning subtests on Stanford-Binet, 49–50, 52–53, 55–56, 58–59
Verbal scale on MSCA, 104–105, 108, 110
Verbal subtests of WISC-R, 33–34
Verbal subtests on WPPSI, 69–71
Verbal subtests on WPPSI-R, 75–77, 79
Vernon, P., 37–38, 130
Vineland Adaptive Behavior Scales
  adaptive behavior composite, 175, 180, 182–184
  adaptive behavior subtests
    communication, 173, 182
    daily living skills, 173, 180
    motor skills, 173, 180
    socialization, 173, 180
  classroom edition, 172, 174–175, 178–180
  description and administration, 172–174
  deviation social quotient, 181
  estimated performance, 175
  interview edition
    expanded form, 172–175, 177–180
    survey form, 172–175, 177–180
  maladaptive behavior subtests, 173, 182–184
  norms, 177–179

Index

observed performance, 175
purpose, 172
reliability, 179–180
scoring and interpretation, 175–177
Spanish form, 174
summary, 183–184
survey form, 172–180
validity, 181–183
Vineland Social Maturity Scale, 172, 181
Visually impaired, 26, 63, 123, 143, 155
Visual-motor integration, 162–163
Visual-spatial perceptual skills, 33–35
Visual-spatial tests, 150–163
VMI. *See* Developmental Test of Visual-Motor Integration

WAIS. *See* Wechsler Adult Intelligence Scale
Weatherman, R., 184, 186, 189–190
Wechsler Adult Intelligence Scale (WAIS), 38, 56, 91, 101
Wechsler, D., 32, 39, 68, 74–75
Wechsler Intelligence Scale for Children (WISC), 32, 115, 122, 146
Wechsler Intelligence Scale for Children—Revised (WISC-R)
  academic achievement, 39
  description and administration, 33–35
  full scale IQ, 36–38
  and Hiskey-Nebraska, 116
  and K-ABC, 42, 45, 47
  mental retardation, 39
  and Motor-Free Visual Perception Test, 158
  and MSCA Test, 110
  norms, 36–37
  other considerations, 38–39
  performance IQ (PIQ), 36–38
  performance subtests, 62
  purpose, 32
  reliability, 37
  scaled score differences, 38
  scoring and interpretation, 35–36
  selecting intelligence tests, 6–65
  and Stanford-Binet, 47–48, 56
  test ages, 36
  true scores, 37
  validity, 38
  verbal IQ (VIQ), 36–38

and VMI Test, 153
and Woodcock-Johnson, 93, 101, 103
and WPPSI-R, 80
Wechsler Preschool and Primary Scale of Intelligence (WPPSI)
  description and administration, 68–71
  full scale IQ, 71–73
  and K-ABC, 45
  and MSCA Test, 110
  and MVPT, 158
  norms, 71
  other considerations, 73
  performance IQ, 71–73
  performance tests
    animal house, 70
    block design, 70–71
    geometric design, 70–71
    mazes, 70
    picture completion, 70–71
  purpose, 68
  reliability, 72
  scoring and interpretation, 71
  and Stanford-Binet Test, 56, 58
  test ages, 71
  validity, 72–73
  verbal IQ, 71–73
  verbal tests
    arithmetic, 69, 71
    comprehension, 69, 71
    information, 69, 71
    sentences, 70
    similarities, 69, 71
    vocabulary, 69, 71
  and VMI Test, 154
  and WAIS, 38
  and WISC-R, 38
  and WPPSI-R, 80, 82
Wechsler Preschool and Primary Scale of Intelligence—Revised (WPPSI-R)
  description and administration, 75–76
  full-scale IQ, 77, 79–81
  and MSCA Test, 111
  norms, 78–79
  performance IQ, 77–81
  performance subtests, 75–76
    animal pegs, 76–77
    block design, 76–77
    geometric design, 76–77, 79, 82
    mazes, 76–77, 79

Wechsler Preschool and Primary Scale of
    Intelligence—Revised (WPPSI-R)—
    Continued
  object assembly, 76–77
  picture completion, 76–77, 79
  purpose, 74
  raw scores, 77
  reliability, 79
  scaled scores, 77
  scoring and interpretation, 77–78
  summary, 81–82
  test ages, 78
  validity, 80–81
  verbal IQ, 77–81
  verbal subtests, 75–76
    arithmetic, 75–77
    comprehension, 75, 77, 79
    information, 75, 77
    sentences, 75
    similarities, 75, 77, 79
    vocabulary, 75, 77, 79
  and VMI Test, 154
Wide Range Achievement Test—Revised
    (WRAT-R), 56
Willson, V., 45
WISC. *See* Wechsler Intelligence Scale for
    Children
WISC-R. *See* Wechsler Intelligence Scale
    for Children—Revised
WJ-R COG. *See* Woodcock-Johnson
    Psycho-Educational Battery—
    Revised
Woodcock-Johnson Preschool Scale, 101
Woodcock-Johnson Psycho-Educational
    Battery, 5, 46, 56
Woodcock-Johnson Psycho-Educational
    Battery (Part I: Tests of Cognitive
    Ability)
  academic achievement, tests of, 99
  age-equivalent scores, 99
  average cluster score, 99
  broad cognitive ability, 95–96
  cluster difference score, 99
  cluster scores, 95, 99, 102
  clusters, scholastic aptitude, 99
  cognitive factors, 95–96, 101
  description and administration, 95–99
  expected achievement cluster scores,
    99

expected grade scores, 99
full scale cluster, 101
functioning level, 100
grade-equivalent scores, 99
norms, 100–101
other considerations, 102–103
part scores, 99
percentile rank range, 99
percentile scores, 100
perceptual speed factors, 101
purpose, 94–95
relative performance index, 100
reliability, 101
scholastic aptitude, 95
scoring and interpretation, 99–100
standard scores, 100
subtest profile, 100
subtests
  analogies, 97–98
  analysis-synthesis, 97–98
  antonyms-synonyms, 96–99, 102
  blending, 96–98, 102
  concept formation, 97–99
  memory for sentences, 95, 97–98
  numbers reversed, 97–98
  picture vocabulary, 95, 97–98, 102
  quantitative concepts, 96, 98, 102
  spatial relations, 95, 97–98, 101
  visual-auditory learning, 95, 97–99
  visual matching, 96–98, 101
summary, 103
validity, 101–102
Woodcock-Johnson Psycho-Educational
    Battery—Revised (WJ-R ACH), 82
Woodcock-Johnson Psycho-Educational
    Battery—Revised (WJ-R COG)
  age/grade profile, 88
  basal level, 87
  broad cognitive ability, 85
  cluster scores, 88
  description and administration, 83–87
  difference score (DIFF), 88
  extended percentile ranks, 89
  extended scale, 85
  extended standard scores, 89
  intracognitive discrepancies, 90
  norms, 90
  oral language cluster, 85, 91
  other considerations, 92–93

Index   211

purpose, 83
Reference W score (REF W), 88
Relative Mastery Index (RMI), 88
reliability, 91
rote memory, 93
scoring and interpretation, 87–90
standard battery subtests, 83–87
  analysis-synthesis, 84, 86–87
  incomplete words, 83, 86–87
  memory for names, 83, 86–87
  memory for sentences, 83, 86–87
  picture vocabulary, 84, 86–87
  visual closure, 84, 86–87, 91
  visual matching, 83, 86–87
standard scores, 88, 90
summary, 93–94
supplemental battery subtests, 84–87
  concept formation, 84, 86–87, 91
  cross out, 84, 86–87
  delayed recall-memory, 84, 86–87
  delayed recall-visual-auditory
    learning, 85–87
  listening comprehension, 85–87
  memory for words, 84, 86–87
  numbers reversed, 85–87
  oral vocabulary, 84, 86–87
  picture recognition, 84, 86
  sound blending, 84, 86
  sound patterns, 85–86
  spatial relations, 85, 86
  verbal analogies, 85–87
  visual-auditory learning, 84, 86–87
validity, 91–92
W score, 88
Woodcock-Johnson Psycho-Educational
  Battery Scales of Independent
  Behavior (SIB)
  adjusted scores, 188
  average cluster score, 188
  broad independence clusters, 185, 189

cluster scores, 188
community living skills, 189
description and administration, 185–187
early development scale, 187
maladaptive behavior indexes, 189–190
  asocial, 189
  externalized, 189
  general, 189
  internalized, 189
motor skills cluster, 189
norms, 189
other considerations, 190–191
percentile rank profiles, 188
problem behaviors profile, 188
problem behaviors scale, 187
purpose, 185
relative performance indexes (RPI), 188
reliability, 189
scoring and interpretation, 188–189
short form scale, 187
subscale profile, 188
summary, 191
training implication profile, 188
validity, 190
Woodcock, R., 82–83, 86, 94, 102–103, 184–186, 189–190
WPPSI. See Wechsler Preschool and Primary Scale of Intelligence
WPPSI-R. See Wechsler Preschool and Primary Scale of Intelligence—Revised
WRAT-R. See Wide Range Achievement Test—Revised

Yow, B., 139
Ysseldyke, J., 100

Z scores, 7